MR. CHINATOWN
THE LEGACY OF H.K. WONG

WESLEY R. WONG
WITH CATHERINE LENOX

WRITE
CONTACT

Seattle, Washington, USA

MR.CHINATOWN
THE LEGACY OF H.K. WONG

www.MrChinatown.com

Published by Write Contact
www.WriteContact.com

Book cover watercolor painting by Allison M. Wong
Book cover layout by Sonja L. Gerard

Book design by Sonja L. Gerard

Chapter divider bamboo/scenery watercolor paintings by H.K. Wong

Printed in the United States of America.
Paperbound edition of this book originally printed by:
Ingram Spark/Ingram Content Group, One Ingram Blvd., La Vergne, TN 37086
www.ingramspark.com

ISBN 978-0-578-90191-6 (pb)

10 9 8 7 6 5 4 3 2 1

CONTENTS

FOREWORD

By United States Senator Dianne Feinstein

In 1970, while President of the Board of Supervisors, I attended a banquet at the Empress of China Restaurant in San Francisco's Chinatown. Six stories high, with a sweeping view of downtown San Francisco, the landmark restaurant on historic Grant Avenue was co-founded by H.K. Wong.

At the time, I was impressed to learn that H.K. had not only established the restaurant but had been the energy behind the Chinese New Year Festival and was actively involved in many organizations that promoted San Francisco's Chinatown. His gracious, lively, friendly personality had made him a popular member of the business community.

In 1980, as Mayor of San Francisco, it was my honor to appoint H.K. to the San Francisco-Shanghai Friendship Sister City Committee, where he served on the Host Subcommittee. The City's "sister-city" association with Shanghai was the first to be established between American and Chinese cities and was entered into at the very highest levels of both governments.

During the time I served as Mayor, H.K. served on the committee that brought *Treasures from the Shanghai Museum: 6,000 Years of Chinese Art* to the San Francisco Asian Art Museum. It was the first exhibition ever organized with an established museum in China and grew out of our Shanghai Sister-City relationship. Additionally, he was an active participant in the "Save the Cable Cars" campaign, raising funds to match federal dollars for the system's restoration. Always eager to promote Chinatown and the city, he was a member of the Board of Directors of the San Francisco Convention and Visitors Bureau.

I valued his friendship and admired his commitment to building community spirit in San Francisco. Others took notice too. In 1987, in celebration of the *San Francisco Examiner* Centennial, H.K. was selected as one of the most memorable 101 San Franciscans of the previous 100 years. The recognition was well-deserved. H.K. Wong's contributions to Chinatown, to San Francisco, and to the State of California will be remembered for years to come.

INTRODUCTION

"The greatest legacy is that which benefits
the widest number of people for the longest
period without limit to value."

– **Yusuf Cat Stevens** (British singer-songwriter)

My dad, Henry Kwock Wong, better known as H.K. Wong, was a second-generation Chinese American who became such a popular and influential personality in San Francisco's Chinatown from the 1930s to the 1980s that he was nicknamed "Mr. Chinatown" and "Mayor of Grant Avenue" by the Chinese Chamber of Commerce and residents of Chinatown. He was a businessman, entrepreneur, restaurateur, sportsman, journalist, author, promoter, historian, technical director, watercolor artist, and family man who left an indelible mark on San Francisco and his beloved Chinatown.

Merriam-Webster defines the term "Renaissance man" as a man who has acquired profound knowledge or proficiency in more than one field – and is an outstandingly versatile, well-rounded person. With his extroverted, upbeat, enthusiastic personality, and infectious laugh, my dad was just such a man. In addition to having a wide, diverse range of skills and interests, he had a wide smile for everyone he met. People loved him. In 1978, he received the Jefferson Award from the American Institute for Public Service. A native San Franciscan, he devoted his entire life to community service and support of civic organizations. He was avid about building a positive image for Chinatown. In 1987, the *San Francisco Examiner* posthumously selected him as one of the 101 most memorable San Franciscans over the past hundred years, in celebration of the newspaper's centennial.

In fact, my dad's influence on San Francisco and Chinatown cannot be overstated. It could be said that he laid the foundation for today's Chinatown. From acting as a one-man press bureau for the entire Chinese community, building the Chinese New Year Festival and Parade, and co-establishing the landmark Empress of China Restaurant, to working as a technical advisor for the movie *Flower Drum Song*, my father worked tirelessly to promote San Francisco's Chinatown and its cultural traditions.

He strove to build bridges of understanding between Chinatown and mainland China. To that end, as Coordination Chairman of the Chinese American Committee, in June 1975, he facilitated bringing the first major international exhibition to travel outside of China since the end of World War II to the U.S.: *The Exhibition of Archaeological Finds of the People's Republic of China.* He was the reason that this exhibition was seen in San Francisco rather than only in Washington D.C. and Kansas City, Missouri. Through his efforts, the exhibition made a stop in San Francisco before returning to China and was seen by nearly 900,000 visitors at the Asian Art Museum, a wing of the San Francisco De Young Museum. The curators of the exhibition were from Peking and became friends with my dad, sparking other notable exchanges. Two years later, he was instrumental in bringing the People's Republic of China's 2,000-year-old Han Tang Murals to San Francisco.

In 1980, he served on the San Francisco-Shanghai Friendship committee and the committee that brought *Treasures from the Shanghai Museum: 6,000 Years of Chinese Art* to the San Francisco Asian Art Museum. It was the first exhibition ever organized with an established museum in China and grew out of the San Francisco sister-city relationship with Shanghai, which had started on Jan. 28, 1980, one year after China and the United States established formal diplomatic relations. Senator Dianne Feinstein, then Mayor of San Francisco, had formed the sister-city relationship, which is still active today. My dad had agreed with Mayor Feinstein's belief that it was important to bring the two cultures closer.

H.K. was dedicated to unifying the Chinese community with the rest of San Francisco, the country, and the world. His belief in the inherent goodness of humanity is why he became the liaison officer between the Chinese and City Hall for the visit of Madam Chiang Kai-Shek to America in 1943. In 1958, he founded the Miss Chinatown USA Pageant as a part of the Chinese New Year celebration to encourage participation from

Chinese communities nationally. Between 1940 and 1984, he worked tirelessly for numerous associations, among these as Secretary of the Chinese Consolidated Benevolent Association (known as the "Chinese Six Companies"). He served on the Board of Directors for the Chinese Chamber of Commerce and the San Francisco Convention and Visitors Bureau. He was also a journalist for numerous publications, including the *Chinese Digest, Chinese World, East/West, and Asian Week*. Plus, in 1963 he was one of five founders of the Chinese Historical Society of America and served as its President and Director from 1967 to 1971.

His energy was boundless. An avid tennis player his entire life, in 1935, he was a charter member and President of the San Francisco Chinese Tennis Club. For the next 25 years, he promoted tennis in the Chinese community. He actively brought the club into the Northern California Tennis Association and had the club's annual tennis tournament sanctioned as a Chinese National Championship. Under his direction, the San Francisco Chinese Tennis Club won the Pacific Coast Chinese Club championship in Vancouver, B.C. He was also Chairman of the Northern California Tennis Association Inter-club competitions during the 1950s, which ran over a thousand interclub tennis matches in Northern California, and was also the first Chinese American to serve on the Board of Directors of the Northern California Tennis Association. He was posthumously inducted into the Northern California Tennis Association Hall of Fame in 1992.

His enthusiasm extended to other sports, too. In 1936, he was Manager of the San Francisco Rice Bowl Football team, an all-star Chinese team that represented San Francisco annually. In 1947, he co-founded the San Francisco Chinese Basketball Club, which won several national championships. Also, from 1956 to 1957 he was the San Francisco Publicity Chairman for the Sports Car Club of America.

His wife, my mom Honey, shared his love of tennis and racing sports cars. She was one of the few women he knew who drove sports cars and had a zest for adventure, and my dad was drawn to her wit, spunk, and easy, joyful spirit. They had met in 1940 on Grant Avenue during a festival but did not marry until 1957. They later adopted me from Hong Kong in 1963.

For LaVay,
Without whom I would not be
the person I am today.

"H.K. Wong was truly a Renaissance man. His involvement in major milestone events and activities that transformed Chinatown from an insular, overlooked, neglected community to a vibrant part of San Francisco was truly extraordinary. Involvement by Chinese Americans in local, national and even international events, has become the norm. Projects like the construction of Ping Yuen, Portsmouth Square Garage, Empress of China, establishing the annual Chinese New Year parade, formation of the San Francisco-Shanghai sister city committee, bringing exhibitions from China to S.F. emphatically demonstrated the scope and breadth of Chinese American capabilities to promote San Francisco. He was also generous in giving credit to the many unsung Chinese American heroes who worked with him to make meaningful and effective involvement in these endeavors."

Sue Lee
Chinese Historical Society of America
Executive Director, 2004-2017

"H.K. Wong was a man about town and was involved in so many things that helped to develop San Francisco's Chinatown and other Chinatowns in North America. Wesley Wong's biography of his multitalented father provides a glimpse into his life and some of his contributions. Reading *Mr. Chinatown* reminded me of the events of my youth, the importance of history, and how one man could do so much for future generations."

Sue Fawn Chung, Ph.D.
Professor Emerita, University of Nevada, Las Vegas
National Trust for Historic Preservation, Advisor Emerita
Author of *In Pursuit of Gold: Chinese American
Miners and Merchants in the American West*;
Chinese in the Woods: Logging and Lumbering in the American West,
and other books

H.K. had a longstanding interest in Chinese American history and culture. He and his friend, William Hoy, liked to visit gold mining sites of the late 19th century, abandoned Chinatowns, and old Chinese temples, often collecting artifacts that served as the foundation of the Chinese Historical Society of America (CHSA) Museum collection. He thoroughly enjoyed doing oral interviews. Some of his favorite interviews are collected in the book, *Gum Sahn Yun* (Gold Mountain Men), published posthumously in 1987. Creatively drawn to the arts, he was also a prolific watercolorist. One of his paintings was featured on the cover of *Travel Holiday Magazine* in November 1978, a national publication of food and travel, and another is on the cover of his oral history book.

My dad was a consummate businessman and promoter. With a twinkle in his brown eyes, he would say, "When I start to talk, I can be convincing. I am a good salesman because I believe in my causes." Personally, I believe he was also a good salesman because strong, trusting relationships came naturally to him. Before he passed on January 13, 1985 in San Francisco, he had successfully owned two businesses, the Ti Sun Company Hardware & Furniture store, and the Polk/Pacific Building Supply. He had also helped found a third as co-owner of the palatial showcase restaurant, the Empress of China. It was fitting that he was a founding director and vice-president of the City of San Francisco Portsmouth Plaza Parking Corporation, a nonprofit firm that funded construction of a public garage underneath Portsmouth Square, because that structure was located next to the Empress of China Restaurant he'd established and underneath a park in which he'd been born (in a cottage on that site).

In writing this book, in addition to paying homage to my dad's significant contribution to San Francisco's and Chinatown's history, it is my intention to honor the integrity of who he was, which can best be summed up in his own words: "I believe in doing what you can in the sense of being able to help, particularly when something can enhance life for all of us."

This is the story of how my dad, Henry Kwock Wong, enhanced life in San Francisco and its Chinatown and why his legacy will continue to do so for many generations to come.

1

THE EARLY YEARS

Charismatic leader Henry "H.K." Wong was born April 29, 1907 in Cottage B-25, in Portsmouth Square, a one-block park in Chinatown, San Francisco, California. Years later, while being interviewed by *San Francisco Examiner and Chronicle* journalist Mildred Hamilton, he jokingly said, "Portsmouth Square is the birthplace of the City of San Francisco – and me too." He was right. Many historical events happened at Portsmouth Square, not the least of which was H.K.'s birth.

Portsmouth Square is historically significant because it was the center of Chinatown and located near the waterfront. California's first public school was built there in 1847. On May 11, 1848, one block away from Portsmouth Square, Sam Brannon also announced to an enthusiastic crowd that he had discovered gold in the mountains, at the American River. This launched a surge in population to San Francisco, among these many Chinese men. Between 1849 and 1853, drawn by the prospect of gold, Chinese immigrants flocked to California by boat. The trip was arduous, taking anywhere from six to eight months. Most left their wives and children behind in China, sending home whatever money they could save. In 1852, a serious crop failure in Southern China caused more than 20,000 Chinese immigrants to come to California in search of gold. Tending to live together in groups, they quickly discovered that many Americans were resentful of their arrival. Rather than being allowed to prospect on their own, Chinese immigrants were allowed to work only mines that had already been abandoned. Also, in 1852, the state wielded a heavy tax on foreign miners, targeting Chinese immigrants. By the end of the 1850s, Chinese

H.K. Wong

immigrants accounted for one-fifth of the population of the southern mine counties. Some worked for a short while and returned home. Others continued to prospect for gold and found niche employment in laundries, restaurant work, boarding houses, and other places, especially as house servants (this was very fashionable until the 1910s).

From 1863 to 1869, approximately 15,000 Chinese manual laborers helped build the transcontinental railway. They were largely responsible for constructing nearly 700 miles of train track between Sacramento, California and Promontory, Utah. Paid less than their American counterparts, they lived in tents while other workers lived in train boxcars, and they shoveled 20 pounds of rock over 400 times per day. Their conditions were brutal too, often involving rock avalanches, severe snowstorms, and accidental explosions, which killed hundreds of workers.

By 1870, there were 63,000 Chinese in the U.S., mostly living in San Francisco. Few people realize that they also built levees on the Sacramento River and helped found the state's fishing, wine, and cherry industries. The Bing cherry is named for Ah Bing, a Chinese foreman who worked for Seth Lewelling, the horticulturist who developed the Bing cherry and established an orchard in Oregon. By that time, a quarter of the miners in California were Chinese. Following the Gold Rush, Chinese miners were hired to work in low-paying agricultural and industry jobs. In 1874-1875, Chinese workers also helped build the earthen dam on Lake Chabot in the Castro Valley, a primary water source for the East Bay.

Few Chinese women came to San Francisco and the U.S. before 1880. Until the passage of the 1875 Page Act, which essentially meant that Chinese wives had to prove that they were not prostitutes to immigrate, any Chinese woman could immigrate. However, most found the lifestyle too harsh – especially those accustomed to having servants (this was common in Guangdong) – so many of them returned to China. After 1882, the only Chinese women who could immigrate were wives of merchants, diplomats, and students.

Early Chinese immigrants called America "Gum Sahn," or "Gold Mountain," and sought their fortune in the gold mines. Women in China who were married to successful miners became known as "Gold Mountain wives." They lived well. But for peasant wives whose husbands did not return with gold or send money home, the story was often sad. These women were left behind to farm their land on their own, raise their families, and live like widows for many years. Word of the discrimination and backbreaking work their Chinese immigrant husbands faced rarely made its way back to China.

When the gold mines were no longer productive, many Chinese immigrants settled in San Francisco and worked as merchants or cooks, opening their own businesses: restaurants, laundries, and other services. Due to their cultural upbringing in China, they knew how to persevere through hardship and apply diligence, savvy, and hard work to build their businesses to prosperity. The result was that Chinese businessmen successfully competed with white-owned businesses, inciting jealousy and even more racism and hatred. This feeling spawned riots and intense coercion to block Chinese immigrants from entering the United States. Even a group of white women, the Workmen's Party of California (WPC), protested the presence of Chinese laborers by claiming they were a threat to white women because "their bodies were diseased, they were sexually perverted, and competed with them economically." Though these stereotypes were patently untrue, white women argued that the Chinese took jobs that they used to have, driving them into prostitution. California, with the largest Chinese population in the U.S., the bulk of which lived in San Francisco, led this push. The result of this resentment was the Chinese Exclusion Act of 1882, which ended Chinese immigration for nearly sixty years. It was the first immigration law ever to ban a race from entering the U.S.

Although historical facts are known about early Chinese immigrants, the Chinese Historical Society of America notes that most were not able to leave written records. Literacy in traditional China meant passing the civil service exam, but you could read and write and not be considered literate. Almost everyone knew how to write their names and hometowns and could read and recite a Chinese poem that was printed on Keno tickets (Keno was played in the 1850s and 1860s in Chinatown), but they could not write a scholarly or literary essay. However, my relatives were educated and did know how to write. It is to their credit that I can trace my family line and relate its history as seen through their eyes.

With a family tree dating back to 1125 in China, my dad came from a long line of successful scholars, prestigious lawyers, politicians, community leaders, and respected citizens. His first known ancestor was Guey Jing, the eldest son of Cheng Lok, who migrated from Fukien Province, Po Tin County, to Kwangtung. Guey Jing later settled in the Chew Ging area. He became involved in both law and politics, attaining high honors in the Imperial Examination, a civil-service exam given in Imperial China to choose administrative officials. He then became Magistrate of Ying Duck County. Thus began hundreds of years of relatives who ranked high in the Imperial Examinations and who became high city officials, industrious scholars, teachers, and community leaders. To hold this lengthy, proud lineage and dignity of spirit but be treated as an inferior in America had to have been sobering.

In June of 1984, Arthur K. Wong, my uncle, compiled a massive account of our family lineage. In it, he noted that most people in China are of the Han race, but there are also many minority races. One of these is the Manchurian from North China. In 1644, the Manchus, a largely tribal group, took advantage of the Han Chinese Ming Dynasty's political in-fighting, low morale, and declining loyalty in the military. In 1644, they overthrew the Han Chinese Ming Dynasty and established the Ch'ing (Qing) Dynasty, which ruled from 1644 to 1911. Chinese loyal to their fellow Han people of the Ming Dynasty resented the Manchu's minority-race rule and control. Marriage between the Manchus and Hans was strictly forbidden. One of the first laws the Manchus passed was for Chinese men to wear the hairstyle of the Manchus – a shaved forehead and queue (pigtail)—that they considered a mark of subservience. Chinese rebels defied this regulation, but if they were caught without the queue, they were immediately beheaded. Consequently, there were riots and rebellions against the Manchu rule everywhere in the country.

The servant class took advantage of the opportunity and revolted against their masters. One night, they locked their masters' doors with chains and killed them. This was called the "Servant against master war." Two of my forefathers, Gung Kuan (20th generation) and Nee Guey (21st generation) were killed in the uprising. Gung Ding (20th generation) escaped the massacre and fled with all the deeds of the family farm with him. He hid from his assailants in the Bo Kwok Temple. He was so grateful to the Temple for saving his life that he gave the deeds to them. That is why my family was given pork offerings at Fete (a ceremonial gathering to honor family) each year from the temple priests.

Six months after Nee Guey (21st generation) was murdered, his only son, Yow Guey (22nd generation) was born. Four months later, the baby's mother died. Yow Guey was then raised by his uncle, Nee Won, thus saving the only direct bloodline of my family to the present day. Otherwise, our branch of the family tree would have been terminated at the end of the 21st generation, in the 1600s.

My great-grandfather, Wong Kee Own (27th generation), came from the village of Foo Shan Toy, Shan County, Kwangtung Province. One of his sons, Wong Kim Wey (28th generation), disappeared in 1894 after an argument with Lee Ming, the manager of an herb store where Kim Wey had been employed for three years. Rumor has it that Lee Ming was a vicious person, and after the argument, Kim Wey died of his injuries. His body was never found, but a few months later Lee Ming fled the country. Kim Wey's brother, Kim Lun, investigated the incident, but was unable to prove anything. Wong Kim Lun, my grandfather, and his brother, Wong Kim Tson, continued the family line.

My grandfather, Wong Kim Lun, was born July 12, 1860 in Fu-shan Toon, Toisan district, South China. He grew up in his family home on a narrow, crowded lane in the village, close to the school he attended. His family had additional land, where they grew rice, taro, Chinese *lo bok*, sweet spuds, sugar cane, and peanuts, for which the town was famous. He later pursued higher education in Canton. Like his relatives before him, he took the Imperial Examination and passed on the county level. A highly intelligent man, he became a *"show choy"* – a lawyer and magistrate in Canton City. Shortly before leaving for San Francisco, he also became an educator.

In 1877, when relatives in the U.S. sponsored Wong Kim Lun and he came to San Francisco, he arrived as a merchant. As the story goes, after arriving and settling in San Francisco, one day my grandfather was standing on a Grant Avenue street corner in Chinatown (then Dupont Street) during a New Year's celebration. He saw a beautiful young girl and was captivated by her. Intent on seeing her again, he asked his friends if they knew who she was. He found out her name, and later with his friends went to visit her parents to arrange a match. His ardor was rewarded. The beautiful girl he had seen and pursued was none other than my grandmother, Shee Gee (Gee Ah Tie), daughter of merchant Gee Yick Lee. Born in San Francisco's Chinatown on August 17, 1887, her family lived at 723 Dupont Street. My grandfather later referred to her as "a date from heaven." When he met Shee Gee at age 40, he was a widower. In a family photo when my dad was around five years old, my grandfather appears to be much older in the photo than my grandmother. But his first marriage is not documented in our family tree.

That same street corner also played a big part in my parents' life again. Years later, my father saw another entrancing young woman, the very strikingly pretty Honey Quan, also at a New Year's celebration on Grant Avenue. Honey became his second wife on April 15, 1957. In later chapters, I will tell more of their story.

An educated man, Wong Kim Lun was of medium height, with a discerning, intelligent face and sharp eyes. On April 29, 1936, when he spoke with William Hoy (a longtime friend of my dad's, student of Chinese, a journalist, and Chinese artifact collector), Hoy was struck by Kim Lun's composed disposition. My dad and Hoy had often roamed the streets of Chinatown together, meeting and chatting with friends over many cups of coffee at Fong Fong's Bakery Fountain or the restaurant, Sun Wah Kue. Conversations with the elders never ceased to interest Hoy. Talking with my grandfather was no exception.

The history my grandfather had lived was substantial and not always easy. However, at 76, although his serious face, salt-and-pepper hair and slight, graying mustache showed his years, his eyes lit up like a young man's when he talked about his past. Speaking in Toisan dialect, my grandfather unveiled his memories, interspersing the interview with quotes from the classics, Chinese history, and the traditions and geography of ancient Cathay. Hoy listened intently and penned notes from my grandfather's conversation. I am deeply indebted to him for capturing my grandfather's words in such detail.

Following WWII, Hoy lived in the basement of my dad's home and stored a lot of his written work there. Though he died young, he was a prominent journalist. What he wrote about my family's history is a precious time capsule, and its value cannot be underestimated.

My grandfather had twelve children. Kim Lun's first-born daughter's Chinese name, Ah Fung, meant "beautiful phoenix." His first-born son was my father, Ah Ding Kwok, whose name means "control the country." The children later adopted English names: Ann, Henry (my dad), Harry, Edith, Fred, David, Arthur, Robert, George, Clara, Pearl, and Phoebe. As the eldest son in his family of 12 siblings, my dad looked after his siblings.

Before the 1906 earthquake in San Francisco, my grandfather said, "life was a song for his new bride." She wore elegant silk garments, accented by exquisite jade jewelry, pearls, and gold bracelets. She sewed clothing of only the finest materials for her young daughters. But on that fateful morning of April 18, 1906, at 5:12 am, the family's life changed forever. The earth shook fiercely, and much of San Francisco burned, reduced to rubbish overnight. All of Chinatown went up in flames, taking with it all my grandparent's properties, their stores, and every dollar of their life savings. Shortly after, my father was born.

After the earthquake, raising their many children became a huge challenge for my grandparents. In those days, it was hard for people to recover their losses. My grandfather's dark days intensified when he was forced to take any job he could find, however menial, just to feed his family. For the next thirty years, he worked tirelessly to operate numerous businesses, liquor stores, restaurants, and laundries in San Francisco, with limited success. Later, he worked in laundries from California to New Mexico to make ends meet. He clerked in stores and worked as a bookkeeper. He taught school and worked on farms in Oxnard, California. It is hard to imagine moving a family with twelve children so many times, but he went where there was opportunity.

When Hoy asked my grandfather if he had any entertaining anecdotes about my father during that time, my grandfather laughed, and with a sparkle in his eyes, said, "In 1914, I took my eldest son, Henry [my dad], then seven years old, to Carlsbad, New Mexico, where I would be taking over a cousin's laundry, and where we would also live. My cousin was planning to return to China for a year and needed a trusted person to handle his business. I was chosen. We took a train ride that appeared to wander around the Old West country, and it took a week to get to our little town. On one of those days, we looked out our coach window and saw the Grand Canyon below us. We later made the final train change in El Paso, Texas. That is when my son saw his first real live alligator in the El Paso Park plaza. Carlsbad was only a small hamlet in the hot desert with tree-lined streets that were flooded with water from the nearby river at 4:00 pm. It was so hot there we could not eat much; a quart of canned tomatoes over warm rice was our meal. We used to walk over the bridge on Sunday and watch the gold coin turtles at the bottom of the stream, but it was too hot to eat. My little boy (H.K.) helped when he found lots of loose coal on the nearby railroad tracks, which fell from the fully loaded engine tenders as they rattled by. A small wagonload was good for at least two hours of heating up the flat iron stove."

Carlsbad also made an impression on H.K. "The weather was always hot. We would go barefoot. Each afternoon, the town would flood all the ditches by the street to irrigate the shade trees. I would play in the cool water. I would often take my little cart and pick up coal that dropped from the overloaded bunker of the train engine. It was easy to get ten tons of it."

In 1915, after returning to San Francisco from Carlsbad, New Mexico, H.K. attended the Oriental Public School from first to fourth grade. Founded in 1859, it was set up as a segregated school for children of Chinese descent due to the anti-Chinese bias that had emerged in the United States in the late 1800s. Japanese and Korean students also later went to school there.

H.K.'s early memories included an interest in sports. His first tryout for the track team proved unsuccessful when a guy put his foot behind the other contestant and gave that guy a running start. But in my dad's next race, an All-Star meet, he won second place. As he described it, "I placed second and got a red ribbon, but all the rest of the competition got carsick and couldn't run. So, there were only two runners, another guy and me. I was a dozen yards behind him." This unlikely outcome did not faze my dad, though, whose enthusiasm for sports lasted his entire life.

That same year, my grandfather took my dad to the Panama-Pacific International Exposition (PPIE), otherwise known as the 1915 San Francisco World's Fair. The event celebrated the completion of the Panama Canal and highlighted San Francisco's recovery from the 1906 earthquake and revitalization as a global city. In April 2015, to commemorate the 100th anniversary of the PPIE, the Chinese Historical Society of America presented an exhibition, *Underground Chinatown–Racism at the Fair*, which focused on one of the exhibits at that fair--"Joy Zone." Though it was popular with fair attendees, it portrayed Chinese culture falsely.

As an adult, through his businesses, travel, and community outreach, my father worked tirelessly to bring true understanding of Chinese heritage and culture to the U.S. At eight years old, he had seen his heritage misrepresented at the PPIE. I have often wondered if that memory inspired him to share a different view about Chinese culture to the people living outside Chinatown when he became an adult. Remembering studying Chinese classics during his early school days in San Francisco's Chinatown, my dad recalls, "Fung Sin Sang droned on and on, and we would usually fall asleep." But as an adult, his passion to share traditional Chinese culture outside Chinatown changed his interest in it forever.

My dad had a paper delivery route. Starting at the waterfront at 5:30 am, amid dark, wavering, smelly gaslights, he would trudge up to the doorsteps of tenement rooming houses to deliver the morning paper. Then he would go to school. In the afternoon, climbing up countless steep stairs to the 5th, 6th, or 8th floor, he would deliver the evening papers to the swanky Nob Hill district. After that, he would go back to Chinese school from 5:00 pm – 8:00 pm. As my dad said, "It's a wonder that we had any time to study or to eat."

Three vignettes that he jotted down on a piece of paper give a glimpse of H.K.'s view of San Francisco Chinatown as a child. They are a colorful look at days gone by, quoted verbatim.

- The little old man who walks up and down the street and into all the buildings with two huge baskets slung from a bamboo pole on his shoulders. He is selling Chinese sweet (sic) cakes. He usually shouts, "Roo-sie ah cake, moo-ey for bang – rose cake and fig cookies."

- The peanut man on Pacific Avenue and Wentworth Street, whose family lives in the basement. Somewhere in the premises, he has stored and roasted all varieties of peanuts. Outside on his steps going down to his place, he has a charcoal roaster, with peanuts being roasted and filling the air with aroma. He sells a large bag of several varieties of peanuts for five cents.

- The coon man, the animal man, who sells live animals that he traps in the mountains. For a dollar or two, the right kind for a gourmet Chinese meal - "makes the blood walk faster."

In the early days, Grant Avenue between Broadway and Pacific was the boundary between Italian town and Chinatown. My dad wrote, "Grant Avenue was an area of small shops, herb stores, and butcher shops. At the south end there was an arts supply shop, the king of which was Sing Fat Company, the biggest and most famous importer and exporter of Chinese art goods. There, you could find vases 'worth a king's fortune' or cheap curios for a few cents. There were many gaps on Grant Avenue, empty lots filled with debris and rubble of the 1906 earthquake and fire. Part of Grant Avenue, and much of Clay, Washington, Jackson, Pacific, and Sacramento streets, were paved with cobblestones. Horses pulling heavy freight wagons up and down those streets often slipped. It was particularly treacherous in the fog and rain. There was a little shop on Grant Avenue near Jackson that used to be a lottery center. But since the crackdown on lottery centers, it is now used as a place for old timers to cook up soup to 'build our bodies.' One day they cooked up snake soup, which was an instant hit when the word got out. The place was crowded with people eager for a taste of the snake soup, but this 'goldmine' petered out when the health department caught wind of it. The little shop on Grant Avenue had no permit to operate a public eating place – and thus one of Chinatown's instant success stories went down the drain. But up until the 1950s, live ducks were delivered to the Grant Avenue poultry shops by Tom, the old duck delivery man. He would hand those quacking ducks to the shop worker, who would weigh them, put them in a cage for sale, and kill each one for the buyer. Tom also brought double and triple duck eggs, which he would save for a few of his personal friends and favorite poultry shop owners. These eggs were three times the size of a grand chicken egg. My mother used to salt them for three months and 'ho la' we would have triple duck eggs, a prized addition to a good dish of ground pork."

H.K. lived at the Porcelain building, *gong gwah low*, at the corner of Pacific and Grant Avenue, upstairs on the third floor in two rooms, with a common bathroom. His mother picked shrimp and delivered it to a shrimp company to keep the family going. In an interview with the *S.F. Sunday Examiner & Chronicle*, my dad would later tell journalist Mildred Hamilton, "We were quite poor, but I had a marvelous boyhood. I always worked - we all did. One of my first jobs was picking shrimp, the little bay shrimp on Commercial Street. I was about seven or eight years old – and I was a champion shrimp picker."

Grandmother Gee Ah Tie around 12 years old, San Francisco, circa 1899.
Photo by Peerless Studio.

Grandparents Wong Kim Lun and Shee Gee (Gee Ah Tie), circa 1915.

H.K. attended the Oriental School
in San Francisco Chinatown
from first to fourth grade.
It was a segregated public school
for Chinese, Japanese, and
Korean students.

H.K. (front row, third from left) at the Pleasant Valley School in Camarillo, CA, circa 1917.
He was the only Asian student, and wore a suit and tie. It was a farming community, and
most of the other boys wore overalls. The practice of wearing a suit and tie stayed with
H.K. his entire life.

2

OXNARD

When H.K. was ten years old, the entire family took a train to Oxnard, where they settled for three years. H.K. attended grades 5 through 8 there. A small farming community 60 miles from Los Angeles, California, Oxnard had a smaller Chinatown. The family house was located between Savier Road (later changed to Main Street) and A Street in a tiny passageway. This alley of smaller houses and shacks for Chinese and Mexican residents was called "China Alley." Chinatown's business area was located on Savier Road, with three Chinese restaurants, several stores, a few gambling houses, and a Chinese school. H.K. attended the Chinese school, as he had also done in San Francisco's Chinatown. It would be years before he attended a non-Chinese school. My grandfather was able to send sons David and Arthur to China to get an education, but his deepest regret was that all his children did not get higher education because of the family's poverty. As the eldest son, my dad was expected to go to work to help support the family, so he did not receive a formal education beyond the 8th grade. However, he was self-taught in everything he did and did so with a tenacious spirit and relentless drive that brought him great success.

Of their life in Oxnard, my grandfather said, "The period we moved to Oxnard was a togetherness one. My wife wisely guided the kids and made them into an active Work Corps." He also noted that his children were quite resourceful. "These kids, city-bred youngsters, were excited to be out in the country and to see animals and growing things. They walked along the road and chopped down young trees and cut them down to firewood size for our cooking. Their little wagon was more useful as they pulled it

H.K.Wong

to freshwater creeks five or more miles away to gather watercress. They would tie the watercress down in neat bundles and sell them for five cents a bunch or three bunches for a dime. Some Sundays, my uncle would drive his horse and laundry delivery wagon to the Ventura seashore, a ten-mile one-way trip. The kids would spend the whole day gathering rich Pacific Coast seaweed, highly prized for soup. When these were washed and dried, they would sell them to the Japanese growers, as well as Chinese restaurants and stores. They would also find choice lima beans that had been lifted and thrown into the bushes after the threshing machines had finished their work in the lima bean fields. They would pack them up in a 100 lb. sack and get a tidy sum for the lima beans. Food was highly precious in those days."

H.K. also said, "Because of World War I, food was expensive, and beans were in great demand for the fighting force. Usually, the threshing machines would come along and pick up and thresh the crop, and in one marvelous operation, also sack it in one hundred-pound sacks. Always on the topsoil of the bushes, the best beans were dropped. That is where we came in. We followed the operation from field to field and as soon as they vacated the place, brother Harry, sister Edith, and I would pull our little wagon into the field. Armed with gunny sacks, we would pick up all that remained on the topsoil. A good field and quick eyes and fingers would gain us a sack full by evening, which we could sell to the bean cooperative at $5.00 a sack, a good source of income for a family. After school, we would eat fried hard-boiled eggs with *ho yow* [oyster sauce], strips of meat in marinade, and steaming rice, or Eagle sweetened condensed milk on fresh baked bread...yum yum...and so filling. Another menu item we enjoyed was thinly sliced potatoes, deep-fried to a crisp with pork chops covered in brown gravy and *see yow* [soy sauce] - nothing like it. It was one of our most treasured dishes." With my father's early appreciation of food, it is no surprise he later became a noted restaurateur.

H.K. joined other Chinese workers who picked lima beans and hoed weeds between the rows in the surrounding agricultural fields. Always persuasive, even though he was only ten years old at the time, he talked himself into getting a man's job hoeing by suggesting to the foreman that he could go twice as fast as an older man. He got the job and the same pay, $5.00 a day. (By today's economy, that was worth about $100 a day, which was big money for a ten-year-old.) During this time, he also worked at a big ranch as a helper to Yee On, a husky young man who gave him the job because he had eyes for H.K.'s sister and haplessly wanted to marry her. H.K. noted, "Ranch cooks usually hired another man to help cook for the crew of 60 to 70 men. Before going to sleep at night, I would set the main table. Waking at 5:00 am, I would slice 50 to 60 loaves of fresh 'sweet-smelling and soft' baked bread and finish setting the tables. I would run around and serve food to the hungry bunch. Then, by 7:30 am, I would clean up, hop on my bicycle (a present from the cook), and pedal nine miles to school in Camarillo. Kids called me "China," as I was the only Asian there. After school, I would usually pump the bike westward, which was hard work as the stiff Western ocean wind was always blowing from 10 to 20 mph. I got to know a couple of Irish farm boys who rode to school on their horse (2 to a horse). They longed to ride a bicycle, so I made my first advantageous trade. I let them ride my bicycle while I rode their horse! At the ¾ mark, we would exchange modes of transportation and they would go on their separate way home." From day one, my dad was a savvy businessman, while making certain that everyone he did business with was happy.

Oxnard was also home to a sugar beet factory at the time and had a small Chinatown of Chinese people who worked seasonally on the many large farms, or as cooks on the farms. In 1917, the town also had its own fire department, and the Chinese had one of their own. Paid for by the Chinese and manned voluntarily by Chinese citizens, the fire department answered calls from all over the city. Cooks, gamblers, teachers, waiters, and laundrymen alike would rush to help when they heard the fire siren. Housed in a tiny shed in China Alley, the Chinese community's firefighting equipment was one small hand-pump water cart with iron wheels and a huge coil of hose. The China Alley #1 Volunteer Fire Department's youngest volunteer was my dad, who served as mascot for the firefighters.

My grandfather said, "He added his small strength to the long tow rope when the town fire alarm sounded."

My dad remembers going to his first American school in Oxnard. A Wong man, who was wealthy, had a spoiled son about my dad's age (all of ten). My grandmother would pack sandwich lunches in a Prince Albert one-pound oblong can for my dad. One special day, she added a piece of fresh baked apple pie. H.K. was delighted when he opened his lunch can and offered some to the Wong boy, who took one look at it, and chucked it to the ground. My dad never spoke to that boy again. H.K. was also harassed and attacked by Mexican kids at school. His older sister, Ann, would protect him by "whipping them in their butts with a horsewhip until they hollered."

During that same time, my grandfather's spirits were lifted by the offer of a job teaching Chinese to a local leader's son. Though the pay was not much, it gave him a wonderful chance to teach Chinese traditions, culture, and language. He was also earning money hoeing weeds. His younger son also got a job as a cook's assistant during a potato harvest. He worked in a 50-foot long cookhouse wagon pulled by a team of 20 horses. He peeled 300 pounds of spuds each day and sliced baked bread for 40 hungry white workers.

When H.K. was fourteen, my grandmother bought a minor share in a cousin's hardware store and permitted my dad to eat there during evening meals, provided he set the table, cleared the dishes, and swept the floor afterward. He often helped the family at the store, sticking around longer than required due to his curiosity about the merchandise. His interest later led him to work as a translator and buyer, and inspired him to eventually work full-time there. My grandmother's hardware store would close for a week during the Chinese New Year for gambling until dawn, the telling of village folk tales around the dinner table, and midnight snacks. This early experience no doubt laid the foundation for H.K.'s management of a hardware store in his adult years. As H.K. later said, "At the store, they always celebrated good times. The cook would get extra good fish and fowl, friends would join us until late, and the oldsters would tell risqué jokes."

During the time H.K. lived in Oxnard, however, my grandfather lost his teaching job. By necessity, he had to take a job in Alhambra, California. His new work at Alhambra Hospital was more than fifty miles from Oxnard, and about eight miles from Los Angeles.

H.K.'s Indian 4 motorcycle in Oxnard, December 1929.

3

LOS ANGELES

From 1929 to 1931, my grandfather operated the entire Alhambra Hospital laundry by himself. He had his own quarters with a cot, sheltered from his workspace by only a paper wall. The hospital provided most of his meals.

When H.K. was twelve years old, he was sent to Chinatown in Los Angeles to attend the Wing Lee Chinese School, as well as an American school. He attended both schools Monday through Friday. For some months, he boarded at one of the Wong clans' rooming houses. Later, he lived behind the school classroom with his teacher, Mr. Lee, in a small alcove on North L.A. Street. The old man generously cooked H.K. hearty meals for only $1.00 a week. When my dad's father came to visit, Mr. Lee fed him too. One time he took them both to lunch at a swanky L.A. downtown hotel, the Rosslyn. Built in 1923, this vintage Beaux Arts style hotel is now designated as a historic landmark. Back then, a full roast beef lunch and a dish of ice cream cost Mr. Lee fifty cents. My dad gobbled the meal quickly.

Since Oxnard was sixty miles away from Los Angeles, on Saturday, H.K. would spend 10 cents to take a big red train to Alhambra, where he would stay the weekend to help his father run a mangle electric ironer that was used in the 1930s to iron clothes quickly. The backyard of the laundry had a huge orange grove with a few lemon trees. In the evening during blossom season, my dad could smell the blossoms for miles.

Going from Oxnard to L.A. in those days was a full day's trip. H.K. said, "It was considered quite an adventure to drive one's private car to L.A. from Oxnard. Ma went with me, and once, Uncle Yee On. She had to pack along a huge Army-issue 45 pistol. The Buick performed well for its days, sometimes even venturing up to 60 mph, but mostly in the 30s. Then we had a flat tire. Poor man (Uncle Ye On) had to walk miles to a lone ranch house and seek help. Eventually, he got some tire patches from the rancher and fixed it up himself. In the meantime, it was getting darker and darker, and we heard strange animals crying in the dusk. Big sign! Ma uncocked the 45 when we got home."

H.K. also shared colorful accounts of his time at the laundry. "Sometimes Pop would remove the tumbler from the washer and I would take a good soaking bath, as there were no bathing facilities at the Chinese School, only a toilet and a wash basin. Also, the doctor who ran the hospital had a young son, at that time a youth just going to college. They had a huge Marmon automobile that could go at a tremendous speed. He took me out riding one evening, and when the speed hit 60 miles per hour, a huge alarm bell rang. We didn't hit that speed too often!" My dad became a competitive car-racing enthusiast in his later years. There is no doubt in my mind that the then speedy Marmon automobile had something to do with his later passion for racing fast cars. He also wrote admiringly of an uncle, who worked in Alhambra. "It was quite a sight to see him run for the big red train, which sometimes didn't wait long at the stops. He was over 60 years old and sprinted like a college student track star in his black Chinese slippers!"

H.K. could visit the family home only once a year. He recalled, "In those days, I would go home only at Christmas or Thanksgiving. Once I was unable to go home and spent Thanksgiving Day alone. Mother sent to me by mail a box full of walnuts, almonds, pecans, two turkey wings and whole legs, cranberries, and buttered sweet potatoes. I took the package and went back to the lonely school and just sat on the schoolhouse sidewalk to eat it, all the time with tears coming down my face, which salted the turkey and cranberries. Lonesome boy..."

However, he wrote happily of his time in Los Angeles. Sometimes he would catch a ride on the tail end of the trucks that were loaded with grapes on Alameda Street. He would nibble along the way and, jumping off at the stop sign, grab a fistful of them for the road. Chinatown was also separated from the rest of Oxnard by the Southern Pacific main track. Often, freight cars would be shunted back and forth, holding up pedestrians for ten or more minutes. With an athletic spirit, my dad would take this opportunity to jump on the freight trains as they went by.

Los Angeles' old Chinatown used to be mainly on Alameda Street, opposite the Los Angeles Union Station, which was built in 1939. The railway station tracks sliced Chinatown into two halves. On one side, where the station is now, some of the restaurants and rooming houses were located. The other side housed herb shops, more restaurants, and poultry stores, as well as residences. Ferguson Alley ran down the center of this section. A Chinese temple was just off this small alley. Other businesses of the Chinese community were located on the east side of North L.A. Street, directly opposite the plaza. On a blocklong area of North L.A. Street were general merchandising stores, the Chinese School H.K. attended, a church, and an auto garage at the extreme southern end. Across the lot from the Chinese School was a hay market filled with truckloads of baled hay. The trucks parked there overnight, and H.K. and his friends would play there, sliding up and down the ropes. They also played softball. H.K. said, "Luckily, the best hitter was a Wong boy, whose father was one of the richer merchants. We had no problem paying for the broken windows, which ran about 25 to 50 cents per smash or home run."

Chinatown back then was somewhat large, with many lottery places and gambling houses. One of my dad's most vivid memories was of a time when a Wong man, sleepy from long hours at the gambling table where he worked as a dealer, decided to head back to his room for a nap. He inadvertently crossed in front of one of those freight trains and was killed, or, as in my dad's words, "ground to pieces of human flesh and blood." When my dad and his friends walked to school the next morning and saw the man's grisly remains, they were so unnerved that they could not eat for the rest of the day.

It would not be the last time H.K. would see blood, though. The next time, it did not bother him since it was in a hospital setting. One day before leaving Alhambra after visiting his father at the hospital, the janitor quit. H.K. was offered the janitor's job at greatly reduced pay. Since it was summer vacation and the family needed money, he took the job. Each morning, he scrubbed the surgery table, which was full of blood and more. He also swept, mopped, and dusted patient rooms, "each one of them pleasantly decorated." He said, "Several times, I would take an amputated foot or leg of a patient and chuck it down the incinerator to a roaring fire. Mopping the blood and stuff was not bad. The only time I got scared was the day before going back to school – the last day. All the time I had been working there, not one person had died, except that morning. A lady died - and when they took her away, I had to mop and clean the room. Gosh, I was scared nearly sick. But I whizzed through the chores in no time flat, packed up, and went back to L.A. for school." When there was a job to be done, my dad rose to the occasion without complaint.

That same year, my grandmother sent two of my dad's siblings, David, and Arthur to school in San Francisco. In a letter written later in his life, dated July 29, 1934, David reminisced about that time. "I remember particularly, dear brother, of the happy time we enjoyed together, particularly of the time when all the family was in Oxnard, while you alone worked hard at Wing Lee. I was then sent out by Mother to San Francisco for school. You met me at the San Francisco train station and took me to the Chung Wah School (Chinese Central High School) on Stockton Street. We played radio at night and went to the movies. One day I was ill, and you were so worried that you had to run in and out for doctors, medicines, and thousands of little things. Your affections were so great then, no less were my admirations and love toward you."

In 1919, H.K.'s eldest sister, Ann, then 17, married Yuen C. Yee in an arranged marriage in Oxnard. The couple moved to Kingman, Arizona, where they managed a store that sold products to local miners. My dad remembers jumping onto the running board of their train to go with them until his mother called to him to get off.

The following year, in 1920, my grandmother bought their house in Oxnard for $10. My dad was thirteen years old. There, my grandmother raised chickens and gathered eggs in the backyard. From 1942 to 1945, my grandmother also operated the Wong Poultry Farm in Niles, California. The farm was sizeable, with three barns, a tractor, water tank, gas tanks, and two plots for vegetables and fruit. A dog named Captain Daniel McGrew MacGlue, nicknamed Danny, was also part of the family. The family sold eggs that (by the receipt of their first sale of a dozen eggs to Walter Wong, made payable to El Wong Rancho del las Grande Heuvos y Fresno) shows they were paid $1.20 per dozen. By October 1943, eggs were being harvested from more than 6,000 chickens. In 1943, America and its Allies had also been in World War II combat for several years. That same year, my dad received a Class 2 military draft exemption, "deferred because of occupation." The family farm had grown substantially, and his mother could not manage it alone.

Even as an adult, my dad never lost his sense of commitment to his family and volunteered to help when they needed it. My grandfather noted that H.K. came to his assistance when he was in the hospital, bringing him Chinese herb soup to speed up his recovery. H.K. drove by himself from San Francisco to Los Angeles, which was an 850-mile round-trip, for four consecutive weekends to tend to his father.

H.K.'s first car, a 1917 Ford Model T Roadster, Los Angeles, August 1929. The car was started by the hand-crank in the front of the car.

H.K.'s Jaguar SS100 Roadster, July 1932. It was his fourth car, but the first of many Jaguars he owned in his lifetime. His love for sports cars suited his personality.

Alameda Street, Old Los Angeles Chinatown, circa 1933.

H.K. inoculated the chickens against chickenpox at the Wong family poultry farm in Niles, CA., in October 1943. He vaccinated 2,000 chickens in one day.

4

SAN FRANCISO CHINATOWN

My grandfather moved the family back to San Francisco in 1920. This time the family stayed there, living in Chinatown. He invested in a restaurant and worked as a bookkeeper until he retired in 1937. Two of his youngest daughters, Phoebe and Pearl, aged 12 and 16, were still at home during that time, as well as some of the boys.

They all attended the Chinese school, Chung Wah. Money was still very scarce for the family. My grandmother, however, was very resourceful. In addition to being housewife and mother to a large family, she was a savvy investor. She bought property in Oxnard, and San Francisco (at Clayton Street and Bernard Street). She also invested in the Cathay Market (Oakland) and the Acme Fish Company (Los Angeles). The family experienced discrimination on Bernard Street, too. H.K. wrote in his notes that one neighbor grumbled, "Get that durn Chinaman out of here. I don't want to see no chink."

In 1930, a year after the stock market crash, along with many others, the family struggled to make ends meet. H.K.'s parents decided to send his brothers, David and Arthur, back to China to go to school. In a letter dated July 29, 1934, that David had sent to H.K., reminding him of their earlier times together in Oxnard and San Francisco, David wrote woefully of his departure from America. "When I clasped your hand amid the blowing whistle, my eyes were full of tears and my heart was with you. You then comforted me thus: 'Go back to China and study hard. I will certainly get you boys back to this country. If you ever need money, write me and I will support you. Don't worry!' I could only nod and try my best to force back

H.K.Wong

the tears. My heart was broken! I was then only 13 and Arthur 10. Just imagine, such small children had to leave their parents and brothers and cross the immeasurable great ocean while they were in the greatest need of motherly love and care!"

By then, hard times had also hit China, and David and Arthur were forced to drop out of school to look for jobs in the city. Both believed that a better life with more opportunity was waiting for them in America and pleaded with H.K. to send them $100 in gold for a ticket to San Francisco. However, the Great Depression rendered it impossible.

The hard times in China, however, did not go unnoticed by San Francisco's Chinatown. By 1937, China struggled against the Japanese invasion in the Second Sino-Japanese War. In addition to the racial discrimination Chinese Americans faced in the U.S., many of them felt abandoned by the international community. The war against Japan in China was all but ignored by the rest of the world. However, it was important in Chinatown, especially for those with relatives in China. Stories of starving children suffering from the war inspired the community to launch the first San Francisco Chinatown Rice Bowl parade down Grant Avenue on June 19, 1938, to raise relief for China. Hanging out windows, leaning from balconies, and crowded together on the sidewalk, Chinatown residents threw money to the parade. In its first year, the Rice Bowl raised $55,000. The day's festivities included sporting events, music, theater, fashion shows, a simulated air raid, and a dragon dance. Attendees were also asked to purchase a "Humanity button" for fifty cents. Those caught not wearing the button risked a mock "trial by kangaroo court," involving voluntary judges and fines of up to $100. Locals dressed as pseudo beggars, and children riding on floats also carried alms bowls, "begging" for donations to "fill the rice bowls of China." Due to his commitment to Chinatown and philanthropic heart, as well as his love of sports, my dad served as manager of the Chinese Rice Bowl football team from 1937 to 1939. The success of the first event inspired a second one in 1940 (raising $87,000) and a third one in 1941 (raising $93,000). Later Rice Bowl games assisted regional nonprofits, including the Chung Mei Home for Chinese Boys, located in El

Cerrito, California. In the late 1930s, the Rice Bowl Club donated proceeds from its game to the Chung Mei Home's permanent scholarship fund.

Though Chinese at the time were not permitted to buy real estate in some parts of the city (especially in the Nob Hill/Russian Hill area), in 1941, Mr. and Mrs. H.M. Buckley, an Italian couple and friends of my dad and grandmother, bought a house on their behalf on Russian Hill in San Francisco. They transferred the deed to H.K.'s mother in 1945. Having grown vegetable gardens in Oxnard, after moving back to San Francisco, my grandmother continued to enjoy gardening. She grew Chinese vegetables in a side yard next to the house where she and my grandfather spent the rest of their life. She was popular with the neighbors, who affectionately nicknamed her *Lo Wong Mo.*

H.K.'s first marriage, to Lily Leong in September 1942, ended in divorce in October 1953. Lily Leong was an attractive, desirable woman with a good family background whom H.K. had regularly dated for some time. Due to this long association, H.K. felt that marrying her was a good idea. But the couple was a mismatch from the start. Though they stayed legally married for eleven years, shortly into the marriage, they both realized they had made a mistake. They had few interests in common, which in H.K.'s words, "were a continual source of irritation." They were separated many years before making the divorce final. It is not surprising that their marriage did not survive. H.K. was perpetually upbeat and positive. Constant irritation and bickering bothered him greatly. As one writer of that time described my dad, "Enthusiasm is probably the best one-word description for this ever-moving man. From the moment he hops out of bed in the morning until he drops off to sleep, he bubbles from every pore. He has almost instant recall of names and faces and often can give a name if a person is described to him. He snaps photos without flash or motor drive as fast as any newsman. He cannot remember the dollars he has loaned to many though they meet him on the street and look each other in the eye. He never brings up an unpleasant moment...any friend would readily admit that he's more bubbly than champagne and if you're engaged with him in conversation, the sooner the spontaneity rubs off, you might very easily be volunteering on his latest project."

H.K. and Lily Leong divorced in 1953, but H.K., always considerate of the welfare of others, made a provision in their divorce settlement that allowed her to live in the downstairs unit adjoining his house. Lily lived there her entire life, even after my parents' marriage. That arrangement made for some tense encounters when I was growing up because my mother and Lily Leong never got along. After my father died, Lily Leong lived in the house for 20 more years until she died as well. My parents generously never charged her rent. I never interacted with Lily Leong because she was mean-spirited, did not seem to like children, and had two huge, ferocious dogs.

In 1946, my dad purchased an apartment building with 15 units on Leavenworth Street. My future mother, Honey Quan, and her brother, Bill, were tenants there. By the early 1950s, Honey had become an apartment manager for the building. H.K. and Honey had known each other since he first saw her on the Grant Avenue street corner in 1940. They had begun to play tennis together and shared many common interests, including a fondness for sports cars. Unlike Lily, Honey was spirited and smart, with a strong, lively personality. My mother had been romantically interested in my dad since the first day they met. On September 5, 1942, the day he married Lily Leong, she wrote in her diary, "Mr. H.K. Wong was married to Lily Leong today. It was a sad day for me."

Fifteen years later, however, on April 15, 1957, Honey married H.K. She was 39 years old and he was 50. By that time, my dad was so well-known in Chinatown that to have been married there would have required an enormous wedding at considerable expense. Instead, they decided to quietly slip away with two friends and got married in Hawaii. H.K.'s youngest sister, Phoebe, was their maid of honor. Dooley Kam, a Bank of Hawaii executive and regional tennis champion, was their best man. Peter Abenheim, known for his role as "Captain Fortune" in a popular 1950s KPIX children's television show, "The Captain Fortune Show," escorted Honey down the aisle. H.K. and Honey spent their honeymoon on Maui. On their return to San Francisco, they had a second reception for their friends at the Kuo Wah Restaurant.

H.K. at Portsmouth Square, San Francisco, November 1934.

H.K. and first wife Lily Leong at the Bal Tabarin Theater Restaurant, San Francisco, September 1943. The Bal Tabarin was a popular nightclub on Columbus Avenue in the 1930s and 1940s. Their marriage lasted for eleven years, but they were a mismatch from the start.

San Francisco Chinatown, for *Chinatown News*, January 1938. Plans to repaint all the bamboo-shaped streetlight standards like this one in the Chinatown section of Grant Avenue were announced by the Downtown Association in conjunction with the general campaign to beautify San Francisco in preparation for the Golden Gate International Exposition.

H.K. and his brothers at his home on Bernard Street: (back, L-R) Robert, David; (front, L-R) George, Harry, H.K., Arthur. Circa 1950.

H.K. and Honey in my dad's Jaguar XK120 at the Palace of Fine Arts, circa 1954. My parents' love of sports cars drew them together.

H.K. and Honey after playing tennis in Golden Gate Park, circa 1955. My parents' love for tennis also attracted them to each other.

H.K. and Honey's wedding at the Hawaiian Village, April 15, 1957. Peter Abenheim (Captain Fortune) walked Honey down the aisle, H.K.'s sister Phoebe was maid of honor, and Dooley Kam was best man.

H.K. and Honey were married on April 15, 1957 in Honolulu, Hawaii. On their return to San Francisco, they had a second wedding reception at the Kuo Wah restaurant.

5

THE QUAN FAMILY

When he was only seventeen years old, in 1898, Honey's father, Quan Chin, arrived in San Francisco from Canton, China. Honey said that in reflective moments, with a shot glass in hand over a bowl of rice, he would recount his story of crossing over the Pacific on the Japanese ship Maru, and the "hardships, loneliness, and courage" he faced leaving home. Though he spoke no English when he arrived, he stayed abreast of current affairs by reading Chinese newspapers and magazines. Working as a family cook, he also saved money and survived the 1906 earthquake. He returned to China, where he was matched with a Chinese girl, Talana Wong. She lived in Hong Kong with family servants, was five feet tall, and had jet-black hair and extremely fair skin. Talana was schooled in the traits of being a "lady" and hoped to meet and marry a wealthy gentleman. Her marriage was likely arranged to Quan Chin because he was viewed as a man of means (as he had been to what they thought of as "Gum Sahn," Gold Mountain). The opposite was true, but there was no turning back when they left China in 1910.

Arriving in the U.S., at age 17, Talana had to quickly learn housekeeping skills. She had never even used a broom. The years of scrubbing, washing, and ironing that followed gave her strong muscles. These proved useful in San Francisco - she was able to fend off muggers.

Returning to the U.S. with his new bride, Quan Chin was rehired by his former employers, the Schmidt family, as the family cook. They lived in a large house on Selby Lane, Atherton, California, an area known for its wealth. At the Atherton estate, a winding driveway led past the house to

H.H.Wong

a large barn that housed a black electric car with glass windows and their Hupmobile. Old photos show Honey's dad in a starched white shirt and dark pants standing on the running board of the impressive automobile. Quan Chin's employer renamed Honey's parents James and Kate Quan. James had three brothers and one sister. His older brother also came to the U.S. and became the cook for a family in Woodside, California.

The Quan's first son, Charles (Chaz), was born in 1914; then William (Bill) in 1916; daughter Honey in 1918; Atherton (Hap) in 1920; and Richard (Rich) in 1923. In notes my mom kept, she said that she considered herself the "ham" in the family, sandwiched between two brothers on each side. As for the origins of her name, she wrote, "Father felt sorry that I was a girl-child, so he favored me with Honey. In China in the old days, they used to drown girls because girls would grow up, marry, and leave home, thus no help to the family."

Honey's mom, Kate, raised pigs in the backyard for a few extra dollars. Sometime in the mid-20s, the employer's son bought the Quans a lot on Nimitz Avenue. Shortly after, they built a small bungalow with a detached garage. The need for money was always present. Kate got a summer job at Chew's Cannery in Mayfield peeling fruit. Every day, she and the other women workers would climb up a short ladder into a wooden covered wagon, bundling together on its wooden slats. From the employer's home, James and Kate Quan would also take the family to San Francisco on the train, go to dinner, attend Chinese Opera, and stay overnight. Every two years, they would have a family portrait taken at May's Studio on Sacramento Street in San Francisco, dressed in their finest clothes. Honey's mother made beautiful dresses of Chinese silk, sewing them on a treadle sewing machine. She would accent them by wearing shiny black patent-leather heels. Her talent as a seamstress later led her to employment in a sewing factory.

James Quan was a fine self-taught cook. On any given day, the aromas wafting out of his kitchen would entice everyone to move in that direction. He made roasted turkeys doused in cranberry sauce, crumbly pies, light ladyfingers, and mouth-watering meringue popovers topped with melted butter and strawberry jam that were, as Honey would say, "this side of heaven." Quan passed his cooking skills to his second son, Bill, who would bake delicious pumpkin pies for the extended Quan family every year for our holiday gatherings.

In 1931, Honey was the only Chinese child to graduate from Las Lomitas Elementary School in Atherton. She then attended Sequoia High School in Redwood City, graduating at the top of her class in June 1935. One of Honey's treasured mementoes is a panoramic photograph of her entire student body in 1935, with her sitting front and center, and the back of the photo signed by 30 of her classmates.

Her academic achievement qualified Honey to continue her education at U.C. Berkeley. She was able to have access to higher education and attend these fine schools due to her father's employer. Prejudice and bias were words Honey never knew until she attended U.C. Berkeley and went looking for housing. At 16, after being turned down or having doors slammed in her face, she was one of two young women accepted at the International House. The other student was Japanese.

For a couple of years in the early 1940s, Honey was Secretary to Charlie Low, owner of the Forbidden City night club. During WWII, Honey worked as a clerk and administrative assistant at the Alameda Naval Air Station to support the war effort. She learned touch-typing and stenography, skills that served her well in later years. Her diary and notes were filled with numerous shorthand notations.

At the end of WWII, Honey decided to pursue a career in merchandising, first at H. Leibes on Grant Avenue, handling mail orders and complaints, and then as a clerk in the shoe department at Saks Fifth Avenue across the street. She was shortly promoted to an assistant in the dress/gown salon on the second floor, which included managing inventory, mark-ups, mark-downs, and transfers. She also conducted weekly fashion shows at the Fairmont Hotel in San Francisco, Circus Club in Menlo Park, Meadow Club in Fairfax, and with Sophie's, Dior, and other designers at various local hotels – plus Elizabeth Arden's on Sutter Street, with its famous big red door. A huge black iron gate and a well-tended flower garden flanked each side of the brick walkway to the entrance of Elizabeth Arden. Customers spending a day there got a special beauty treatment from head to toenails. Honey's niece, Sue Fawn Chung, remembers the high standards held by Elizabeth Arden. Laughing, she reminisced, "Whenever I'd join my Aunt Honey for lunch, I couldn't meet her at Elizabeth Arden without wearing a shade of Elizabeth Arden lipstick. When I asked my aunt why it was important that I always wear Elizabeth Arden lipstick, she said, 'They know their colors.' It surprised me that they knew their product well enough to tell if I was wearing it or not."

As Honey later said, "Elizabeth Arden was a jewel box boutique, housing her cosmetics, accessories, dresses, a body department/exercise pool on the second floor, and hair salon. Elizabeth Arden was also a great lady in every sense – her dress, her demeanor, and her expectations of our behavior were nothing less than her standards for herself. For me, it was a great learning experience, especially the switchboard that nearly cost me my job. I would inadvertently push the key in the wrong direction – and either listen in on a conversation, ring in someone's ear, or pull a cord and disconnect my boss. These systems of the '50s and '60s have been replaced by automated ones."

Honey took a break from the fashion business from 1959 to 1968 to assist my dad as a bookkeeper at the Ti Sun Company Hardware and Furniture Store. She re-entered the fashion business in 1969, starting as a head cashier at Peck and Peck, a woman's specialty shop that had just opened in downtown San Francisco. By 1972, she became manager of the store, reporting business operations to the headquarters in New York City. It was during her years of working in the fashion industry that my mother developed her sophisticated style. Her wardrobe was filled with elegant clothes, and she was always fashionably dressed for events and parties.

Though my father was probably well acquainted with the prejudice of his time and encountered discrimination, he never let it quell his enthusiasm for bridging the gap between all people, regardless of race or background. Writing this book tells my father's story and pays homage to his legacy; it is also my way of unveiling the 800+ years of my heritage, as well as shedding light on what is likely a similar story for many Chinese American families. Sorting through countless boxes of articles, letters, interviews, and memorabilia evokes memories of my early years and the annual family gatherings we would have with my closer aunts, uncles, and cousins. Eventually, the family just got too large to get together. Now, all the elder generation has passed on. As my mother would say, "Some people have greatness…some people have greatness thrust upon them…and some people find greatness." My father had all of these, tenfold.

Grandfather Quan Chin, AKA James Quan,
circa 1915.

Grandparents Kate and James Quan with daughter Honey (my mother, age 2), circa 1920.

Kate and James Quan with
Atherton (Hap, age 2),
Charlie (Chaz, age 8),
Honey (age 4),
and William (Bill, age 6),
circa 1922.

Las Lomitas Elementary School 8th-grade class: Honey, the only Chinese American in her class (2nd row, 3rd from right), circa 1931.

Honey Quan, circa 1943. Photo by Raymond's Studio.

6

THE ADOPTION

"I was chosen, I was wanted,
I was cherished, I grew in their hearts,
I was the missing piece, I was loved,
I was adopted."

- Unknown

An aged document, yellowed with time, tells the story of my adoption by H.K. and Honey on August 15, 1963. My date of birth is listed as September 22, 1957; place of birth, unknown; present address, Children's Institution; and Custodian, Superintendent of Institution. I have no information about where I was born, nor any recollection of my birth parents. What I do know is that on the afternoon of August 19, 1959, when I was about two years old, I was found by the police wandering the streets of Kowloon, Hong Kong, and taken to Po Leung Kuk orphanage in Happy Valley. For three months, efforts to trace my birth parents through radio broadcasts and newspaper advertisements were unsuccessful. I was declared abandoned.

Clinical psychologist LaVay Lau, Ph.D., a social worker at the orphanage, remembers my story vividly. She said I was distressed, crying, and terrified when they found me. Thin and weak, with sores covering my head, I was first admitted to a hospital for treatment. About a month later, I was discharged and placed in a children's orphanage, in a ward with thirty-three boys and girls, ages four to six. The matron of the orphanage named me Kwong Wah Bun. The ward was crowded, severe, and dimly lit. We rose at 7:00 am for a breakfast of milk, bread or crackers, and congee, a pudding-like rice porridge. Kindergarten started at 8:30 am, with lunch at noon, and a required nap at 3:00 pm. The ward's beds were nothing but mats on a wooden plank, with only a foot of space between each bed.

H.K.Wong

Children dressed alike, in baggy blue-denim uniforms. While in the ward, we were not allowed to mingle or play freely, but if the weather was good, we had an hour of free play outside. Supper was served at 5:00 pm, after which we were confined to our beds for two hours before bedtime. A housemother with no previous training or supervision policed us, often shouting to keep us docile, quiet, and obedient. Apparently, I did not have a warm relationship with her because she did not encourage closeness. Given no resources to manage the ward, she resorted to policing and discipline.

The orphanage had more girls than boys. Abandoned Chinese boys were rare. It was by the stroke of good fortune or fate that Dr. Lau first met me. She was checking on a little girl who was on her case list for adoption. That little girl was in the bed next to mine. I locked eyes with Lau, and she took an immediate interest in me. My first request to her was for a toy telephone.

When Dr. Lau first inquired about my adoptability, the orphanage staff told her to forget about me. They said that I had bloody stools, was malnourished, and cried inconsolably for hours for my lost family/ caregiver. I was apathetic and unhappy. When workers visited, rather than respond to them, I would just dolefully stare at them or answer questions in an emotionless way. I also had difficulty sleeping, disturbed by nightmares that would wake me in the middle of the night. I ate poorly and was irritable, losing my temper easily. To their way of thinking, I was unadoptable.

However, it is to Dr. Lau's credit that I was adopted into a loving family and am writing this book--because she believed otherwise. She took a risk and requested instead that they release me to her. She told the orphanage staff that she was going to take me to the park. The orphanage agreed to release me to her. Instead of the park, Lau took me to the hospital. She told me when she carried me to the hospital, I was so weak, I could barely walk. She said, "You were as light as a feather, weighing not much more than 25 pounds at age four. It is good that you have no memory of this nightmarish experience." She immediately arranged a meeting with the chief of pediatrics at Queen Mary Hospital because the doctors at the orphanage had been either uninterested in treating me or incapable of knowing how sick I was. Dr. Lau told the doctor that she had a desperately sick boy and mentioned that she was from the orphanage but could not pay for treatment. The doctor generously agreed to do a diagnostic. It turns out that what was thought to be a systemic disease was simply rectal polyps, easily removed.

On May 29, 1961, I was declared eligible for adoption, but it would take another year before I was truly ready. The ward's documentation notes that my disposition and social interactions were lighter and happier by November 1962, when the Social Welfare department referred me to the International Social Service (ISS).

"His speech is clear and distinct, and he is very verbal. He is an interesting child – sensitive, intelligent, and very responsive and affectionate. He plays well with other children. One of his good friends is a six-year-old girl in the same ward. If the others make fun of her for any reason, he shows concern for her feelings and tries to comfort her. He is very enthusiastic about learning to write, and his first request when he saw a worker was to ask for a pencil and paper so he could show her a new Chinese character that he had learned. He has an excellent appetite and demonstrated when taken to lunch that he can eat as much as an adult. However, he is not eating to his capacity since the institutional food is not always palatable or adequate. He is very enthusiastic about the possibility of adoption, although his concept of what this means is limited because of his age."

That same year, Marjorie Montelius, executive director of the United Crusade-supported International Institute in San Francisco, took over as director of the Hong Kong office of the International Social Service (ISS). The purpose of the Hong Kong office was to find adoptive homes for Chinese orphans ranging in age from infancy to adolescence. These children, of which I was one, were abandoned by the poorest of the three million Chinese refugees who were streaming at the time into Hong Kong and left to fend for themselves on the street. They were then taken into institutions until homes could be found for them by the ISS. Montelius noted during the time period in which I was adopted, "The adopting parents include humanitarian people in all walks of life who have been moved by the plight of these children."

Initially, Dr. Lau placed me temporarily in foster care with a British couple who had two young children of their own. When she checked up on me during a follow-up visit a week later, she noted that I was not only sturdier, I was more animated and emotionally expressive. I had smiled brightly at her and said, "Miss Lau, I am happy."

On March 6, 1963, Dr. Lau wrote, "Wah Bun is a loveable, appealing youngster, who is warm and accessible to relationships. He enjoys physical attention and is openly affectionate. He is an intelligent child who displays no special problems at present and is suitable for adoption."

Looking through files of prospective adoptive parents, Dr. Lau had found H.K. and Honey. At the time, she had no idea that they were friends with her brother, Merton, and sister-in-law, Claire. Though H.K. by that time was already quite involved in public activities, my parents' primary motivation for adopting me was not humanitarianism. In fact, it was highly personal. Honey could not conceive children. She and H.K. were looking for a boy, ideally not a baby. I was a perfect fit. My healthier, happier self was renamed Wesley Robert Wong and sent from Hong Kong to live with the Wongs in San Francisco. I was given the nickname, "Waby," I believe as a contraction of Wesley Robert that sounded close to my Chinese name. I also had difficulty saying my English name. I quickly outgrew this nickname.

At the time of my adoption, Honey was 45 and H.K. was 56. Though the home study conducted by the ISS noted that they were older than most adoptive parents, it also noted that they were energetic, unusually resilient, and had great stamina - or as my mother put it, they were "young in spirit." In an assessment of their suitability for adoption, one writer said of my father, "it is difficult to believe that he is 56 because of his childlike nature, vitality, energy, and enthusiasm."

One reference for H.K. and Honey as good potential adoptive parents read, "I could go on and on saying why I think the Wongs are ideally suited to become parents, but I am afraid if I do, the sheer volume of praise would discredit and 'water down' statements I have already given. I do not wish to appear someone who deals in superlatives, because I am not. The Wongs are wonderful people who would make wonderful parents...." As their child, I can unequivocally say that this was true.

Shortly after I was adopted, my mom noticed that I kept mentioning Lau's first name (LaVay) to her. I had become quite attached to LaVay at the orphanage and missed her. Puzzled why I was so fixated on one specific person, my mom wrote to the orphanage to find out who LaVay was, but by that time, she had already returned to the U.S. and was living in Hawaii. So, the orphanage forwarded the letter to her. When LaVay wrote back, my mom looked at the return address from Hawaii; to her surprise, she realized it was the address of Merton and Claire Lau, close friends who my parents had known years before the adoption. Merton was LaVay's brother. This unlikely connection signaled to my mom that my adoption to her and my dad was destined.

In Chinese culture, elder men are often referred to as "Uncle," so H.K. had always been known as "Uncle H.K." In his daily diary in 1963, directly following my adoption, my dad made an entry in his diary that read, "I no longer have to refer to myself as 'Uncle H.K.' Now I can call myself 'Dad.'" He was proud of the new distinction.

My parents considered adopting a second child. They had installed a bunk bed at the house. When I was about seven years old, my mother asked me if I would like a brother or a sister. Matter-of-factly, I told her no, that I was a "lucky boy" and did not need either. She listened to me, which is why I remained an only child. Due to my parents' large network of friends and their involvement in the community, I got to do a lot of things growing up that my friends did not get to do. My parents treated me as an adult. I attended many community events and dinner parties and interacted with a lot of adults. Whenever we went out to dinner, I ordered off the adult menu. My parents were amazed at how much I could eat and remain skinny. I was happy with my new life.

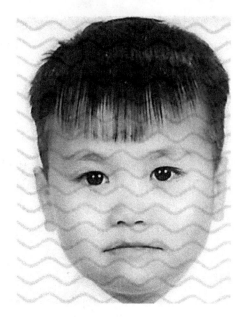

Wesley's passport photo as Kwong Wah Bun, August 1963.

I met my dad for the first time at the San Francisco International Airport on August 15, 1963, and picked out a Mickey Mouse coloring book that night.

My family celebrated outside the San Francisco courthouse after my adoption to Honey and H.K was finalized on February 15, 1964. It was a cold day, and my parents were very stylish. Photo by Sid Tate, *S.F. Nob Hill Call Bulletin*.

With my mother in Sacramento, sitting on my dad's Jaguar XK150 coupe, circa 1964. I rode in the back well of that car for a couple of years until I got too big, and my dad sold it for a Ford Thunderbird.

7

BUSINESSMAN
AND
ENTREPRENEUR

After its establishment in 1848 as the oldest Chinatown in the U.S., San Francisco Chinatown was captivating to curious outsiders. It also gave insular comfort to residents. Following a visit to Dupont Street (now Grant Avenue) in the 1880s, novelist Rudyard Kipling had called San Francisco Chinatown "a ward of the city of Canton set down in the most eligible business quarter of the place."

My dad was a consummate businessman, a focus that began when he was quite young. Whenever opportunity knocked, H.K. was always the first to "answer the door," especially in his beloved Chinatown. From 1921 to 1932, he worked for Wing Lee Hardware and Furniture Store in San Francisco, first as an apprentice and clerk, and later as a buyer. For a short while, from 1938 to 1939, he also worked as a teller at the Bank of Canton. Located in the oldest Asian-style structure in Chinatown and decorated with a three-tiered pagoda, the Bank of Canton was a stately place. Its president thought a career in banking would be a good match for my dad because H.K. was a gifted salesman. The bank president offered to train my dad, who told him that if after two years he still liked the job, he could continue in banking. But as H.K. neared two years in banking, he realized it was not a good fit for him. He told the bank president, "I like business, but I would rather count money that is mine than other people's money." The Bank of Canton president told him he could return at any time for more pay, and if there was anything he needed, to come back and ask for it.

H.H.Wong

Six months later, H.K. returned to the bank, but not as an employee. My dad asked for his first loan of $4,000 to buy his mother a house – and he received it. This knowledge of finance would become a cornerstone for the success of businesses my dad later built.

On March 16, 1940, H.K. became co-owner of the Ti Sun Hardware Company, where he worked for the next thirty years. An article in *Hardware Age*, July 1942, wrote glowingly of H.K.'s new endeavor. "H.K. Wong, in age and spirit a member of the young Chinese colony welded to the American tradition, quit his job as a teller in the local bank. With four other principal partners, some of them older, G.W. Wong, D.H. Po, Der Sang, and B.H. Chan, he has formed the Ti Sun Company to deal in hardware, housewares, and furniture."

In Herb Caen's column on February 18, 1947 in the *San Francisco Chronicle*, Caen mentioned that H.K. was interviewed on a national radio broadcast and was asked what Ti Sun meant in English. H.K. had explained, "It means The Big New Store." Caen also wrote, "The other day Wong received a letter from Texas delivered promptly. Written on the envelope was simply: 'The Big New Store, San Francisco.'"

Opening first as a small store, Ti Sun Company was located at 1005 Grant Avenue. In addition to living- and dining-room furniture, the company carried bedding, radios, television equipment, floor coverings (including imports), rugs, and lamps. It was successful and quickly outgrew its location. Within six months, a second store at 1123 Grant Avenue was opened for the company's expanding furniture business.

My dad and his staff worked long hours, from 10:00 am to 9:00 pm, but closed at noon for half an hour and at supper time for an hour. All store employees could eat free meals provided by the store cook. Snacks were also provided after hours. Of the wide selection of furniture and appliances sold at Ti Sun Company, home appliances were the most widely sold. Within one year, the company was highly prosperous. One journalist for the industry publication, *Hardware Age*, likened the Ti Sun Hardware Company to "Jack in the Beanstalk on Vitamin B-1." Why was Ti Sun Company such an immediate success? I believe it was due to my dad's likeability, ingenuity, and understanding of people and their needs. Contributing to my dad's success was also his constant contact with business associates, customers, and friends. In his daily diaries, almost every page contained a phone number or business card of the people he needed to call.

In the article, "Ranges to Chinese Americans: San Francisco's Ti Sun Company Combines Occidental and Oriental Know-How in its Successful Store," written by H.O. Andrew for the July 1950 magazine, *Gas Appliance Merchandising*, H.K.'s success in marketing and selling gas ranges to Chinese Americans was featured. Editor H.O. Andrew noted that H.K. Wong and his partners had many "firsts" in Chinatown. The Ti Sun Hardware Company was the first store in Chinatown devoted exclusively to appliances and home furnishings. It was the first to stock rugs and have a children's nursery department. It was also the first appliance dealer in Chinatown to implement installment-plan buying – and it was the first business to offer free delivery service on appliances, extending as far south as Salinas and Watsonville, and as far north as California's capitol, Sacramento. Consistent advertising was also placed in the *Chinese Press*, America's only English-language Chinese newspaper at the time, and aired on radio KSAN during its Chinese hour.

My dad knew that after WWII, modernizing homes was becoming a trend in the Chinese American community. Gas furnaces were replacing hot-water tanks, and new kitchens were being remodeled with gas ranges. Chinese families were moving outside Chinatown, but they still frequented the shops and food markets there. In the past, Chinese cooks had not needed refrigeration because they bought and ate everything the same day. But some of their new homes were now outside Chinatown, making buying fresh produce every day difficult. This meant that refrigerator sales increased--and, though Chinese cooks did not bake cakes and pies, they did cook large roasts, the top of the range being their main cooking area. At first, the elder Chinese cooks did not like the flat grill on the Wedgewood range top. They had no need for it, since they did not fry steaks and chops, nor make pancake breakfasts. With some instruction and persistence, however, H.K. taught Chinese cooks that the grill could be used to simmer soups, steam vegetables, and keep food hot. Since Chinese soups could simmer up to 12 hours, the grill became quite handy. My dad's salespeople and maintenance workers understood and sold their products well – and my dad was a great salesman. He could give any objection a positive result. One industry magazine article drew attention to his business philosophy. "Mr. Wong is a stickler for service and, even though the manufacturer's guarantee may have run out six months before, he is always more than willing to send his service men out on calls because he says it shows Ti Sun Company's good will and his customers will think kindly and well of his firm, and return for other merchandise when they are in the market again."

H.K. recognized early on that Chinatown was ripe for social and economic development. By the early 1950s, the Ti Sun Company had become an anchor business in Chinatown. As a co-owner of the company, H.K. was keenly interested in building his business as well as elevating the image of Chinatown as a safe place to shop and dine. To that end, in 1953, he became Director of the Chinatown Chamber of Commerce, a position he held in 1953-1954, 1956-1957, and 1959-1960. Since he was inspired to build success for all of Chinatown, H.K. decided that cooperation between businesses there would be a good idea. Larger businesses could lend marketing savvy, business acumen, and support to the smaller ones. As Director of the Chinatown Chamber of Commerce, in 1954, H.K. founded the Upper Grant Avenue Merchants Association.

In an article written by Irene Hammond Corpe in 1958, the journalist also observed that winning a prize in a gas range competition required knowledge of selling techniques and products. This was certainly true of the awards my dad won in hardware marketing, promotions, and creative window display design.

In the fall of 1951, the Ping Yuen Housing Project was approved for funding under the Housing Act of 1949 at the cost of $3.4 million. A three-building project on Pacific Avenue between Kearny Street and Powell Street, Ping Yuen was the first U.S. federally funded housing project for the Chinese in America. The Ti Sun Company was given the opportunity to outfit a model apartment with Heywood-Wakefield Modern furniture at the newly completed Ping Yuen building. My dad received top recognition for furnishing and decorating its model apartment. On October 21, 1951, the first building designated as Central Ping Yuen was completed and dedicated in a ceremony. H.K. welcomed the Mayor of San Francisco, George Christopher, and his wife with a cup of tea at a housewarming during the dedication ceremony. A full-page spread in the December 1951 issue of Heywood-Wakefield's company magazine includes photos of the model apartment, elegantly appointed with Chinese decorations and accessories. Ti Sun furnished many of the apartment units, as the furniture store was conveniently located just around the corner from the housing complex. Much to the delight of the Heywood-Wakefield Modern Company, thousands of people visited the model apartment. East and West Ping Yuen were completed in 1956, and a fourth building, Ping Yuen Annex, was added in 1961 at the cost of $2.3 million. H.K. also commissioned a mural depicting one hundred years of Chinese American history, 5 ft. x 1.5 ft., to be placed at the Ping Yuen housing project. In 1952, the Chinatown Committee, an organization founded to better conditions in Chinatown, awarded my dad a "Pailou Award" for his work on the Ping Yuen Housing Project.

That same year, H.K. was appointed Director of the Gas Appliance Society of Northern California, Pacific Gas and Electricity (PG&E). He was the first Chinese American businessman to receive this distinction. The role gave him firsthand knowledge of a two-month campaign in 1955 that the organization launched to acquaint the public with their new line of 1955 gas ranges. In May of that year, in conjunction with its "Around the World Free with T.W.A. Contest," the Gas Appliance Society of California sponsored a window display contest for all appliance dealers. The San Francisco unit of the Gas Appliance Society of California invited area gas-range dealers to participate in the contest, among them the Ti Sun Company. My dad was delighted. He loved competitions, especially ones that exercised his creativity. Dealers were challenged with "calling the public's attention to the quality, beauty, performance, economy, and time-saving qualities" of the new gas ranges. Major gas range manufacturers were pouring big money into the "Around the World Free with T.W.A. Contest" to induce people to go into dealers' showrooms. To enter the drawing, people went to any gas range dealer displaying the "Around the World" sign, selected the range model they wanted, wrote the model number on an entry form, and gave it to the dealer. First prize for one lucky winner was an around-the-world free trip via TWA and a deluxe gas range. Second prize was a new kitchen, complete with a range, refrigerator, and dryer, plus painting and redecoration of the kitchen. Ten other winners would receive a new deluxe gas range of their choice.

The Ti Sun Company, in addition to showcasing the new Rheem-Wedgewood gas ranges in its window display, contrasted them with cooking equipment from around the world. My dad took charge of designing the display, with artwork help from Peter Lewis of the Repair Department and my dad's brother, Arthur Wong, of the Stove Sales Department. Chinese characters were brushed by Tom Wong of Furniture Sales, and the background and other details were coordinated by Warren Lee of the Appliance Department. Sand filled out the display, scooped off the beaches of San Francisco. My dad even put my young cousin to work finding empty crates on the street, which were crafted into the stove of India. Gas Appliance Society posters, TWA travel posters, bilingual signs, and brushed Chinese characters were placed throughout the display. Paintings of Chinese and American food cooked on the range were also displayed. Four red Chinese lanterns hung above the exhibit, with the words, "Fly Around the World" superimposed on them. The window display featured a Chinese brick- and straw-burning stove, a type still used at the time. Another part of the window displayed a Japanese charcoal-burning hibachi, a traditional cookstove of Japan. A third part showed a mud-covered, dung-burning stove used in the villages of India, and a fourth, a Hawaiian rock pit surrounded by fresh fruit, vegetables, a waving palm tree, oriental jug, and other accessories. The realistic replicas were carefully constructed by Ti Sun Company staff and rendered with full attention to detail. The cost of making the display was negligible: 50 cents for a can of paint; 20 cents for plaster; 20 cents for a wire screen;

and $1.00 for Chinese vegetables, which were replaced every three days. But Campbell-Ewald, the advertising agency for Rheem-Wedgewood Gas Ranges, was suspicious about the Chinese characters my dad had added to the giant billboard on Columbus Avenue. One Campbell-Ewald advertising executive on his way to lunch in Chinatown was surprised to see Chinese characters inscribed across a billboard the agency had prepared entirely in English. My dad and a friend had sneaked out in the night and written the Chinese characters on the billboard. Suspecting foul play or sabotage, Campbell-Ewald contacted a translator, who assured them the characters read, "Ti Sun Company – Your Chinatown Agent – Very Reasonable Prices." According to H.K.'s philosophy of Confucius, "Good local tie-in gets more mileage out of manufacturer's campaign." My dad was very savvy, because half of Chinatown's population did not read English. The inscribed message was bringing in customers.

When the top dealer window display award was announced, the Ti Sun Company had won it due to their "selling value, originality, arrangement, and adherence to campaign theme and contest rules." The top dealers' prize was an all-expense-paid weekend trip to Las Vegas, Nevada, courtesy of Trans World Airlines (TWA). Arthur Wong (H.K.'s brother and a department manager for the Ti Sun Company), and his wife, Linda, accepted the award. In a letter written June 1, 1955, the General Manager for Rheem Wedgewood Manufacturing Company wrote to H.K., "We hope your award will bring additional success to your sales efforts."

As an enthusiastic journalist at the time for the newspaper, the *Chinese World*, H.K. wrote in his longstanding column, "H.K.'s Corner," about Arthur and Linda Wong's trip. His observations were characteristic of his vigorous, colorful writing style.

> "The hot sun and ever-present sand outside are in direct contrast to the clean, cool, air-conditioned interior of the many famous establishments in Las Vegas – an atmosphere of opulence, plush, plush, and swank. There, the curious, the hopeful, the reckless, and the experts try to match their skill and luck against the house. Casually dressed

folk, suave gentlemen, gingham-dressed housewives, and exquisitely Dior-gowned women rub elbows at the tables. They wander in and out of the big casinos with gleams in their eyes for a hopeful grab at Miss Fortune. Into this mad, gay whirl recently went Appliance Manager Art Wong and his wife, Linda...they were given the royal treatment...a merry-go-round of reception, entertainment, and sightseeing that left them starry-eyed during their stay at the booming city."

The following month, in July 1955, the Ti Sun Company also took first place in a national linoleum window display, the Congoleum-Nairn National Gold Seal Window Display Contest, garnering "Best in the Far West," which covered seven western states. The staff had imaginatively arranged rolls of linoleum flooring against a Chinese background, which had immediately caught the judges' eye. The Ti Sun Company was presented with a $250 check and a trophy. Additionally, Congoleum-Nairn Inc., New Jersey, awarded H.K. with a 21-inch RCA Compatible Color TV set for also winning its best display photo contest.

Another impressive window display that generated attention in 1955 was one that featured the tools and products of *Popular Mechanics* magazine advertisers, resulting in record sales in those lines. The Ti Sun Company was sent a window-trim kit by *Popular Mechanics*. A poster with images of salespeople selling the tools and products of *Popular Mechanics* advertisers was in the trim set. The Ti Sun Company altered the clerks' faces on the poster, turning their images into Chinese salesmen wearing mandarin hats. In the background of the window display, the Ti Sun Company posed a giant figure of Confucius--an oil painting made by one of its clerks. In keeping with H.K.'s business focus, the Chinese saying, "Confucius says, He who wishes to do better work should first possess the best tools" was brushed in bold, black Chinese characters on orange paper and placed next to the image of Confucius, whose fingers pointed toward a *Popular Mechanics* "Do It Yourself" poster.

In a letter dated August 29, 1955, H.K. wrote to Mr. Clover L. Perkins,

Advertising Manager of *Popular Mechanics*, that 40% of the 30,000 people living in Chinatown did not speak English, and of those who did, the majority were bilingual. He said that this was why his window display had exhibited Chinese characters alongside the English signs provided by *Popular Mechanics*. Thousands of people visited Chinatown daily, and many of them only spoke Chinese, while others who were bilingual preferred it. My dad was a sharp businessman and knew his audience and how to reach them. Following installation of the window display, Ti Sun Company staff noticed an increase in the number of inquiries about the products. Out of 2,000 entries, the Ti Sun Company won an Excellence in Hardware award for this display.

The July-August 1950 issue of *Ford Truck Times* praised my dad's decision to buy one of their trucks in an article on the Ti Sun Company with a photograph of my dad in the truck along with four Chinese showgirls. "Henry K. Wong started his Ti Sun furniture and hardware company 10 years ago in a small cubicle in San Francisco Chinatown. Since that time, Wong has built his firm into being the largest of that type in the colorful community, and at one time or another has served every one of its 30,000 inhabitants. For years Wong thought contract haulers were the most economical means of moving his merchandise – that is, until a salesman from S&C Motors, San Francisco Ford dealer, sold him on a trim van. Now he considers the truck his number one advertisement as well as a big money saver. The letters on the truck are trimmed in fluorescent gold and glow on the darkest nights. The young women are from Charlie Low's famous Forbidden City, a Chinatown night club."

Hoffman Television was one of the early developers of the color television for the U.S. market. In 1955, Hoffman selected the Ti Sun Company for the premiere display of their latest and most advanced color television because of the large number of TV set owners in San Francisco and their intense interest in color TV. Color TV was a novelty, and color broadcasts were quite limited in the 1950s. Sales for color TVs did not take off until the 1960s, when NBC greatly expanded their color broadcasts.

On April 29, 1964, H.K. renovated and re-opened the Ti Sun Company as a hardware, homeware, and furniture center with twenty employees. Realizing how valuable his pickup truck had been to the company, my dad bought a second one.

Business was prosperous from the 1950s through the mid-1960s. By the end of the 1960s, U.S. economic growth was slowing, and inflation was rising. People were spending less on home furnishings. In 1968, the Ti Sun Company was downsized, and the furniture portion at 1133 Grant Avenue was leased to the Three Star Bakery. My mother, Honey, was manager of the bakery for two years and assisted them in setting up the shop, ordering supplies, and handling the main sales and promotions. I have fond memories of rushing to the bakery after school at Jean Parker Elementary to sample all the pastries. After 30 years of success with the Ti Sun Company, my dad sold his share of the business to a dedicated employee, Leland Dea, and his wife, May Dea.

From 1972 to 1980, my dad partnered with H.M. Frank Lim as co-owner of the Endico Corporation, the parent corporation for a building-supply business. The company developed and operated the Polk/Pacific Building Supply at 1555 Pacific Avenue, San Francisco, the first Chinese-owned large-scale building materials supplier in the U.S. The Polk/Pacific Building Supply served the whole range of buyers, from individual do-it-yourself home-repairers to apartment managers and giant contractors. It was twice the size of the Ti Sun Company, with 10,000 sq. ft. of retail space. The Endico Corporation also leased space to commercial clients one block away at 1476 Pacific Avenue. On the second-floor mezzanine of the warehouse building, they leased office space – and, on August 8, 1975, except for a small area reserved for offices on the ground floor and a walk-in refrigerator space in the basement, they leased much of the ground floor to a then little-known wholesale bakery called "Just Desserts." The baked goods company grew into a famous San Francisco icon, serving up unparalleled, mouth-watering desserts baked 100% from scratch. Their chocolate fudge cake and carrot cake covered in cream cheese frosting, and their sponge cake slathered with a cherry-liquor-spiked dark-chocolate ganache, were legendary. To this day, Just Desserts is still in operation.

In keeping with modern times, it now serves organic, nut-free, and vegan bakery products.

My dad had a magnetic charm, and people gravitated to him. He leased studio space at 1476 Pacific Avenue to musician/performer Boz Scaggs in 1973. In the summer of 1976, I was with my dad when he was at the Just Desserts bakery discussing property matters with one of the bakery's partners, and in walked Boz Scaggs, who recognized H.K. My dad struck up a friendly conversation with him and introduced me. Before we left the bakery, Boz invited my dad and me to tour his house, which was located directly across the street from the bakery. It was a very narrow eclectic three-story house. While we were going up the stairs, I remember seeing Boz's guitars and his gold record on the wall. There was also a watchtower on the top of the house with a spectacular view of the city. Touring his house was amazing. My dad was quite a character and very charming and charismatic. This shows how easily he made friends.

Customers lined up on opening day of the Ti Sun Co. Hardware and Furniture store at 1005 Grant Avenue, March 16, 1940.

Customers shopping in the fully stocked Ti Sun Co. Hardware store on the opening day, March 16, 1940.

H.K., co-owner of Ti Sun Co., was ready to greet customers at the cash register on the opening day of the store, March 16, 1940.

Ti Sun Co. furniture showroom, March 1941.

H.K. created the store window display promoting the "Around the World Free with TWA" contest in conjunction with the Gas Appliance Society of California. Ti Sun Co. won first place for the window display showcasing the new Rheem-Wedgewood gas ranges. May 1955, photo by Kem Lee.

A Ti Sun Co. window display featured the tools and products advertised in *Popular Mechanics* magazine. The display included a giant figure of Confucius pointing toward a *Popular Mechanics* "Do It Yourself" poster, along with the Chinese saying, "Confucius says, He who wishes to do better work should first possess the best tools." August 1955, photo by Kem Lee.

In a clever sales scheme, an old refrigerator was placed on a flatbed truck outside the Ti Sun Co. hardware store, welcoming customers to see the new models inside the store. Circa 1959.

H.K. with actor/dancer/comedian Danny Kaye and restaurateur Johnny Kan at the Ti Sun Co, checking out the new woks. Circa 1959.

H.K. demonstrating the broiling pan of the new Rheem-Wedgewood gas range. Circa 1955.

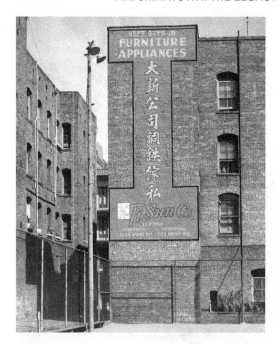

Advertising display for Ti Sun Co. on the building next to the Chinese Playground tennis court. The sign was contracted for 3 years, but remained on the building for over 15 years. Circa 1945.

Ti Sun Co. billboard on Columbus Ave. near Chinatown, promoting Hoffman televisions. Chinese characters were added to the billboard to attract more Chinese customers, half of whom spoke and read only Chinese. Circa 1954; photo by Kem Lee.

S.F. Mayor George Christopher enjoyed a cup of Chinese tea at a housewarming with his wife Tula, H.K, and a hostess during the dedication ceremony at the Ping Yuen Housing project. The Ti Sun Co. furnished the model apartment for the housing project. October 1951.

Model apartment at the Ping Yuen Housing Project furnished by the Ti Sun Co. H.K. received a "Pailou Award" for his work on this project. October 1951.

H.K. seated in his Ford truck that he considered his number one advertisement and big time saver in delivering appliances and furniture to his customers. The young women were from Charlie Low's Forbidden City night club. Photo by Bev. Washburn, for *Ford Truck Times*, July-August 1950.

Wesley making popcorn at the grand opening of the Three Star Bakery on January 22, 1968.

Ribbon-cutting ceremony at the Polk/Pacific Building Supply, with Jack Lee Fong, H.K., Frank Lim, Lili Lim, Ron Pelosi (S.F. Supervisor), John Yehall Chin, Wendy Kwan (Miss San Francisco Chinatown), and Lim P. Lee (S.F. Postmaster), July 29, 1972. Photo by Kem Lee.

Opening-day reception at the Polk/Pacific Building Supply, July 29, 1972. Photo by Kem Lee.

8

RESTAURATEUR - THE EMPRESS OF CHINA

H.K. was always on the lookout for opportunities to participate in new business ventures and to help his friends. His first foray into the restaurant business began in 1961 as an investor in the "7 Chefs," a food-court-style Chinese restaurant owned and managed by his good friend, Peter Chun. Located in the newly developed Foothill Square Shopping Center in Oakland, California, the restaurant operated for about ten years. It was a treat for me as a youngster to visit the shopping center, roam through the stores, and then sample the food in the food court.

In 1962, Mr. Tom Do Hing, a pioneer merchant and community leader and head of one of the largest and oldest import firms in Chinatown, purchased an old four-story brick building on Grant Avenue, erected after the 1906 earthquake. Tom had conferred with his eldest son, Stanley, on the eventual use of the building. Standing next to them was H.K. and restaurateur Kee Joon, who suggested to the Toms, "why don't you tear it down and build the tallest building in Chinatown and let us put a restaurant on top?"

Eleven months later, the Tom family decided to turn the property on Grant Avenue into a world-class retail and office complex in the heart of Chinatown. It became the tallest building in Chinatown. The building, known as the China Trade Center, cost $1 million to construct. The bottom two floors and basement contained an Oriental import store and a mini mall of shops. The middle two floors contained offices – and the top two

H.K. Wong

floors were designed specifically for a restaurant, including an extra-tall ceiling for a grand ballroom. It cost $750K to design and build the space for a "roof garden" restaurant.

My dad's crowning achievement in business partnership, fundraising, and public outreach resulted in the opening and subsequent promotion of that "roof garden" restaurant, San Francisco Chinatown's landmark Empress of China. In partnership with managing director and nationally known restaurateur, Kee Joon, H.K. became the enthusiastic public voice of the restaurant and its corporate secretary. Joon had presented the idea of the restaurant to his friends, all key community leaders, and the idea had taken hold. Leading merchants, including my dad, pledged three-quarters of a million dollars in capital. Joining Joon's forces were also Philip H. Fong, Fay S. Tom, Stanley S. Tom, attorney Emma P. Lum, and realtor Daisy C. Wong. To raise funding to build the restaurant, the Chinese Restaurant Associates, Inc. was formed with nine founding directors, eight of which were challenged with securing private investors and selling stock to them. Each director signed personal financial guarantees of $10,000. My dad also convinced about 80 of his friends to invest in the restaurant, which was amazing considering the fact he was running the Ti Sun Company at the same time. In total, the directors sold over $500K in corporation stock. A small stockholders' conference room was built on the fifth-floor mezzanine above the grand ballroom, and special gold keys were made for each of the initial stockholders as a token of their investment.

By 1966, corporation directors had secured 277 shareholders. Most of these were Chinese, but in that sea of original shareholders, the first non-Asian shareholder name to stand out to co-author, Catherine Lenox, was #139, Mr. Lionel R. Lenox, II. A banker from Santa Cruz, California, Mr. Lenox believed and invested in the Empress of China Restaurant. An admiring friend of H.K. with a keen sense for good investments, Lionel "Bud" Lenox was also Catherine's father. He knew that the Empress of China Restaurant would be a success.

A master Chinese chef with restaurant experience, Joon became a key member of the founding group. Like H.K., Managing Director Joon was a native Californian, born and raised in Santa Barbara. He had gained his culinary knowledge at his father's knee, working at his parents' 15-table restaurant when he was nine years old. Both H.K. and Joon came by cooking naturally. They also came from a heritage of scholars. Joon's grandfather had come from China to America in the 19th century as a letter-writer for Chinese laborers working on the railroad, many of whom could not read or write. Workers dictated their letters to Joon's grandfather, who sent the letters back to China, and then read the replies when they arrived back in California many weeks later. Joon was already recognized for his affiliation with the well-known restaurant Imperial Palace. Part owner and manager of it, Joon had a dream of starting his own restaurant that would reflect the true elegance of China. He envisioned a bigger one with a banquet hall that would serve authentic Chinese cuisine. The Empress of China would become the realization of Joon's dream. The top two floors of the new pagoda-style China Trade Center building would be a natural setting for it.

Located at 838 Grant Avenue in the heart of San Francisco Chinatown, the Empress of China's six-story building was an impressive architectural masterpiece. Designed by the architects Worley K. Wong and Peter Rocchia of the architectural firm Campbell and Wong, it featured antique décor brought back to the U.S. from Taiwan and was regarded as one of the most beautiful restaurants in San Francisco. From its pillar gateway on Grant Avenue, painted aged-red like temples in China, to the 170 steps that led up to the sixth-floor Garden Pavilion and spacious dining room and ballroom, the architects spared no expense in building it. Its 100-seat upper floor made it the largest restaurant in Chinatown, and its authentic cuisine gave it distinction. Everything in the Empress of China honored Chinese tradition, pageantry, and culture.

The Garden Pavilion, constructed and assembled by descendants of the original Peking Palace craftsmen in Taiwan, was inspired by the classic lines of the famed Nan Hai T'ing in His Yuan, the royal park in Peking. It took over two years to complete in Taipei. Its eight massive columns, sixteen heavy cross-beams, scores of arches, carved works for the pavilion, marble fountain, and many hand-tooled panels and carvings for the dining room and lobby were taken apart in Taipei and then shipped to the Empress of China in San Francisco. The pieces arrived, packed in 35 gigantic crates and boxes, on June 6, 1966. The shipment was so heavy, it required a crew of men and a forklift to unload and uncrate it. The 24-foot-diameter octagonal pavilion was then reassembled at the Empress without using a single nail.

The lobby leading to the Pavilion Room boasted centuries-old palace chandeliers crafted from extremely aged wood in beautiful shades of green, bronze, and gold. Made just before the 1906 earthquake and fire and delivered to San Francisco just after the fire, the chandeliers' original cost was $40,000 in gold. As a young boy, Joon had seen such a chandelier in China and knew that these ones were rare and valuable. The people at the place he discovered them had never known they were there, as they had never been turned on. One of these chandeliers graced the front entrance on Grant Avenue, leading into a lobby with a 20-foot ceiling, where the restaurant's name was etched in Chinese characters. Also precious to the restaurant were the rare inlaid mother-of-pearl accent and marble tables, too valuable for dining but used as room decorations. The main dining area was decorated in painted and carved Chinese panels, 12 to 17 feet tall by 2 feet wide. Some had open teakwood carvings and some were carved only on one side. They weighed about 200 pounds each.

The Empress Ballroom, the largest in Chinatown, had a double-high ceiling and breathtaking panoramic views of the city. Its architecture was designed to resemble that of the Han Dynasty. The Empress Room, the main dining area, also had impressive views, with tall windows facing North Beach and Telegraph Hill. Four rare gilt carvings representing the four seasons hung against its walls. Brocaded jade-green silk walls, palace chandeliers, and peacock feathers also graced the room. Close by, the Golden Court area offered a stunning view of the East Bay. Antique gold-painted Peking puppet shadow boxes trimmed in kingfishers' feathers framed this room's mirrors.

Perhaps the most intriguing feature at the Empress of China Restaurant, however, was its massive 10-foot framed tapestry of Empress Lü, "Empress of the Earth," hanging on the wall of the Pavilion entrance. Of the Han Dynasty, Empress Lü was the first woman to become Empress of China. In Chinese tradition, the "Earth Empress" represents transformation and change. Stately and regal, Empress Lü's eyes seemed to calmly watch over everyone who entered her realm. As H.K. would say at the time, "She watches over us."

At the Empress, while the décor was decidedly traditional, the kitchen was state-of-the art and fully modern. Joon had already built a successful restaurant and knew what he wanted. He hired top kitchen designer Bob Yick, who had already designed 80% of all Chinese kitchens in the U.S. and nearly all the Chinese restaurants in the San Francisco Bay Area and the rest of California. When completed, Yick's huge kitchen complex had 131 feet of Chinese stove ranges and was the first Chinese restaurant to use 38"-diameter woks. Cooks could steam 60 chickens at the same time! Joon also brought his own recipes, knowledge from other chefs, and research from Hong Kong to the sizeable menus. Thousands of unusual dishes of old China that were the Emperor's favorites were included on the Empress' menus. Westernized Chinese blends, such as chop suey, which was created by early immigrants who could not find the ingredients needed for traditional Chinese dishes, were never served to Empress of China diners. Prices were moderate, too. Lunch, including delicious Dim Sum, was a mere $1.95. A full-course dinner was $4.95. After finishing the kitchen that he designed for the Empress, Yick declared it "the finest kitchen he had ever designed in his entire history of 55 years of making kitchens."

The cuisine was top-notch. The restaurant's associate, Stanley Tom, went to Hong Kong for four months to contact top chefs in the restaurants and hotels there and bring two of them back to the Empress of China kitchen. By the time he reached Hong Kong, his search had been so publicized that every restaurant and head chef in Hong Kong wanted to meet with him. Tom was successful, and in addition to a local Executive Chef and a large crew of top chefs from across America, Empress of China opened with two top chefs from Hong Kong.

The Empress also featured exotic beverages from around the world at its Empress cocktail lounge, an appealing area with a spectacular view of Coit Tower, decorated in Han Dynasty 15-foot panels and a teak canopy. Three tanks filled with Koi fish graced its balcony. Next to the main dining room was The Emperor's Chamber, a separate VIP room that seated 20 and was reserved for private dining. With its mandarin-red brocaded-silk walls, mirrors reflecting Han period grilles, a temple carving, and smaller antique chandeliers, it was elegant and cozy. The VIP room also featured two mother-of-pearl display cases exhibiting museum-quality antique Chinese artifacts. Eating there was like dining in a museum gallery. Many dignitaries dined in that room.

When it first opened, my dad was still owner and manager of the Ti Sun Company, juggling his everyday responsibilities with the work required of him in his new position as Corporate Secretary and fundraising executive for the Empress of China. In addition to raising money for the restaurant, he also helped purchase the furniture, carpeting, and tableware through the Ti Sun Company. When I think of my dad, it is hard to imagine how he managed to succeed at so many jobs at the same time. The truth is, he seemed to be 20 people bundled up into one. His energy was boundless.

Opening on August 15, 1966, the Empress of China invited stockholders to a private banquet, complete with an enticing menu featuring "the superb cuisine of ancient Imperial China." In an article in their World of Business column titled "Elegance on Grant Avenue," the *San Francisco Examiner and Chronicle* noted the occasion. The throngs of media reporters that attended the opening were most certainly inspired by my dad's tireless publicity of the event. Columnist Sidney P. Allen wrote, "Business can, upon occasion, be the dream of a lifetime come true. We give you the case of Kee Joon, bon vivant, restaurateur par excellence, and a man who knows what makes this biggest Chinatown in America tick. A few months ago, most of San Francisco's '400,' the carriage trade, poured out for what society columns described as a wildly successful opening. Familiar faces dotted the throng – like Mayor Jack Shelley, attorney Mel Belli, beautiful model Pat Montandon, lovely actress Shirley Temple Black, the 'old crooner' Bing

Crosby himself, his glamorous Kathy, and many, many more. The press – publishers, editors, columnists, and photographers – were on hand for the occasion too, for this was an historic moment. It was a preview party to mark the completion of the heralded Empress of China Restaurant. Now, such a response – reporters estimated there were 1,600 on hand to clog Grant Avenue traffic for hours – might seem like a hysterical welcome for a sophisticated community. The Empress of China Restaurant, though, is by no means just another eating house in a city famed for its excellent cuisine. Nobody was regarding this as simply a new ribbon cutting. Interest obviously was at a fever pitch. The reason for this great big hurrah is simple enough. This establishment may well stand, as the man who conceived it expects, as the 'break-through' point for San Francisco's Chinatown in renaissance, the supreme mark of Chinese elegance and beauty by which all else will be judged."

No one could have been made happier by these words than my dad. He had been working for Chinatown, and its "breakthrough," for years. A fortune cookie accompanied the article. It read, "Confucius says best wishes." As Joon would say, smiling, "No woman need be fearful her costume will clash with our subtle décor. It sets every guest off as a star."

I was eight years old when the Empress of China opened its doors. At the Grand Opening, I recall throngs of people, but the most glamorous person I remember was Rosie Fang. In 1962, she had come from Hong Kong to study at City College of San Francisco. Only 19 years old at the time, she had won the title of Miss Trade in Hong Kong and a scholarship to study in the U.S. My parents became her guardians, and she lived with them for a while. She became part of our family and was like a big sister to me. Years later, I was a junior usher at her wedding to Sam Ong, and my dad walked her down the aisle. Rosie was stunningly attractive and 5'8", which was tall for an Asian woman. At the Empress opening, she wore a special semitransparent dress with sequined brocade and a wreath of flowers on her head, especially designed for her by Mr. Richard Blackwell, a famous designer with the House of Blackwell known for his "10 Best and Worst Dressed Women" list, which ran from 1960 through 2007. Rosie was one of the first Chinese models for Mr. Blackwell and traveled extensively for his fashion studio. A lot of eyes were on her that day. To my eyes that day, Rosie made it to my best-dressed list. That dress was unforgettable. Ada Tom, who always looked impeccable, doubtlessly also showed up at the event looking like a star.

Ada, now in her eighties, still has fond memories of Opening Day at the Empress of China. Her late husband, Fay Tom, was one of the founding directors of the restaurant. He was also one of the brothers of the Tom family that owned the China Trade Center, where the Empress was housed. Ada reminisces, "Herb Caen was there, as well as lots of dignitaries." A third-generation San Franciscan, Ada is now the only one of her family still living in San Francisco. She says, "I have family in London, New York, and Hong Kong. But whenever my eleven children, and countless grandchildren and great-grandchildren came to visit San Francisco, we never ate anywhere but the Empress. It was a family restaurant."

The Empress of China was a popular destination for many locals, tourists, and celebrities over the years. Later, in the San Francisco Magazine *Diner's Choice*, 1968-69, an article featuring the Empress read, "In less than two short years, this magnificent roof garden retreat, the only high-rise Chinese restaurant on this continent, has won more honors than most dining places in Chinatown combined. President and Managing Director Kee Joon's achievements have been saluted by *Institutions Magazine*, *Esquire*, and by *Holiday Magazine*, which in its envied Award, states, the city's newest and most beautiful Oriental restaurant, high in a tall Grant Avenue building, with a sweeping view of the hills and the Bay... Mr. Kee Joon is the smiling genius who made this all come true."

When the Empress of China was being built, I was about seven years old. Many of my childhood memories are linked to it. I remember when the ornate gilded teakwood mirror frames were delivered to the Ti Sun Company hardware store. They consisted of many pocket windows decorated with a bird motif, with tiny bird feathers sealed in glass. The frames had apparently been in storage for many years and were heavily encrusted with dirt and grime. I spent hours helping my dad carefully scrub the glass with soap and water, delicately vacuuming the pocket windows. The Empress was great for my parents. My dad gradually diminished his involvement in the hardware and furniture store after 35 years of business there to concentrate on the restaurant. He set up a small office for himself and worked there for a few hours every day. He loved the place. The view of the city skyline from his office was an inspiration for many of his watercolor paintings in later years.

Whenever any of his friends or acquaintances came to San Francisco for business or travel, my dad would host a dinner at the restaurant. It goes without saying that we ate at the restaurant quite frequently. This suited my mother, because she did not like to cook at home, and she was not a great cook. She got distracted easily and would often burn the rice boiling on the stove, but if she caught it before it got too charred, my dad would add hot tea to the pot and eat the crispy rice with the tea. He was a good sport.

Shortly after the restaurant opened, I had joined the Cub Scout Pack 3, which met at Jean Parker School. I then advanced to the Boy Scout Troop 3, based at the American Legion Cathay Post on Powell Street. Troop 3 was established in 1914 by eight Chinese boys in Chinatown and is the oldest Boy Scout troop west of the Mississippi River. On the troop meeting nights when my parents were hosting a dinner at the restaurant, I would wear my full scout uniform for dinner and then excuse myself from dinner to walk seven blocks to my troop meeting. The restaurant staff got used to seeing me in my scout uniform. The troop had a couple of milestone anniversary parties in the Grand Ballroom. I presented my Eagle Scout project at the troop's 60th anniversary party. Being involved in many of my parents' social activities, I did not have a lot of friends, so the scout troop allowed me to do many outdoor activities, serve the community, and build valuable life skills. I also got to travel to the National Jamboree in Idaho, and the World Jamboree in Norway.

Through many of the dinner parties I attended at the restaurant, I picked up a few tricks from Walter Wong, a headwaiter at the time, that to this day impress my friends. He taught me how to deftly handle two serving spoons with one hand and how to debone a whole steamed fish. Steamed fish was one of my favorite dishes (my dad always ordered it at the Empress), and I was often allowed to debone the fish at the table. Walter was also an amateur photographer. He sold me his Nikon SLR camera before our trip to China in 1975 and gave me a few lessons on color slide photography.

After its first year of operation, the restaurant was recognized for its interior design and cuisine in many national and international magazines. Every year, to celebrate the restaurant's success, all shareholders were invited to an elaborate shareholders' banquet in the ballroom. These parties were extremely popular and memorable for the shareholders but were discontinued after a few years because the event had grown too large. Many of the shareholders were bringing large numbers of extended family members and friends to the party. As the restaurant was receiving numerous awards and international recognition, demand for the bookings for the grand ballroom grew too. The ballroom had a stage and a dance floor and could accommodate up to 600 people. It was one of the larger venues in the city for dinner parties. During its heyday in the 1970s and 1980s, its price was hefty as well, commanding up to $20,000 per event. Bookings for wedding and family association parties on the weekends were the most popular. With only a limited number of weekend dates available each year, bookings were often made many years in advance. On the day that I got married in August 1982 at the Old Saint Mary's church, with 400 guests, the ballroom was already booked for a dinner party. We had to settle for a lunch buffet that day. Even with inside connections, my dad could not rearrange that one!

The Empress received the first of its Outstanding Restaurant Awards from *Holiday Magazine* in 1967 and continued to receive more awards for the next 35 years until the magazine went out of business as the *Travel-Holiday Magazine*. Every year, the magazine hosted a gala awards party for all the winning restaurants. My parents were able to travel to some exciting locations such as Mexico City and Montreal to represent the Empress of China, while I stayed with my Uncle Hap and Aunt Gladys in

Santa Rosa.

To maintain its high standards of elegance, ambiance, and decorum, the Empress in its early years had a dress code. Gentlemen were required to wear a coat and necktie, and the women were required to wear a dress. Shorts and sandals were strictly forbidden. Sports coats and neckties were available for men who came without them. The policy started to ease up as the tourist trade increased. My dad's wardrobe contained over 100 neckties, as he felt it was important to always be professionally dressed.

My dad was always thinking of ways to improve the menu. Green tea ice cream originated in Japan but had not become widely available in the U.S. until the late 1970s. My dad thought it would be a good idea to serve it as a refreshing dessert. H.K. was a friend of Earle Swensen, the founder of Swensen's Ice Cream. I was around 12 years old when my dad took me to meet Swensen at his Hyde Street shop. Swensen was a kind man and would offer treats to children. After a tour of his shop and a demonstration of the machinery, my dad asked him to create a recipe for the green tea ice cream to serve at the restaurant. After a few days of experimentation, Swensen sent over a few gallons of ice cream. The ice cream was delicious and was soon added to the menu.

After only two years in operation, the corporation was profitable enough to issue a 2% dividend to the shareholders, and after nine years, more than 100% of the original investment was returned to shareholders. In fact, business was so successful in those first two years that in 1967, the Empress Board of Directors agreed to explore an expansion in Honolulu, Hawaii. H.K. met with Mr. Chinn Ho, president of Capital Investment Company, and his son, Daniel, in Honolulu about the possibility of operating an Empress of China Restaurant in the Ilikai complex. In November 1970, the board discussed the possibility of expanding into New York City. A site in New York Chinatown at Bowery and Elizabeth Street was available and suitable for a large restaurant. In February 1971, the Board also discussed the possibility of expanding the Empress into Mountain View, California. That August, the directors toured the new Pruneyard Towers in Campbell, California, with the idea of expanding the

Empress into the Pruneyard Shopping Center there. My dad developed a site survey, business plan, and prospectus for investors. This was the expansion opportunity that progressed the furthest. Even an embossing stamp for the stock certificates was ordered. However, these plans were eventually scrapped when the corporation was not able to get agreeable terms for the lease.

The Empress of China hosted numerous political figures, including President Jimmy Carter, Vice-President/Senator Herbert Humphrey, Mayor Joseph Alioto, Senator Dianne Feinstein, and Mayor George Moscone. The lobby entrance on Grant Avenue was also lined with many photographs of celebrities who dined at the restaurant, including Frank Sinatra, Dean Martin, Sammy Davis Jr., Mick Jagger, and the famous Carol Doda. As a matter of fact, if you mention any Hollywood celebrity of that time, they had likely eaten there. The Empress was their sought-after place to eat and hang out. Other local and national politicians, princes and princesses, the chancellor of West Germany, countless movie stars, and sport celebrities also frequented the Empress.

I have vivid memories of personally meeting and having lunch with two Hollywood stars. Raymond Burr starred in the TV show "Ironside" from 1967 to 1975. Before the Old Hall of Justice on Kearny Street behind the restaurant was demolished in 1967, some of the early shows were filmed on the fourth floor of that building. One day, my dad invited Raymond Burr to lunch after shooting the show, and I got to join them. I was about ten years old at the time, but I clearly remember Burr's commanding presence and his deep voice. He was a big man but very friendly.

"The Streets of San Francisco" was another TV drama, starring Karl Malden and Michael Douglas. The show was filmed on location in San Francisco between 1972 and 1977. It was at another lunch that my dad hosted at the restaurant that I got to meet Karl Malden. He was a very funny man, and his strawberry-shaped nose was as big and bulbous as you would imagine from his films. The TV show filmed a basketball game sequence at my alma mater, Lowell High School, during my senior year. The school was all abuzz that day, and parts of the school was cordoned off for filming.

My dad was an accomplished marketer. At every opportunity, he promoted the Empress of China through newspaper and magazine articles, radio talk shows, and TV appearances. In 1972, the California State Exposition (CalExpo) included a Chinese heritage show with exhibits of artifacts from the Chinese Historical Society, artwork from Taiwan, and a special table display from the Empress of China. H.K. designed the display in the style of the restaurant's Emperor's Chamber, with two dining tables arranged with ornate Chinese tableware. He created a brochure and postcard for the restaurant and a recipe booklet of 20 of the Empress's famous dishes for Expo visitors. The booklet included recipes such as Empress Egg Roll, Fresh Lemon Duck, and my favorite dessert, Peking Honey Apples. The Peking Honey Apples were coated in a batter, prepared, and served tableside with a crystallized sugary coating that was flash cooled in ice. I successfully prepared the Peking Honey Apples for my college classmates during my studies at Humboldt State University, and they were all impressed. I have not attempted the recipe since.

While still deeply involved with the Empress, my dad found an opportunity to get back into banking from 1975 to 1980, as a bank director of a new El Camino Bank branch in Chinatown, on Stockton Street near Broadway. Lionel "Bud" Lenox, who had banking connections at El Camino Bank and was a lifetime friend of H.K.'s, knew that my dad was highly connected in Chinatown and would be the best possible candidate for its branch director position there. Lenox contacted executives he knew at the bank on behalf of my dad, and H.K. was hired for the position. One of my dad's duties in his new job was developing a Chinese New Year marketing campaign that brought a lot of new Chinese customers to the bank. H.K. used his business and marketing savvy, his connections to the Chinese community, and his experience at the Bank of Canton forty years before to help the El Camino Bank establish a successful branch in Chinatown. The bank has changed names several times and is now the East West Bank.

In an August 21, 1978 entry in his daily diary, my dad wrote of a terrifying incident that happened at the Empress and how he calmly handled the situation. At 10:00 AM, H.K. went to the Empress to check on the staff in preparation for the lunch crowd. As he entered the Empress lobby and the bar, he noticed that no one was around. He sauntered into the office and was suddenly stopped by two masked robbers, each with revolvers pointed at him. The robbers had already forced the bar manager, Eddie Hui, to open the safe and lie on the floor. They then instructed H.K. to lie on the floor alongside Eddie. At that point, Eddie was trembling violently, so my dad patted his leg to calm him down. The robbers grabbed the sacks of money and rushed out the door. The police came within five minutes, and the incident was reported later that night on KGO-TV and in the *San Francisco Chronicle* the next day. I suspect that my dad's duck-hunting experience 23 years before had allowed him to stay calm when confronted by two armed robbers.

In August 1981, a new heating and air-conditioning unit for the restaurant was so large and heavy, it had to be airlifted and installed by helicopter. It was the first time an air delivery was made onto a rooftop in Chinatown. On the day of the installation, Richard Hart and his camera crew from KPIX-TV were on the roof to cover the event for their *Evening Magazine* show.

Business had been going well throughout the 1970s, and the corporation had some cash reserves. In August 1981, the Empress Board of Directors agreed to purchase a mixed-use commercial/residential property on Pacific Avenue a few blocks away from the restaurant as an investment and a tax benefit to the corporation. The mortgage on the property was paid off in five years. The property proved to be a wise investment, as it generated rental income for 37 years and helped bolster the corporation's finances in the leaner years.

In 1985, my mother took over my dad's seat on the Empress Board of Directors. She held that position until 2009, when I took over her seat until the corporation was eventually dissolved in 2019. It was during this process of dissolution that I contacted Catherine Lenox. She and her sisters had inherited her father's Empress of China shares. I had first met Catherine on one of my family's visits to the Lenox family home in Santa Cruz when we were teenagers. When Catherine turned in her shares, we began to talk about where our lives had taken us over the past fifty years. Catherine said that she was now ghostwriting books for a living, many of which were family legacy memoirs. I mentioned that I had long wanted to write my dad's memoir. We decided to honor our fathers and their friendship not only by rekindling ours, but also by writing this book.

In the fall of 2014, after forty-eight years as an iconic San Francisco landmark, date nightspot, and venue for events, wedding receptions, and banquets, the once elegant Empress of China was forced to close its doors. The recession of 2008 had hit California hard, and the China Trade Center never recovered its losses. At the same time, the growth of Chinese residents in the East Bay, South Bay, and Richmond district of San Francisco spawned many Chinese restaurants in other areas. As a result, the Empress lost substantial business.

In September 2014, Empress staff received notice that the building was to be sold and converted to office space. Writer Paolo Lucchesi, in the blog SFGATE, bemoaned the change, terming the Empress "a silent, dusty perch above the chaos of the city streets, where one can slow down and appreciate the splendor of the place we live." He noted the Empress "held back a flood of homogeneity" and that in its closing, San Francisco would "lose a bit of the city's texture." In its heyday, writer Jonathan Kauffman had also said of the Empress, "It's impossible not to love this place." As someone who experienced many happy memories there, this was certainly true of me.

In 2019, the building that once housed the Empress had stood empty for four years. Initial plans to turn the building into office space or a hotel had been discarded. On October 15, 2019, however, the Hakkasan chain's former international executive chef, Ho Chee Boon, announced that he planned to revive 7,500 square feet of the Empress of China space (calling it "Empress by Boon") by early 2020, following a remodel by UK-based designer group LLYS. In addition to his work with the upscale Chinese restaurant, Hakkasan, Boon had overseen the Dim Sum restaurant chain Yauatcha. He said that he planned to manage Empress by Boon through email from New York City, serving "modern Hong Kong-style dim sum." Boon, who was born in Malaysia, owned restaurants in London, Moscow, and Bangkok. In 2012, he moved to the U.S. to open Hakkasan in New York.

Since that time, reopening a restaurant in the top floor of the iconic China Trade Center building that housed the Empress has come under fire from Chinatown Community Development Center activists who view the proposed upscale Empress by Boon as a sign of gentrification. Since its menu prices will likely not be geared to local clientele, residents fear a loss of neighborhood authenticity and inclusion. Proponents argue, on the other hand, that the new restaurant will bring jobs and tourist dollars to Chinatown, and that second- and third-generation Chinese Americans do not frequent banquet-style restaurants as they did in the past.

When I was writing this book, whether new life and Cantonese cuisine would flow back to the iconic Empress of China space remained to be seen. The wake of Covid-19 had left many would-be investors nervous about taking on new ventures. Still, if plans proceed as Boon envisioned, Empress Lü's eyes may again calmly observe diners who enter her realm and, as my dad said, "watch over us" into the future.

The 7 Chefs, a food-court-style Chinese restaurant located in the newly developed Foothill Square Shopping Center in Oakland, CA., circa 1961. It was H.K.'s first foray into the restaurant business as an investor.

Pen, ink, and marker drawing of Chinatown by H.K. with the Empress of China and the China Trade Center building.

The principal directors of the Empress of China reviewed the blueprints with architects Worley Wong and Peter Rocchia. Back Row: H.K., Stanley Tom, Peter Rocchia, Fay Tom, Kee Joon. Seated: Emma Lum, Worley K. Wong, circa 1964. Photo by Kem Lee.

The original board of directors of the Chinese Restaurant Associates, Inc., the parent company of the Empress of China. Back row: H.K., Fay Tom, Kee Joon, Philip Fong, Stanley Tom. Seated: Edna Lee, Emma Lum, Daisy Wong. Circa 1966. Photo by Kem Lee.

The 10-foot tapestry of Empress Lü, "Empress of the Earth," welcomed all guests at the pavilion entrance to the Empress of China. Circa 1967.

The Garden Pavilion, constructed and assembled by descendants of the original Peking Palace craftsmen in Taiwan. It consisted of eight massive columns, sixteen heavy cross beams, scores of arches and carvings, and a marble fountain. The 24-foot-diameter pavilion was assembled at the Empress of China without using a single nail.

The Pavilion Room, with centuries-old palace chandeliers, gilded wood carvings, and an expansive view of the San Francisco skyline and Coit Tower. It seated 120 diners.

The Emperor's Chamber, a private dining room with seating for 20, was decorated with mandarin-red silk walls, two small antique chandeliers, gilded wood carvings, and two mother-of-pearl display cases exhibiting museum-quality Chinese artifacts.

The Empress Cocktail Lounge, decorated in Han Dynasty 15-foot panels and a teak grille canopy, offered a splendid view of Coit Tower, and served exotic beverages from around the world.

A wedding banquet in the Empress Ballroom, the largest in Chinatown, with a double-high ceiling, panoramic views of the city, and a seating capacity of 600.

H.K. with Bing Crosby and Rosie Fang at the grand opening of the Empress on August 15, 1966. Rosie was a model for the House of Blackwell, and wore a custom semi-transparent dress by Blackwell. Photo by Tom Lee.

Emma Lum and Kee Joon with Shirley Temple Black at the grand opening of the
Empress of China, August 15, 1966.

Karl Malden at the
Empress Lü tapestry,
circa 1975.

Diane Feinstein campaigned for Mayor of San Francisco in the Empress Ballroom, circa 1979.

H.K. designed a special table display representing the Empress of China at the California State Exposition (CalExpo). He created a recipe booklet of 20 famous Empress dishes for the Expo visitors. Circa 1972.

The new HVAC unit for the Empress of China was airlifted onto the roof of the China Trade Center building, August 1981. The installation (by helicopter) was covered by Richard Hart of KPIX-TV for the *Evening Magazine* show.

9

RECIPES FROM THE EMPRESS OF CHINA

The Empress of China was famous for its award-winning and scrumptious dishes from many regions of China: Canton, Szechuan, Hunan, and Mongolia. Some of the Empress signature dishes were the Peking Duck, Flaming Baby Quail, Ginger Crab, Mongolian Lamb, Roasted Duck Noodles, and Winter Melon Soup. Flaming of the baby quail at table side was discontinued in the late 1990s due to fire regulations prohibiting the use of open flames. The winter melon soup was served inside the carved whole winter melon itself. The ginger crab was my dad's favorite dish, and during Dungeness crab season he would invite his friends to the restaurant for a crab feast. Paper bibs were provided for guests, as the ginger crab was a messy affair. One of my favorite dishes was the smoked tea duck that was prepared by smoking it in tea leaves for a day beforehand.

Many of my dad's friends asked him for recipes for the dishes. The chefs were reluctant to share their recipes. After spending many hours in the kitchen observing and talking to the kitchen staff, the chefs slowly revealed their recipes. The recipes provided in this chapter are from the recipe booklet that my dad compiled for the 1972 California Exposition as a giveaway from the display booth showcasing the Empress of China table setting, "Empress Recipes of Chinese Dishes."

The Master Chef of the Empress of China had several hundred rare recipes in his repertoire. He shared his expertise on some of the dishes served at the Empress and added a few other popular requested recipes.

H.H. Wong

There are two hundred ways of cooking a chicken, so just persevere and in time you will be delighted at your own skill and talent for the time-honored art of Chinese cookery.

EMPRESS OF CHINA
R O O F   G A R D E N   R E S T A U R A N T

America's only high-rise Chinese roof garden restaurant
Distinctive Cuisine of all China
Amidst Oriental Splendor with Enchanting Vistas
International Gourmet Honors & Holiday Awards Since 1968

HAPPY COOKING DAYS - THE EMPRESS OF CHINA!

SEI SEEGAI – CHICKEN SALAD THE EMPRESS STYLE

1-3 Lb. Whole Chicken

4 Tablespoons of best grade Chinese soy sauce

4 Tablespoons of oyster sauce

1 Tablespoon of sugar

1 Tablespoon of sesame oil

1 Tablespoon of honey

4 green onions

1 bunch of Chinese parsley

¼ Lb. of chopped, roasted almonds

¼ Lb. of Chinese fun see (Chinese vermicelli)

One small crisp lettuce

Clean chicken. Then hang to dry. Deep fry until well browned. Bone and cut into shreds. Mix soy sauce, oyster sauce, honey into bowl. (Do not put in the refrigerator.) Cut onions to 2" long shred. Cut lettuce into shreds. (All of this should be prepared before cooking chicken.) Mix shredded chicken with sauce first. Then add in the onions, Chinese parsley, chopped almonds, fried fun see, and the lettuce. Toss well and serve warm.

CHINESE CHICKEN SALAD - AN AUSPICIOUS APPETIZER

1-3 Lbs. of whole chicken
Brush chicken with Chestnut flour
Deep fry chicken for ½ an hour
When chicken is thoroughly cooked, remove from the pan and let it cool
Shred whole chicken and place in a large bowl

Mix together:

4 Tablespoons sesame oil
½ cup plum sauce
4 Tablespoons light soy sauce
1 teaspoon sugar
1/3 cup shredded ginger (either red or white)
Sliced Chinese pickled onions
Shredded green onions and Chinese parsley
Toss with shredded chicken
Add one head of shredded lettuce
Sprinkle with slightly browned sesame seeds
Serve cold. (Serves 6)

EMPRESS EGG ROLLS – A NOTEWORTHY APPETIZER

¼ Lb. bamboo shoots, shredded (comes in cans, already shredded, in Chinese grocery stores)

¼ Lb. dried black Chinese mushrooms (soak in cold water, drain, then wash and dry)

3 stalks of celery, cut in 1-inch thin strips

1 medium onion, finely chopped

¼ Lb. cooked prawns, cut into small pieces

1 Lb. fresh bean spouts

1 teaspoon salt

2 Tablespoons sugar

¼ cup best grade Chinese soy sauce

1 egg, beaten

¼ cup vegetable oil

8 egg roll skins (obtained in Chinese grocery store)

Heat vegetable oil in skillet. Sauté all ingredients except egg until half cooked. Drain thoroughly. Place filling on skins and roll each up. Dip in beaten egg and fry in deep fat until golden brown. Cut each egg roll into four pieces. Each egg roll will be 5 inches long and one inch in diameter. Makes 8 rolls.

EMPRESS BEEF - A DELICACY OF THE PEKING ROYALTY

¼ Lb. sirloin beef steak, cut into shoestring strips
3 stalks celery, coarsely chopped
1 large white onion, thinly sliced
1 small can button mushrooms, thinly sliced
½ can small water chestnuts, coarsely chopped
½ Lb. snow peas, cut each piece once diagonally
(for substitute, French-cut string beans)
1 Tablespoon cornstarch
5 Tablespoons best grade Chinese soy sauce
½ Tablespoon sugar
½ cup water

Brown the beef with several Tablespoons of vegetable oil and ¼ Tablespoon salt in a hot skillet. Add onions, celery, mushrooms, snow peas, and water chestnuts and stir slowly for a few minutes over a hot fire. Then cover the pan, turn down the fire and simmer for about three minutes. Just before serving, stir in a thickening made up of the cornstarch, sugar, soy sauce and water. Serve immediately with fluffy steamed rice.

MONGOLIAN LAMB - A FAVORITE OF KUBLA KHAN'S COURT

2 Lbs. boneless leg of lamb
6 Tablespoons of white wine
5 Tablespoons of light Chinese soy sauce
¼ Tablespoon of sugar
1 teaspoon of cornstarch
6 Tablespoons of vegetable oil
Chinese parsley, green onion and Chinese firm
cut pressed ginger

Trim all fat off the lamb. Cut lamb into 1 square inch pieces. Flatten meat with cleaver or slice thin. Marinate with 6 Tablespoons of white wine. Mix Chinese light soy sauce, sugar, and cornstarch. Marinate for ½ an hour or more. Sauté in hot pan with vegetable oil. Stir quickly until lamb is cooked. Garnish with Chinese parsley, green onion and Chinese fine cut preserved ginger and serve. (Serves 4)

FIVE HAPPINESS PORK - A SZECHUAN DISH

1. Cut ½ Lb. lean tenderloin pork into 1-inch cubes
   Add 1 small can button mushrooms, which have
   been cut in halves (or ½ Lb. fresh mushrooms)
   Bamboo shoots, finely sliced
   1 small can water chestnuts, sliced
   Celery, cut into ½ inch pieces

2. Sauté pork in hot pan with oil, until pork
   turns brown. Cover and cook pork with all
   the above ingredients.
   Add: 2 Tablespoons soy sauce
   1 teaspoon sugar

Cook about 25 minutes. Mix 2 teaspoons cornstarch
in ¼ cup cold water. Slowly add cornstarch mixture,
stirring until it thickens – and then serve.
(Serves 2 to 3)

FRESH LEMON DUCK - A BANQUET MORSEL

One whole young duck thoroughly cleaned. Rub salt around inside of duck, then hang until dried. Wipe Chinese light soy sauce (or if you wish, Worchester sauce) on duck. Place duck in oven and roast for two hours. Baste duck with warm water once-in-a-while.

Squeeze juice from four medium sized lemons. Take out pulp and seeds and cut each lemon peel into six pieces. Put lemon peel in lemon juice with one cup sugar and ½ cup white vinegar and place on low heat to simmer until peel becomes tender.

Pour lemon juice and peel over roasted duck and place in oven for 40 to 45 minutes. Remove pan with duck from oven, drain quickly, then cut duck into bite size pieces, pour gravy back on top of duck and serve. (Serves 4)

WHOLE WINTER MELON SOUP - BANQUET SOUP OF THE EMPRESS OF CHINA

(DOONG GWA-JOONG)

One winter melon, 8 to 8 ½ inches in diameter, 10 to 12 inches tall (Order from Chinatown produce dealers or groceries). Melon must be first washed and the white powder on the skin scrubbed off and cleaned. Then cut the top section off, three inches from the top. This will serve as a lid. Scoop out seeds and pulp, scrape inside surface clean and again wash in cold water.

1/3 cup diced tender bamboo shoots (canned)
1/3 cup small whole young button mushrooms
1/3 cup dried lotus seeds
10 oz. diced fresh white chicken meat

Optional, add:
1/3 cup dried black mushrooms
1/3 cup gingko nuts
½ cup dried smoked ham

(Continue)

Place the entire winter melon upright into a large 4" to 6" deep dish to support the whole melon while cooking and serving. This must be heat proof. Into this prepared whole melon, place the above mixture and pour in Chinese chicken stock to ¾ height of the melon. Cover with the melon lid. Then place the dish-supported whole melon on a large wide-diameter tall utensil with 3 to 4 inches of hot water to generate steam while cooking. Place a small rack or pair of wooden chopsticks between the cooking dish and bottom of utensil for protection of the dish. Cover utensil, steam melon 3-4 hours until translucent and tender but still firm. (length of time depending on size and age of the melon). Add hot or boiling water to the pot after the first hour for a continuous steaming action. During the last ten minutes, put in ¾ cup of parboiled green peas, salt to taste, and add more hot chicken stock to fill the melon up to the original ¾ level mark. Keep in utensil until ready to serve. Then carefully remove the steaming hot, whole melon with its supporting dish and place on table. To serve, ladle soup into individual bowls with some of the ingredients and bits of the melon meat. Delicious! (Serves 6 to 8)

HO-SEE LOHAN CHAI - A VEGETABLE MONK'S DISH

½ cup oyster sauce
½ cup red bean curd
1 Tablespoon best grade Chinese soy sauce
2 teaspoons salt
½ cup cornstarch
½ teaspoon sugar
½ cup Keoling or Shew-hing wine (or cooking wine)
A few drops of Sesame oil
1 cup water
4 Tablespoons vegetable oil

Combine above ingredients and set aside for use when cooking.

2 oz. bamboo shoots (sliced)
2 oz. water chestnuts (chopped)
1 oz. vermicelli (soaked)
1 oz. black mushrooms (chopped)
1 oz. whole straw mushrooms (chopped)
1 oz. whole small button mushrooms

(Continue)

½ cup gingko nuts (shelled)
4 oz. Chinese cabbages (cut in 2-inch sections)
2 oz. dried oysters (pre-cooked 4 hours in warm water and drained)
2 oz. dried bean curd skin (pre-cooked)
2 oz. hair seaweed vegetable (pre-soaked)
4 oz. lily flowers (soaked)
4 oz. chestnuts (chopped)

In Chinese wok or a large skillet, bring oil to a boil in intense, high heat. Put in Chinese cabbage and stir-fry for one minute. Drain oil from cabbage and set aside ready for use. Add 2 ½ Tablespoons of oil into the same wok or skillet and bring to the same high heat. Put in the ingredients – bamboo shoots, mushrooms, dried oysters, bean curd, etc. and stir fry for 8-10 minutes. Salt to taste and pour in the combined mixture of (as in the first paragraph) oyster sauce, soy sauce, cornstarch, wine, etc. Quick stir fry for four to five minutes until moist-dry and it is ready for serving. Best when served hot with steaming "wok hay" or pan flavor. (Serves 10)

CHUNG KWONG SQUABS – EPICURE'S DISHES FROM ANCIENT CHINA

2-1 to 1¼ Lb. young dressed squabs
3 thin slices fresh ginger root
1 teaspoon cinnamon
1 small piece dried tangerine peel
(soak in water, wash, and use in softened condition)

1½ teaspoon salt
2 cloves star anise
1 fresh garlic clove
a sprinkling of Five Fragrant spices

Mince ingredients very finely and mix thoroughly.
Lightly rub and spread mixture over squabs and
piece a scallion stalk over each bird. Steam cook
for 45 minutes, rinse off under cold running water.
Carefully dry squabs with absorbent paper towel,
brush lightly outside of squabs with best grade
Chinese soy sauce. Roll whole squab in cornstarch
until evenly coated. Steam cook squabs in pot for 10
minutes. Remove from pot and let cool.

(Continue)

Keep covered and put in refrigerator overnight.

To prepare to eat, use large deep-fry utensil or Chinse wok, with sufficient vegetable oil to cover squab with ½" over. When oil is brought to intense high heat, gently place squabs (one at a time) in oil and deep fry for 5 minutes or until golden brown. Remove from utensil, place on paper towel to drain. Chop and serve with fresh lemon quarters for garnishing. (Serves 4)

THREE PRINCESS CHICKEN IN OYSTER SAUCE – A NORTHERN DELIGHT

One 3½ Lb. whole chicken which has been boned. Pan fry chicken in fryer pan until brown. Add water to cover chicken, place cover on pan and cook for 45 minutes or until tender. When chicken is thoroughly cooked, cut into 1" cubes. Place chicken on warm plate.

Use broth from chicken, add 1/3 cup oyster sauce, 1/3 cup Chinese light soy sauce, 2 teaspoons sugar, but no salt. Cook to boiling point and stir in pre-mixed thickening of 2 Tablespoons cornstarch with ¼ cup water. Stir while cooking for one minute, pour over chicken and ready to serve. Garnish with parsley and finely cut green onions. (Serves 4 to 6)

FRESH PINEAPPLE CHICKEN AND FRESH PINEAPPLE LICHEE CHICKEN –

FROM KWANGTUNG PROVINCE, HOME OF LICHEE FRUIT

Cut one fresh pineapple into halves with leaves on and remove the inside fruit from shell. Place shell on plate for use in serving. Dice pineapple into one-inch cubes. Leave aside.

Bone 1½ to 2 Lbs. chicken, then cut into one-inch square cubes. Dip chicken into chestnut flour, deep fry in very hot oil until brown and well-cooked, about 5 minutes.

Have prepared sweet and sour sauce ready.

Pour one cup sweet and sour sauce into fry pan with chicken and pineapple (and if pineapple and lichee), ½ cup lichee fruit and bring to boiling point. Boil one minute and stir in pre-mixed thickening of 2 Tablespoons cornstarch in ¼ cup water. Cook one more minute and ready to serve. (Serves 4)

PHOENIX AND DRAGON – A SOOCHOW FAVORITE

One 2½ Lb. young chicken thoroughly cleaned. Bone chicken and cut into 1-inch cubes.

Mix:
4 Tablespoons Chinese soy sauce
2 Tablespoons Chinese white wine
1 small clove garlic, finely chopped
1 small fresh ginger, finely chopped
1 stalk fresh green onion, finely chopped

Marinate the chicken in above mix for two hours.

One Lb. fresh prawns, shelled, cleaned, and deveined, cut back, and boiled in water for three minutes. Drain. Sauté chicken and prawns in hot pan of oil. Salt and pepper to taste. Cover pan and cook about 25 minutes. At the end of this period, stir in thickening of pre-mixed 2 Tablespoons cornstarch with ¼ cup water. Cook 30 seconds and remove from fire and serve. (Serves 5 to 6)

CHINESE MUSHROOMS AND ASPARAGUS – DELICIOUS AND NON-FATTENING

Soak ¼ Lb. Chinese black mushrooms for 1½ hour. Wash thoroughly, change water repeatedly until mushrooms are cleaned. Place in covered saucepan and simmer for 45 minutes. Do not add salt. Then remove cover and cook for 30 minutes in low heat. Drain water, place mushrooms on serving plate. (If large mushrooms, slice into small pieces)

Add:
1 Tablespoon sugar
¼ cup oyster sauce
¼ cup light soy sauce

Sprinkle one Tablespoon of cornstarch into mushrooms together into wok or large frying pan. Stir fry mushrooms and asparagus together 10 to 15 minutes. Stir in pre-mixed thickening of cornstarch and water, cook one minute and it is ready to serve. (Serves 4)

SNOWFLAKE SHRIMP BALL – A BANQUET APPETIZER

Shrimp paste: 1 Lb. shelled and cleaned prawns, mash into paste (use Osterizer), then place in bowl.

Add 1 teaspoon white wine, some white pepper, ½ teaspoon salt and egg white
Whip prawn paste until smooth.
Do not add water.

Cut and dice 10 slices white bread into ½" squares. Roll 1 Tablespoon shrimp paste into a ball and cover same with the squares of bread. Heat vegetable oil to boiling in deep fry pot. Place shrimp ball in and deep fry for 20 minutes or until shrimp balls turn golden brown. Watch carefully so shrimp balls do not burn. Serve. One Lb. of prawns makes 10 balls. (Serves 10)

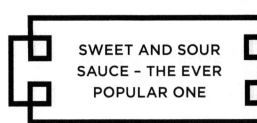

SWEET AND SOUR SAUCE – THE EVER POPULAR ONE

1 cup white vinegar
1 cup pineapple juice
1 Tablespoon salt
1 teaspoon red food coloring
1 fresh lemon (squeeze the juice and put the whole lemon in together; after cooking, take the lemon peel out)
1 cup orange juice
1 cup tomato catsup
1 cup sugar

Cook the above ingredients together until boiling point. When it is cooked, put it aside until it gets very cold before putting in the refrigerator. It is ready for use at any time. Do not keep it for more than two weeks. Use the same sauce for sweet and sour pork, prawns, and chicken.

SWEET AND SOUR PRAWNS

1 Lb. prawns, cleaned and shelled
½ cup flour
½ teaspoon salt

Slice the back on the prawns three quarter of the
way through. Mix with flour and salt. Deep fry in
350 degree until prawns are golden brown. Place
in saucepan and toss cook with one cup Sweet
and Sour Sauce. Stir in thickening, pre-mixed
of 1 Tablespoon cornstarch and ¼ cup of water.
Cook 30 seconds and it is ready to serve.
(Serves 3)

SWEET AND SOUR PORK

One Lb. lean pork, cut into 1-inch cubes
4 Tablespoons flour
2 Tablespoons cracker meal
1 egg
1 teaspoon salt

Mix the above ingredients together with the pork, then deep fry the pork in slow heat until it is thoroughly cooked. Put the pork into a saucepan and toss cook with 1 cup of Sweet and Sour Sauce. Stir in thickening, pre-mixed of 1 Tablespoon of cornstarch and ¼ cup of cold water. Cook 30 seconds. Then it is ready to serve. (Serves 4)

SWEET AND SOUR WHOLE FISH – A CANTONESE DELICACY

5 Lb. whole fresh fish (Rock cod or Sea Bass)
1 cup of pineapple
1 egg
½ pint of light wine or wine vinegar (wine vinegar preferred)
¼ pint of tomato catsup
1 pint of fresh orange juice
½ pint of sugar
1 teaspoon salt
1 Tablespoon cornstarch
½ cup cold water

Clean and scale the fish. Beat one egg and rub over the whole fish. Sprinkle water chestnut flour on it. Deep fry the fish until it is well-browned. Put on plate and garnish with sliced canned pineapple. Mix sugar, tomato catsup, wine vinegar, fresh orange juice, salt, put the mixed sauce in hot pan, cook until it is boiled. Thicken the sauce with pre-mixed cornstarch and water. Pour sauce over the whole fish and serve immediately. (Serves 4 to 6)

PEKING HONEY APPLE – A DELIGHTFUL TIDBIT

(WESLEY'S FAVORITE TREAT AS A CHILD)

2 medium sized crisp apples
1 egg
½ cup flour
1½ cups sugar

Peel and core apples. Cut each into 10 or 12 sections. Beat egg, combine with flour and water to make a smooth batter. Dip sections of apple in batter to coat, dust very lightly with flour.

In cooking utensil, bring oil to high intense heat and drop in coated apples and deep-fry until light golden brown. Drain on paper towels.

Moisten sugar with sufficient oil and heat over low flame. Stirring slowly constantly until sugar dissolves and becomes syrupy. Quickly pour over apple sections, completely cover all parts of each section.

(Continue)

It is important to work quickly at this point. Transfer apples, already coated, to serving dish and allow a moment to cool slightly. Serve accompanied by a large bowl of water with ice cubes floating in it. To eat, pick up each apple section with fork or chopsticks and immerse in the ice water to crystallize the syrupy coating. Eat immediately. (Serves 6)

The Empress of China featured the distinctive cuisine of all of China. Each dish contained a deft mingling of complementary flavors and textures, cooked to perfection, and represented the delicacies of many regions. Every selection on the menu had its own fragrance and appeal and was a treasured dish of past dynasties. It would give H.K. great pleasure to know that readers will be making a few of them in their own kitchens.

EMPRESS OF CHINA

FOWL
家禽類

CHICKEN

手撕鷄 EMPRESS CHICKEN SALAD 5.50
Sai See Gai
(All Dynasty)
Shredded fried chicken with green onions, Chinese parsley, chopped almonds, spices, served cold with Fan See

雙菜鷄丁 ALMOND AND CASHEW 5.25
CHICKEN
(Cantonese)
Boneless diced chicken, water chestnuts, mushrooms, and bamboo shoots

醬爆鷄丁 CHICKEN IN PLUM SAUCE 5.25
(Shanghai)
Boneless cubes of chicken, bamboo shoots sauteed with plum sauce

宮保鷄丁 PRINCE KUN-BOW CHICKEN 5.25
(Szechuan)
Diced chicken, bamboo shoots, mushrooms, green pepper and hot pepper, sauteed in oil

三蒸鳳球 THREE PRINCESS CHICKEN 6.25
(Peking)
Cubes of boneless chicken, Chinese mushrooms, button mushrooms, fresh straw mushrooms sauteed with oyster sauce

荔枝鳳球 LICHEE CHICKEN 6.50
(Cantonese)
Cubes of chicken, dipped in water chestnut flour, butter and deep fried, then sauteed with Lichee fruit, fresh Mandarin orange sauce and pineapple

龍飛鳳球 PHOENIX AND DRAGON 6.95
(Soochow)
Boneless pieces of chicken, fresh shrimps, ginger, garlic, green onion, spices, sauteed with wine. A dish enjoyed by Emperor Ch'ien-Lung who ordered it entered in the Imperial recipes.

相國鷄球 CHICKEN LI HUNG CHANG 5.50
(American)
Cubes of boneless chicken, sauteed in American wine and soy sauce with snow peas, water chestnuts, green pepper and mushrooms. A dish by Lord Li Hung Chang, the first ambassador to the United States from Imperial China, who introduced the recipe from America to the Empress household.

SEA FOODS
海鮮類

SHELL FISH

龍眼帶子 DRAGON'S EYE SCALLOP 5.75
(Cantonese)
Deep fried Eastern scallops, dragon's eye fruit with sweet and sour sauce

生炒帶子 EMPRESS SCALLOPS 5.75
Chow Dai Gee
(Shanghai)
Sauteed Eastern scallops with water chestnuts, mushrooms and mixed vegetables

皇后龍蝦球 EMPRESS LOBSTER 8.50
(Hong Kong)
Sauteed cubes of lobster meat, snow peas, mushrooms, water chestnuts and vegetables

豉汁龍蝦球 LOBSTER SEE JUP 8.50
(Cantonese)
Sauteed lobster meat with black bean sauce

炒雙龍球 EMPRESS LOBSTER AND 7.50
PRAWNS
(Kwan-tung)
Lobster and Prawns with water chestnuts, bamboo shoots, mushrooms and vegetables

蚨蝶明蝦 BUTTERFLY PRAWNS 5.95
(Peking)
Prawns wrapped in bacon, pan fried to golden brown

干煎蝦碌 PAN FRIED PRAWNS 5.95
(Shanghai)
Pan fried jumbo fresh prawns in shell with green onion, Chinese wine and soy sauce

蝦球龍糊 PRAWNS WITH LOBSTER 6.95
SAUCE
(Cantonese)

A partial view of the Empress of China dinner menu, circa 1973.

The Empress kitchen on the opening day August 15, 1966, with 131 feet of Chinese ranges and 38"-diameter woks.

The chefs at work in the Empress kitchen preparing some delicious dishes.

A typical table setting with banquet-style dishes, including winter melon soup, Peking duck, and crispy-skin chicken.

10

SPORTSMAN

M y dad was a lifelong sports enthusiast. From that day in the 1930s when he first climbed into his friend's "fast" Marmon automobile to the end of his life, he loved sports. He was also invigorated by promoting and organizing them. From managing the Rice Bowl Football team and its fundraising for China in 1937-39, to founding an "Old Timers" basketball game charity event in 1952, he enjoyed using sports to generate money for charitable causes. In fact, if you look through the history of Chinatown from the 1940s to 1980s, any sporting event to better Chinatown would likely have been my dad's idea. Or, at the very least, he would have been active in organizing it.

H.K. thoroughly enjoyed getting people interested in sports. To that end, he was co-founder and President of the San Francisco Chinese Basketball Club from 1947 to 1949, and co-founder of the San Francisco Chinese Sports Car Club in 1954. This zeal for sports was a common thread in his life, and his enthusiasm drew others into it with him. But of all the sports my dad took delight in, tennis was his most enduring interest – and the one in which he held the longest and most prominent positions.

H.K. was an avid tennis player. Noted for being the steadiest influence in San Francisco's Chinatown to promote tennis to the Northern California Chinese population, my dad loved everything about the game. From 1932, when he first picked up a tennis racket, through the rest of his life, my dad was passionate about the sport. His lifelong friend, Dr. Walter Wong, a dentist from Capitola, California, was also a tennis enthusiast. In 1934, Dr. Wong had played in an inter-city tennis match between Los Angeles and

San Francisco at the Palace of Fine Arts in San Francisco. After winning a set, he heard a single rollicking cheer of support burst out over the crowd. Though Dr. Wong ultimately lost the match, when my dad bounded up to him and announced himself as the ardent fan and fellow Chinese American who had yelled his enthusiasm, the two became instant friends. From that day forward, H.K. decided to seriously take up tennis – and they played tennis with each other at least once a month. Until two months before he died, my dad regularly played tennis with Dr. Wong.

In the early 1920s, residents of San Francisco Chinatown were troubled that the only place their children had to play was in the Chinese community's tiny streets and narrow alleyways. Efforts to find play space received continuous opposition from the city planners. Plus, there was not a lot of open space in Chinatown for a tennis court. To address that concern, my dad was one of the people instrumental in getting the first public tennis court built in Chinatown in 1925. The first player to win a match there that I am aware of was Minnie Fong. Sister to Alice Fong Yu, the first Chinese schoolteacher in San Francisco (1926), Minnie won top tennis awards for many years. In 1929, she won double titles at Stanford with her tennis partner, Daisy L. Wong. That same year, she won the Chinese Christian Students' Conference singles. Fong and Wong were the two top women players from the 1920s to the 1930s. But short of a select few Chinese tennis players like Minnie Fong who were playing at the time, tennis was uncommon in San Francisco Chinatown. Many years later, tennis player Thomas W. Chinn explained, "A difficult thing for the present generation to understand is why we did not take up the game earlier. One sentence can answer that query: there were no tennis courts in Chinatown, and we were not welcome elsewhere."

The San Francisco Chinese Tennis Club

Recognizing the need for youth in Chinatown to have a place to play tennis and other sports, the San Francisco Playground Commission appealed to the city for funding to build three courts – one each for basketball, volleyball, and tennis. They were successful. Land was purchased to build a Chinese Playground near Grant Avenue. The first Pacific Coast Chinese tennis tournament was played at the Chinese Playground on its small-scale tennis court in 1935, with 200 participants.

By 1935, tennis had become so popular among young people in Chinatown that my dad recognized the need for an organized tennis club. His reasoning went beyond the actual sport, too. My dad already knew that discrimination blocked Chinese Americans from playing in mainstream U.S. tournaments. He felt that organized competitive sports had the power to bridge cultural gaps and build community. In an April 22, 1982 *Asian Week* article, journalist Lim P. Lee quoted H.K. as saying, "Physical contact in sports leads to mental exchange and opens the avenue of communication between people of different ethnic backgrounds. It fosters better understanding of other heritages and cultures." To that end, and with the intention of motivating youth in Chinatown to become involved in playing tennis, in 1936 my dad became one of the first few founding members of the San Francisco Chinese Tennis Club (first called Chitena). With hope of giving rise to an international champion, the tennis club was open only to Chinese players. Dr. Walter Wong became a charter member of the club.

In 1936, H.K. was elected Vice-President of the San Francisco Chinese Tennis Club, and in 1937 its President. As President in 1937, his vision became reality. The Club became known nationwide, and that same year he became an accredited member of the National Capital Tennis Association (NCTA) and the United States Court Tennis Association (USCTA). (The NCTA is a nonprofit organization dedicated to the growth of tennis, and the USCTA is the nonprofit U.S. governing board of court tennis.) In 1949, the club was permitted to upgrade its annual tournament to the National Chinese Championships. The Club grew, and its players excelled quickly.

Until 1960, my dad actively served the San Francisco Chinese Tennis Club in numerous executive capacities, including management of its publicity, as well as public relations outreach to the Chinese communities of the Pacific Northwest. In 1947-48 and again in 1950-51, he was the first

Chinese American to serve on the Board of Directors of the Northern California Tennis Association, an organization at that time of over 130 tennis clubs in Northern California. During this time, he also chaired the Northern California Interclub committee. Though the San Francisco Chinese Tennis Club was initially turned down for membership in the Northern California Tennis Association, in 1947 it was accepted into it due largely to my dad's enthusiastic and active promotion of the San Francisco Chinese Tennis Club. Not only did he actively bring the Club into the Northern California Tennis Association, he also had the Club's annual tennis tournament sanctioned as a Chinese National Championship. In 1949, the San Francisco Chinese Tennis Club won the First National Chinese Championship.

In the 1950s, Dr. Walter Wong introduced my dad to national tennis champion Dr. Ton Jue, an optometrist, who was playing at one of the tennis tournaments hosted by the San Francisco Chinese Tennis Club in Chinatown. Dr. Wong and H.K. were both members of the S.F. Chinese Tennis Club. Like Dr. Wong, Dr. Jue and my dad shared a love of tennis and became fast friends. Dr. Wong and Dr. Jue lived near Aptos, California, located 70 miles south of San Francisco. In 1975, my dad inspired Dr. Jue to build the Imperial Courts Tennis and Swim Club in Aptos. My dad was one of the original investors, and Dr. Wong became a charter member. Bud Lenox, who had helped my dad get the directorship at El Camino Bank and had invested in the Empress of China, also lived near Aptos in Santa Cruz, California. Lenox and Dr. Jue were close friends. In 1975, Lenox and his family also became charter members of the tennis and swim club. To this day, the Imperial Courts Tennis and Swim Club continues to thrive. Dr. Jue, who is now nearly 100 years old, still visits his club frequently.

For twenty-five years, from 1935 to 1960, my dad tirelessly promoted tennis in Chinatown and beyond. Under his direction, the San Francisco Chinese Tennis Club won the Pacific Coast Chinese Club championship in Vancouver, B.C. As Chairman of the Northern California Tennis Association Inter-club competitions during the 1950s, he also oversaw more than a thousand interclub tennis matches in Northern California. He organized tennis tournaments among various clubs in California, Oregon, Washington, and Vancouver.

My dad enjoyed playing tennis for fun and recreation. He was not always the best player in the group, as he considered himself a "hamburger player." In the 1960s and 1970s, he would drive over the Bay Bridge on weekends and play with his tennis buddies at various courts in the East Bay. Whenever we traveled as a family, we would always pack tennis rackets. When we reached our destination, my dad would seek out two things: a Chinese restaurant (to speak to the chef or owner) and a tennis court (to play a few sets for fun and exercise).

My mother enjoyed playing tennis, too, and was frequently a doubles partner with my dad. It was a love of tennis, among other things, that brought them together in the 1940s. One of my mother's greatest thrills was partnering with the Australian tennis legend Rod Laver in 1981, during a practice session at the San Francisco Tennis Club.

At the 50th Golden Anniversary of the San Francisco Chinese Tennis Club in 1985, my dad was honored posthumously with a huge perpetual men's trophy for appreciation of his role in the San Francisco Chinese Tennis Club and for his inspiration to players. During a dedication ceremony that day, he was also honored for his contribution to the Chinese National Tennis Championships. The dedication read, "Known to his friends as H.K., 'Mr. Outside' was one of the charter members of the Club. He served the Club in all capacities: president, director, solicitor, and public relations. He was most effective in arranging inter-club activities with other cities, such as Los Angeles, Portland, and Vancouver. The rivalry not only provided keen but friendly competition for the respective club players, but the matches provided the bridging of fellowship amongst players of Chinese descent many, many miles away. He was a great organizer and motivator. He served as the non-playing captain to the teams that won the NCTA Inter-club Class C and Class B championships in 1947 and 1948, respectively. Because of his knowledge and dedication, he was selected to the Board of Directors, Northern California Tennis

Association, the first Chinese and probably the first minority to hold that position. He was instrumental in elevating the Chinese Pacific Coast Championships to national championship status, and for many years paid the annual sanction/membership fees of the NCTA and USCTA. He never missed the finals on Labor Day as he would brave sun or wind to record the highlights of each event for the newspapers. Although he was not here to partake in the Golden Anniversary celebration, we can be sure that he is with us spiritually. Even during his last moments, he was still thinking of the 50th Annual Chinese National Tennis Championships. Such was the dedication and dynamics of H.K. Wong."

In February 1992, my dad was also posthumously inducted into the Northern California Tennis Association Hall of Fame. He was the first Chinese American to be given that distinction. The presenter, praising my dad's accomplishments, said H.K. was most known for "his tireless efforts and ultimate success in getting his own way." He noted that H.K. "even persuaded the U.S. Marine Corps to allow Allen Tong, then Marine Corps Champion, to play in the Asian games." Tong inspired the USLTA to sanction the National Chinese Tennis Tournament.

My dad had been bothered for years that the San Francisco Chinese Tennis Club lacked a clubhouse. All the club's correspondence was mailed to my dad's Ti Sun Company address. The tennis club also only had one tennis court--at the Chinese playground on Sacramento Street--and the court was a tennis player's nightmare. Though it conformed to USTA standards, the distance from the sidelines to outside obstructions was only about two feet. Serving to the forehand court, if a player wanted to ace another, he/she could aim the ball at the nearby light pole, which was also about two feet from the sideline. Even more troubling was the court, which had a slant of over one foot. As a past director of the Northern California Tennis Association, my dad, along with his longtime friend, Dr. Walter Wong, after 50 years of playing on that frustrating tennis court, was able to influence the San Francisco Parks and Recreation Department to fix the problem. At the San Francisco Chinese Tennis Club, H.K. became known as "Mr. Tennis" of Chinatown. His legacy lives on there.

The "Old Timers" Basketball Game

Though tennis was primary in my dad's life, it was not the only sport to capture his interest. He also liked basketball. Not surprisingly, in 1952, H.K. organized an "Old Timers" basketball game for the Opening of the Chinese Recreation Center and to benefit the Playground and New Center's Children's fund. He raised $701.

In a newspaper article H.K. wrote in the early 1950s, "Grant Avenue Tales of the Game," he noted: "The first Old Timers basketball game turned out to be a tremendous success, both as an evening of hilarious entertainment for all concerned...it was an outstanding success because a group of citizens, classified for this event as "old timers," were actually civic and business leaders of our community who wanted to show how they could work together harmoniously for a good cause. They liked my idea of getting together for a game, enjoying the facilities of the New Recreation Center, and doing a job for the kids. The results were electrifying. Never have we seen such community spirit, comradeship, cooperation, and fun. It was one great big happy party – the old timers and their families, the fans, and the kiddies all enjoyed it to the utmost. The buffet supper after the game was a gigantic reunion for the players, many of whom had scattered to other parts and until the night of the game, who had not seen each other for many years. The key to the success of this unique event were the "old timers" themselves...they smashed and rolled into each other with the strength of youth – and, when they tumbled down, grinned and helped each other up. They may not have had the fast reflexes, shots, or stamina of their heyday, but they could still handle the ball..."

Resident Thomas W. Chinn, an "old timer" in the game, reflected, "As the curtain rose over Old Timers Night at the New Recreation Center, and the roster of players appeared before me on the program, my thoughts ran back over the years to those 'old days.' I refer back to the 'old days,' when many of the boys played on the sandlot of Morning Bell Chinese

School, site of our present Chinese Playground on Sacramento Street; to the hilly lot where some of us roasted spuds, or played marbles on the rough grounds which is today the site of our Chinese YMCA; or those blessed few play spots such as Chung Wah School or the Chinese Institute on Stockton Street. Yes, those were 'the old days'—when a basketball goal was an extreme luxury – let alone any decent area in the whole community. Today, as we review our community assets and the modern facilities not only from a recreational standpoint, but educational, health, living and sanitary facilities, I wonder if I'm not voicing the thoughts of all the old timers in thinking: 'We never had such things, but I'm glad our children have them, and I will do my bit toward furthering the progressive program of our city and community leaders in this respect!' An orchid to the founders!"

The San Francisco Chinese Basketball Club

My dad was also the co-founder and president of the San Francisco Chinese Basketball Club, 1947-49. The all-star team, formed in 1946 when two sports-minded Chinese businessmen took the squad that won the Chinese title, added top high-school and club stars to form a community team representing San Francisco Chinatown. The team competed in several inner-city and inter-league Oriental National championships and were undisputed Chinese champions. Of his role, my dad would say, "It was our aim to promote good sportsmanship and foster friendly relationships between our boys and members of other races in the wholesome atmosphere of this popular amateur sport."

In notes dashed on a piece of paper, H.K. said of their first match in Santa Cruz, California, "We commandeered the Ti Sun Company's furniture van and drove the team down through the curvy Santa Cruz grade. At arrival time, most of the teammates were carsick. They rushed to the gym, drank some 7-Up, and dashed out to play. We lost with honor by one basket in a fine game – and the audience gave us a standing ovation."

Honored by the Chinese Six Companies, the Chinese Chamber of

Commerce, the Chinese community, and the American and Chinese press for their outstanding win in the National Oriental Championship, the San Francisco Chinese Basketball team went on to play far beyond regional games. By 1956, the team, now stronger, went on a six-week Far East tour acting as "goodwill sports ambassadors." Members of the team included a teacher, an insurance salesman, an importer, two government employees, a serviceman, and college students taking a leave of absence from work and school. The team played in Taipei, Hong Kong, Singapore, Kuala-Lumpur, Bangkok, and other locations. In the November 17, 1956 Saturday edition of the *Chinese World*, H.K. wrote: "The San Francisco Chinese Basketball Team National Oriental Championships of the U.S. added a new laurel to their list of athletic achievements. They won the championship of the 5th Presidential Birthday Cup tournament Thursday night at Taipei by a decision 67-47 victory over Bangkok." Returning to the U.S., the team was welcomed by the Chinese Six Companies and the Chinese Anti-Communist League with a lavish celebratory tea that was open to the public.

On March 28, 1956, vying for a U.S. championship, the team then went to Salt Lake City to play against an Oriental basketball team from Hawaii in hopes of winning the 5th Oriental National crown. In the April 11, 1956 edition of *Chinese World*, in his column, "H.K.'s Corner," my dad wrote about the event. "The best Oriental basketball players in the U.S. and Hawaii descended upon the quiet Mormon city of Salt Lake last week. Grouped into eight teams representing various cities of the country, they engaged in a hectic three-day battle to determine the National champion. All the quintets were Nisei except the S.F. Chinese who took the coveted title. A capacity crowd jammed the spic-and-span Judge Memorial Gym each evening to cheer their favorite heroes. Rooting against them was a valiant band, including the players, of less than eighteen Chinese, who pulled for their boys in a strained, nerve-wracking silence. The San Francisco Chinese defending champions played one of their best games to shackle the last-minute frenzied drive of a strong Hawaii All-Stars outfit. Our boys edged them 61-60 in the closest, most exciting championship game in the 21-year history of the tournament."

The San Francisco Chinese Sports Car Club

A flattened orange and white baseball cap with the words, "PRESS, Pebble Beach Sports Car Road Races" inscribed across its rim is a carefully folded piece of memorabilia in my dad's collection, along with three press-pass tags – one dated April 21-22, 1956, and two dated March 17–18, 1956. As Publicity Director for the Northern California Region of the Sports Car Club of America (SCCA) from 1954 to 1957, H.K. attended many races and wrote about them for the *Chinese World*, in his column, "H.K.'s Corner." His stories covered races in Pebble Beach, CA; Santa Rosa, CA; Seattle, WA; Buchanan Field, Contra Costa County, CA; Salinas, CA; and Sacramento, CA., to name a few. In 1955 and 1956, he also received two SCCA appreciation awards.

From the day in 1927 when he bought his first sports car for $70 (a Ford Model T roadster) to the day he died, my dad was excited by sports cars and sports car racing events. My mother also had enthusiasm for racing and race cars. In the early 1950s, she was one of the few women who participated in the sport. This is likely one of the many reasons my dad found her so appealing.

My dad had a competitive side, too. A humorous article he wrote on March 15, 1955 entitled, "What's that bub?" catches his love of racing and competition. He wrote: "I was driving my little car down the street enjoying the firm ride, the light positive steering, and the fresh air coming in from the open roof. I was at peace with the world and my fellow men on this fine spring day. I glided quietly up to the intersection and geared down to a halt. As I hummed a song in tune with the car radio, a loud, harsh voice grated my eardrums, 'What's that you're driving, bub?' shocking me back into the land of questions and answers. 'Mister, this is a car made in Germany – rear engine Volkswagen,' I politely answered. 'Aw – it looks like a scooter with a bug on its back and sounds like a lousy coffee grinder,' he retorted. My temperature rose, but I did not have time to answer as the signal turned to green. Two blocks later, we were again side by side. 'Say fellow,' he yelled again. 'Why do you want such a pile of junk?' Indignantly, I raised my voice and answered, 'This is not a pile of junk! It can go up any hill in San Francisco and can go 70-miles-per-hour!' 'Phooey,' he retorted. 'I wouldn't have it if you gave it to me.' So, when the signal changed to 'GO,' I gave it to him! I stepped on the pedal and zig-zagged my powerful, agile little car through the heavy traffic and left him blocks behind."

From 1953 to 1958, H.K. organized the San Francisco Chinese Sports Car Club (SFCSCC). On June 1, 1953, he and two other sports car enthusiasts, Andy Young and Paul H. Louie, met to form the SFCSCC. They emphasized that the club "would be run in the sports club tradition" with "no red tape in an informal, fun, happy way devoted to the enjoyment of safe, courteous sports car motoring." Within one year, my dad wrote in his column that the fame of the San Francisco Chinese Sports Club had "spread to the four corners of the U.S." H.K. described the club as an "informal, free-acting, freewheeling group, with one minute devoted to club business, followed by sports car talk."

Over 60% of the club members were Chinese American sports car owners or fans from the San Francisco Bay Area, with a large segment of the Austin Healy drivers in Sacramento. Among these were an artist, an engraver, a photographer, a Hollywood cameraman, an accountant, truck drivers, government workers, business executives, a restaurant owner, and several doctors and dentists.

Early members were H.K., Andy Young, Nellie Young, Walter Wong, Paul H. Louie, H. Louie, Harding Leong, George Lim, J. Jang, and Wilbur Dere. The secretary of the club, Nellie Young, was the only young Chinese woman in the U.S. at the time to ever race a sports car. Sterling Moss, the number-two racer in the world at the time, was a member of the club. Another one of the first members of the club was a top West Coast sports car driver, Attorney Bill Pollack of Sherman Oaks, a two-time winner at Pebble Beach. Still another was the Sports Car Club of America Publicist, Peter Abenheim (Captain Fortune). Alan Le May, a Saturday Evening Post writer from Pacific Palisades, also drove a Lotus in the races. Members were registered from as far north as Alaska, to as far east as New York and Pennsylvania, and as far south as Los Angeles. Nearly all makes of popular sports cars were represented in the club – from the ultra-grand Rolls Royce and classic Allard Roadster and Bentley to the sleek Jaguar 120 and 140 and speedy Austin-Healey; as well as the Morgan, Porsche Super, Porsche Speedster, Sunbeam Alpine, Lotus, and popular MG 1500, MG TFs, MG TDs, and MG TCs.

My dad's first MG belonged to a friend of his who was a car salesman. His friend called one Saturday and asked if H.K. might like to take care of an MG for him. Apparently, someone had traded it in for another vehicle and my dad's friend did not know what to do with it. Without the slightest idea of what an MG was, H.K. promptly said, "Why, yes – of course!"

The story my dad later wrote about his experience with the MG is a wonderful look at how tenacious and resourceful he was. H.K. wrote: "Have you ever driven an MG? If you have, you know the joy and delight of handling such a car. If you have not, please permit me to relate how I started to drive one. It was a cold, foggy, wintery twilight night in San Francisco when I arrived at the parking lot. This was the first time I had ever set eyes on the low midget-like car with no top and no space – wondering, do grown men really drive these things? The lot attendant was in another car with the motor running. 'Are you Wong?' he asked, to which I nodded slightly, still gazing at my car. 'Okay, here's the keys,' which the attendant tossed without hesitation at me and roared off. So, with keys in hand, I wandered up to the little car. By now, it was dark, and the streetlights merely cast shadows. I groped around, opened the door, and got in.

"How to start the car? That attendant could have at least told me how to do that! I played my fingers across the dash like someone reading Braille, and finally located the keyway to insert the key. The next few minutes, there was only the dull thumping of my foot on the floor feeling for the starter. Where was it? This was doing it the hard way. Why not find the dash light and simplify everything? At the sound of footsteps, I raised my head and called, 'Got a match, fella?' Well, three was better than none, I mumbled to myself. 'Thanks.' Using one, I found the headlights, and with another match, I managed to locate the dash lights – and, just before the third match went out, a quick, catlike glance disclosed the starter next to the key. I had heard stories that the parking lot was haunted, so I nervously gave it a mighty yank. At first, the car would not start – and then I did nothing, and it started on its own.

"Not being a family man but nevertheless valuing my life, I decided to test the brakes – how to release the hand brake? First, yanking with one hand, then with two hands, and then I accidentally depressed the button, found it, and released the brakes. Now to try the foot brake. As just an average size man wearing size 9 shoes with a crepe sole, I tried the brakes and clutch, only to step on my left foot. After some study, I was partially able to step on the brake. The wind was whistling down my neck, so I decided the top must go up. I got it out on the left and it went up, then it went up on the right, but the left side collapsed. This was almost too much – but I was not going to be beaten by this midget of a car. So, I got inside and kneeled on the seat, pulling both sides at the same time, only to find out that it was three to four inches from the windshield. After much pressure, I had to kneel on one knee and use one foot to straighten the other side. Then it became a simple, albeit gymnastic matter to screw the two knobs tight.

"Then – for the side curtains. These English people who designed the MG make life difficult! Or could it be that I just could not see things their way? That is right. In England, everything is opposite of what it is in the U.S. After trial and error, I matched the right to right and left to left. By now, I had resigned myself to do everything slowly and deliberately. Time to get started for home. The cars were whizzing by, and as I crouched over the wheel, I realized that I could not wear my hat. This inexperienced sports car driver became more frightened at each intersection as I discovered I only had the driving lights on. How was I going to get home with this little monster without killing myself? I wished for my Victoria sedan. A cop flagged me down and helped me turn on the headlights, which helped considerably. I continued to drive and was amazed at the agility and maneuverability of this tiny car.

"After an hour of a trip that was usually ten minutes, I stepped out of that car and felt that to go on living, I should leave this little thing alone. I was still shaking from my harrowing experience. Now at home, I thumbed through the owner's manual and started reading, interrupted by frequent trips to the garage to study the MG's different parts. The challenge to become a good sports car driver was in my blood. Rising the next morning, I drove down to the deserted North Beach district to acquire skill in the correct way of shifting through the gears.

"Block after block, I improved, and finally managed to shift without clashing the gears. Approaching corners at 10-15 mph, and after much practice, I found I liked this little car. A hasty lunch and more practice – with its road handling, cornering ability, and diminutive size, maybe this was the car for city driving. The next morning, I found a gem of a park in the crowded streets of Chinatown. Rushing through my work by 2:00 pm, I overcame my yearning to try the MG on the open road. I informed my associates that I needed a rest and left for the day.

"I felt that it would be a good time to visit my friend, Dr. Walter Wong, in Capitola and drive via the curving Highway One along the coast. I took the first 20 minutes calmly. I then increased my speed to 40 mph on the curves and discovered this car could hit the curves and hold. At Stanford junction, when I turned to go up the twisting Kings Mountain road, I noticed a green light on the dash that flickered on and off. 'Guess I'm not using the proper gear,' I muttered to myself. When the light stayed on consistently, I began to worry – could it be out of oil? I rolled up to a service station just in time. I found out that blinking green light indicated it was time for petrol, and said, 'I'll take a gallon of gas, please.' When I arrived in Santa Cruz, I gave rides to all my friends. Many were impressed with my little car, and the others – men, women, and children were lined up waiting for rides."

In that first drive, my dad discovered the thrill of why "grown men drive MGs." Later, a doctor friend who H.K. called "a god of MG" heard my dad talking about the car. The doctor promptly bought the MG from H.K., after which my dad began driving a Jaguar. My dad loved the Jaguar and owned several models. When I was adopted, he had a Jaguar XK150 Coupe, and I would ride in the tiny well in the back. When I grew too big for the back well, my dad sold the car and bought a Ford Thunderbird to accommodate me. In his later years, he traded it in for a sporty red Mustang. Speedy cars fit his personality.

Although the SFCSCC did not have rallies or races of its own, members participated in other clubs' activities. Several of its members were active officials in the Sports Car Club of America (SCCA). A nonprofit organization headquartered at 2911 Van Ness Avenue, San Francisco, the San Francisco Region of SCCA in 1956 was the administrative center for all car racing in Northern California and most of Nevada. All SF/SCCA races benefitted civic groups' welfare funds.

In 1954, at the Santa Clara Road Race with an audience of 20,000 spectators, SFCSCC member Andy Young raced his impressive MG-TD, its hood decorated with a bold, shiny multicolored dragon. Mechanic Doug O'Brien also raced that car. But it was my mom, Honey, who drove Andy's legendary race car to a top-five finish – she placed second in the MG-class and 5th overall. On Tuesday, July 20, 1955, the *Chinese World* reported, "Sports car fans were amazed when they saw a Chinese girl appear on the starting grid of the Sports Car Race at the Santa Clara County Fairgrounds Sunday at San Jose. She was Miss Honey Quan, the first and only Chinese girl to drive in a sports car contest. Miss Quan drove the 'Kuo Wah Special,' a MG Mark II sports car, owned by Andy Young, to a fifth overall place and to a second in the MG class race of the women's event. Driving under the banners of the San Francisco Chinese Sports Car Club and the San Francisco Sports Car Club, she was awarded a contestant plaque for her fine performance on the 1.3-mile fairgrounds course of 12 turns to a lap." In March 1955, as a member of the San Francisco Lions Club, Andy also served as a Race Official at the Stockton Sports Car Race.

Some areas of the country, though, were not as welcoming as others. When a San Francisco Sports Car Club of America race was held in Eureka, California, even though H.K. was its publicity director, my dad did not want to go. He ultimately did go but was nervous. In the 1890s, a ban had been placed on Chinese staying overnight in Eureka, when they were driven out after a fracas with the local whites.

The club's big event of the year was an annual Chinese New Year dinner, which featured a resplendent array of Far East delicacies. In 1952, SCCA's San Francisco Region (SFR) sanctioned the Concours d'Elegance in San Francisco. The event exhibited restored collector automobiles that were judged for their restoration, authenticity, condition, and operation. My dad, always at the forefront of any idea to promote San Francisco Chinatown, envisioned a future members-only Chinatown Concours d'Elegance as part of the club's New Year's celebration. Though SFCSCC did not ultimately have its own Concours d'Elegance, it is my best guess that their membership enjoyed the San Francisco SCCA event.

The San Francisco region of SCCA was also noted for pioneering many safety measures in the sport, such as snow fencing for crowd control and spectator protection, which resulted in lower insurance rates for sports car races nationwide and increased fire protection. San Francisco was the first to train, maintain, and equip its own fire-control squad trackside during races. Safety was a top priority. No spectators were ever injured at their races. As my father wrote in a 1956 publicity article for Sports Car Club of America, "Before the drop of the starter's flag, every pylon, marker, hay bale, foot of snow fencing, piece of equipment and person is in its proper place. Nothing is left to chance. It is always 100% 'safety first' for SCCA. Under the leadership and guidance of this group, it will grow into America's favorite spectator and participant motorsport."

My dad was right. Today, SCCA has expanded its west coast region north to the Oregon border, with 3,400 members – and its U.S. membership exceeds 55,000. Racing has also become a highly popular spectator sport. The Indy 500 live event had well over 250,000 attendees in 2019, and the average number of people watching the NASCAR Daytona 500 race on television for just one day on February 17, 2019 was 9.17 million. In 2016, the U.S. Grand Prix in Texas also had over 96 million viewers, the highest Formula One television audience of a Formula One race anywhere in the world.

H.K. and other San Francisco Chinese Sports Car Club members took great pride in the Badge Bar he designed for the SFCSCC. Made of brass and enameled in five colors, it was designed to mount on the grille of a race car. It showed the head of a traditional Chinese dragon next to a lamppost with a cable car following a race car up a steep hill. The letters SFCSCC were inscribed in red across the top. A scroll with the letters SFCSCC repeated in Sung Dynasty Chinese characters was on the left side. My dad explained why he chose to use the images. "The centrally placed dragon's head is symbolic of athletic groups in Old Cathay. The dragon portrayed is a gentle one with a white flowing beard and a happy, laughing manner, emphasizing the club's good fellowship, politeness, courtesy, and safety. The small, diagonal line in the right corner of the badge represents California Street, one of the steepest hills in San Francisco, which crosses Grant Avenue. On the steep street, a sports car is seen driving ahead of a cable car. A Grant Avenue lamppost, a landmark of San Francisco's Chinatown, completes the image. Collectors as far away as Australia and England made requests to purchase them as collectors' items." These many years later, I still proudly display mine at home. My dad creatively included some special elements into the design of the Badge Bar. The year 1954 is placed on the side of the cable car, and the Chinese characters of the three founders' surnames are hidden on the lamppost. The specially designed SFCSCC Badge Bar was featured in an article and on the cover of the December 1954 *Badge Bar Journal*, a national publication for sports car enthusiasts.

The San Francisco Chinatown Lions Club was founded in 1952 as Lions District 4-C4. H.K. was not a Lions Club member but had many friends who were. He adapted the SFCSCC Badge Bar design for a new banner for the San Francisco Chinatown Lions Club in the 1950s and 1960s. Since the original SFCSCC design had a dragon's head at the center that closely resembled a lion's head, it was well suited to represent the Lions Club.

Duck Hunting

My dad was always game to try something adventurous, especially when it involved sports. On Thursday, December 16, 1954 in his column, H.K.'s Corner, H.K. wrote about a duck hunting experience.

H.K.'s Corner – by H.K. Wong - "Duck Man, Duck!" - the *Chinese World*

"Have you ever enjoyed a brace of perfectly roasted wild ducks, cooked to your most exacting taste, spiced to perfection and dripping with natural juices? That delicious gamey flavor is out of this world and is something to drool over – a gourmet's delight and food worthy of a King. The problem is, how to get the ducks?

"My good hunter friend, Dr. Merle Kays, invited me to a duck hunt and volunteered to demonstrate just how difficult it is, but also what a sport and how much fun it is too. That is why the writer and his companion were wading hip-deep in the cold dark waters of the Colusa rice fields, one morning at 4:00 am.

"To me, a novice hunter, it was a strange experience and an adventure. We drove to Colusa the night before, had a warming cup of coffee, and quickly left the twinkling lights of Market Street, their main stem, behind. Soon we turned off the paved highway onto a narrow, rutty, dirt road which skirted the winding Sacramento River. For some anxious miles, we traveled on it through the thick tule fog. Though Dr. Kays has driven this same twisting route twice a week for nine years, we were both still apprehensive. He barreled around the curves at speed, just like a Grand Prix driver at Le Mans.

"Boar's Lair – With an audible sigh of relief, we braked to a welcome stop in front of an unpainted, old shack...a one room drafty dilapidated Clubhouse without plumbing but appropriately dubbed Boar's Lair. A few hours of shut eye, and before the first nightmare ended, the Big Ben sounded 3:05 a.m. Still half asleep, like men in dreams, we groped around for our outer clothing to put over our long johns. Many layers of clothing and several pairs of socks later, I stood up to push my feet into a heavy pair of hip boots. These boots that 6'2" Doctor Kays loaned to me came up to my armpits! (well, almost).

"A fast wash – all whiskers intact, hair still tangled, and we gulped down double portions of eggs, bacon, toast, and coffee prepared without ceremony by willing male hands. And then we were off! Incidentally, the dishwasher, a former Navy man, had an easy way to get rid of dishwater. He simply carried the pan to the open door – and he heaved it out. It is a lazy no-trouble method – except once, an unsuspecting friend was just coming in and caught the whole pan of dishwater – right in his face!

"<u>Siamese Twins</u> – Now to return to the start of this little tale. Through the total darkness, we walked, or rather, I staggered, into the water. It felt chilly, looked forbidding and terrifying to one who can swim not more than a single stroke. My friend did not want to get his hunting jacket dunked (I was in it), so he grabbed me by the arm – and thus we were Siamese-twinned through the muddy waters of the rice paddies. A one-mile walk with several rest stops, and we finally arrived at the duck blind, jokingly named the 'Palace' – best in the vicinity. A natural growth of tall tules and carefully manmade camouflage provided perfect concealment for the shooters from above and protection from the elements. We entered through a fancy iron gate, then climbed down into a huge 5'X12' box constructed of heavy redwood, anchored and sunken into the field with the edge a little above water. Inside are all the conveniences and comforts of home – except for beds and plumbing! Covered benches, rubberized cushions, arm rests, and gun racks assured the snug enjoyment of guests, even to a library of Wild West books – for the 'no action' periods. Cooking utensils, tools, and dishes were neatly stashed away. A tidy pantry was fully provisioned with a supply of soup, canned goods and cream and sugar too. No need to guess how cold – a giant thermometer informed you of how many degrees you were from being a frozen statistic. Steaming hot Chinese cha sheu buns and sizzling barbecue strips of pork were our lunch for the day – fit for diners of the Sheraton Palace!

"Nervously, we fingered our weapons and settled for a wait at the 'Palace.' We strained our eyes to pierce the pre-dawn darkness. As if blindfolded, we heard but could not see the flapping of wings, the cry of thousands of wild fowl, the splashes and noises of a great flock awakening and feeding. We checked our luminous Timex dials often for the opening minute. Eerie loud quacks, directly behind, startled this still shaky neophyte. 'Twas only big Dr. Kays warming up his duck call with a few practice blasts! Using the duck call correctly is an art. You must call them with the right persuasive tone, combined with nature's greeting. Then they will heed the call, circle, and swoop right down...right into the gun range. If not, they contemptuously wheel into the upper strata. That's when they're not dead ducks!

"Fire One – Faint booms from neighborhood clubs informed us that the magic moment had come. A whirl of wings close-by - Ernie's gun banged twice. A miss – then down came a big fat mallard! Thirty seconds later, Doc's gun spoke three times, two misses – and then his teal landed with a splash. Another pair of hapless victims flew out of the grey sky on Ernie's side. He triggered twice and bit his first double. A widgeon plummeted straight down on our blind – we had to duck the duck!

"After a half-an-hour of shooting, my friend urged me to shoulder my automatic for action. I aimed at all winging creatures over Colusa County, and succeeded in scaring them away. As my friend pointedly remarked, 'That fellow is so high, he's using his second tank of oxygen!' Then I realized that shooting ducks should be left strictly to the experts – and my two buddies were such. They could tell at-a-glance whether the zooming birds were mallards, spring, or teal. I couldn't even tell the difference between a duck, a mud hen, or a seagull! So, I focused on shooting the hunters – with my Exakta camera – 20 for 20. I concentrated so hard that once when my friend hollered, 'Down,' I sat right down in the water. The seat of my pants was mighty uncomfortable the rest of the morning. A few more hours of productive shooting and we completed our day of sports. The huntsmen quickly defeathered and cleaned their strings without much help from me, and we headed for home. At my house, they stopped – and grinning like Cheshire cats, they presented me with their limit of ducks.

"Have you ever enjoyed a brace of perfectly roasted wild ducks, cooked to your most exacting taste, spiced to perfection, and dripping with natural juices? Well, I have!"

Fishing

My dad was more successful at fishing than duck hunting. His good friend, Andy Young, owner of Kuo Wah Restaurant, would often take my dad fishing on his boat on San Francisco Bay. Frank Yort, another family friend, owned a farm in Calistoga, California that grew several crops and raised peacocks. The farm also had a pond that was stocked with blue gill, trout, and striped bass. Our family made many visits to the Yort family farm in the late 1960s. My dad taught me how to fish and then how to clean and descale the catch. My fondest memories of my dad were the times we went fishing at the Yort family farm. I still enjoy fishing on the river or ocean with my fishing buddies whenever I can.

H.K. caught an 18-pound striped bass in Suisun, CA., circa 1945.

My dad and I had a successful day of fishing at the Yort family farm in Calistoga, CA., circa 1968.

H.K., President of the San Francisco Chinese Tennis Club, with Consul General C.C. Huang at the Chinese Playground for the 1937 Spring Tennis Tournament, May 1937.

H.K. at a tennis match in Salinas, CA., representing the San Francisco Chinese Tennis Club, June 28, 1936.

H.K. chasing a ball on the Chinese Playground tennis court, circa 1941.

H.K.& Honey with the Australian
tennis legend, Ron Laver, at the
San Francisco Tennis Club, April 1981.
Photo by Vano Photography.

H.K. with his Jaguar
XK120 after a tennis
match in Berkeley,
circa 1958.

The San Francisco Chinese Basketball team tipped off against the Berkeley Nisei team at the Civic Auditorium, March 20, 1948. The Chinese team won the game, 53-34. H.K. was co-founder and president of the San Francisco Chinese Basketball Club, 1947-1949.

H.K. designed the special badge bar for the San Francisco Chinese Sports Car Club (SFCSCC). Made of brass and enameled in five colors, it was designed to mount on the grille of a sports car. The badge bar was featured on the front cover of the December 1954 Badge Bar Journal. Photo by Kem Lee.

The three founders of the SFCSCC (H.K, Paul Louie, and Andy Young) with Andy's MG sports cars in front of the Kuo Wah Café on Grant Avenue. Circa 1954.

A SFCSCC gathering in a Chinatown parking lot. Second car from right: Winnie Wong, Eric de Reymer, H.K. Wong, circa 1954.

Honey seated in Andy Young's MG-TD sports car; its hood was decorated with a bold, shiny, multi-colored dragon. July 1955.

H.K. in his newsman outfit. H.K. was the Publicity Director for the Northern California Region of the Sports Car Club of America (SCCA) from 1954 to 1957. He attended many races and wrote about them for the *Chinese World*, in his column, "H.K.'s Corner."

H.K. covered the Stockton sports car race from the press box, March 1957.

The spectators lined the race course for an intimate view of the Stockton sports car race, March 1957.

Duck hunting in Colusa, CA. with Dr. Meryle Kays, November 10, 1954.

11

JOURNALIST

**"It's all storytelling, you know.
That's what journalism is all about."**

– Tom Brokaw

While sifting through my dad's many boxes of memorabilia, newspaper articles, photos, magazines, journals, and writings, one magazine from the 1950s caught my eye and made me smile. It was from the New York School of Writing, circa 1954. A private school dedicated exclusively to "teaching those with an aptitude for writing how to profit by their talent," the school promised students that they would "achieve financial independence with their pens." Owned, operated, and staffed by people actively working as writers and editors, their ad claimed that writing was a well-paid career with abundant opportunity. "Get your share of this endless outpouring of writing money! In this vast field, there is a spot for you." Through individualized instruction, aspiring would-be writers were told they could learn the trade of professional writing. Though he had already by this time been writing for a variety of publications, H.K. knew he wanted to give an even stronger voice to what was happening in San Francisco Chinatown – so he signed up for the school's classes.

After twenty-one writing assignments from the school and nine comprehensive examinations, H.K. continued to write professionally for many years. Though the promise of an endless outpouring of money was likely an exaggeration, my dad wrote prolifically and did give a voice to San Francisco Chinatown. As a self-taught journalist, he wrote articles for the Chinese Rice Bowl, the Ti Sun Company, the San Francisco Chinese Sports Car Club, the Chinese Basketball Club, the Empress of China

H.K.Wong

Restaurant, the Northern California Tennis Association, and countless civic, cultural, political, business, and arts events.

Reporter

H.K.'s interest in journalism began with his writing of a column for the September 4, 1936 issue of the *Chinese Digest*, entitled "Knocking Around." The column was a collection of events in the Sacramento Chinese community. The *Chinese Digest* was the first English-language publication for Chinese Americans. H.K. changed his column a month later, writing under the pseudonym "R.R.: Roaming 'Round" because he was unsure of his writing ability. The magazine published from November 1935 until 1940.

Chingwah Lee, the first American-born son of a Chinese doctor, had inadvertently inspired the *Chinese Digest*. Though Chinatown's underground at the time was no rougher than the western one with its racketeers and gangsters, Chinatown back then was believed to be a chilling place of hatchet men, slave traders, opium dens, and dark passageways. Western tourists were drawn to Chinatown looking for this rumored lurid behavior, which in fact was highly exaggerated. Lee, 12 years old, decided to set the record straight. He followed tourists and the "Chinatown After Dark" tourist guides around at night, loudly contradicting everything the tourist guides said. Inspector J.J. Manion agreed with Lee, noting that "the majority of American Chinese were honest and law-abiding citizens of whom the U.S.A. may well be proud." The *Chinese Digest* grew from Lee's belief that the truth about Chinatown needed to be told, both to educate the American West about the Oriental East and to preserve Chinese traditions in Chinatown. Newspaper journalist Thomas W. Chinn was the *Chinese Digest*'s first editor. Shortly after the *Chinese Digest* launched, Lee was hired as an art consultant and actor for the movie *The Good Earth* and went to Hollywood. He also played the part of Ching, the farmer, in the film. MGM cast him in two other films, *The Rainbow Pass* and *Daughter of Shanghai*. A good portion of his Hollywood earnings subsidized publication of the *Chinese Digest*.

In the December 1937 issue of the *Chinese Digest*, H.K. wrote about the first Rice Bowl football game. My dad was the manager of the San Francisco football team at the time: "A war relief benefit Rice Bowl football game has been arranged between the Los Angeles (L.A.) and San Francisco (S.F.) Chinese...the first game will be played down south this month and the second next month in S.F. The L.A. team, which has been playing together for the past two years and has been winning all its tilts this season, is a heavy favorite to win. Its strong line and fleet backs will be hard for the S.F. boys to handle. However, the latter are being coached by Bill Fisher, St. Mary's All-American guard, and so their hopes are high..."

In the July 1938 issue of *Chinese Digest*, H.K. wrote exuberantly about the Rice Bowl event again: "June 17, 1938 was an unforgettable night in the memory of all San Franciscans, for on that night one and all opened their hearts and purses to help fill the rice bowls of China, and in so doing, enjoyed the greatest festival ever held here in Chinatown. Never has San Francisco seen such a unique party! It jammed and filled every available inch of the streets. It took hours to go from one end of Grant Avenue to the other. They came to see the magnificent parade, to thrill at the glamorous display of Chinese gowns at the two fashion shows, to laugh and give heartily at the 'Magistrate's Court,' to enjoy the Chinese music and plays on the stands and at the theatres, and to take their chances at the street carnival. The huge and gorgeously illuminated Dragon danced as it had never danced before. It writhed, wriggled, and twisted to the appreciative multitude who, up until now, had only seen it walk through its dance. Chinatown that night was magically transformed into a romantic spot of the Far East."

In the May 1937 issue of the *Chinese Digest*, while President of the San Francisco Chinese Tennis Club (Chitena), H.K. also wrote fondly of tennis: "Tennis – a game of universal appeal to men and women, young and old, a game with more than fifty years of brilliant history in the field of competitive sports – is but a comparatively new game to the Chinese community of San Francisco. Notwithstanding this short time, however, this game has grown in popularity by leaps and bounds in Chinatown. And it is a deserved popularity. With the rapid growth of this new sport, a group of enthusiasts formed the S.F. Chinese Tennis Club (Chitena), to foster sportsmanship and competitive tennis for Chinese youths. Leading organizations of the community, notably the S.F. Lodge of the Chinese American Citizen's Alliance, recognizing this ideal, joined hands with this club to sponsor the First Chinese Pacific Coast Tennis Championships in 1936. These championships are henceforth to be held every year."

Columnist and Magazine Editor

In 1941, H.K. wrote for the *Chinese Nationalist Daily,* and in 1942, for the *Chinese News.* He also wrote for the *Chinese Press* from 1938 to 1953, as well as *East/West, Asian Week,* and *Chinese Pacific Weekly.* But it was in the *Chinese World* newspaper that he did his most prolific writing, from 1954 to 1968, in his popular column, "H.K.'s Corner." Printed in both Chinese and English, *Chinese World* was the only bilingual Chinese daily at the time, and the oldest Chinese newspaper in the U.S. Besides writing his column in *Chinese World,* my dad also served as the California editor/ columnist for the Vancouver, B.C. based publication, *Chinatown News,* from 1958 to 1980.

From 1974 to 1982, H.K. was also the Associate Editor of *JADE Magazine,* Los Angeles, a quarterly magazine that focused on the Asian American community. Jerry Jann, the editor and publisher, was a sports car enthusiast and driver, and one of the stunt drivers of Herbie the VW Beetle in the original 1968 *The Love Bug* movie. Henry Tom, a *JADE Magazine* reader in Los Angeles, wrote in a letter to the editor, "I would like to thank you for the fine articles in *JADE Magazine.* They go a long way to building pride in being an Asian. As a member of the older generation who can remember what things were like many years back, it is pleasing to see the progress and achievements of the younger people."

In the Summer 1982 issue of *JADE Magazine,* businessman George Ow, Sr. penned an article, written as an open letter to his children and grandchildren, that appealed to H.K. The power of Ow's story illustrated why *JADE Magazine* was such an important magazine in building Asian pride – and why my dad was proud to be its Associate Editor. A popular philanthropist and extremely successful businessman in Santa Cruz, California, Ow had been born into an impoverished family in the village of Toisan, China. He wrote that his earliest memory was of being so hungry, he ate pebbles. Ow came to the U.S. in 1937 with only $2 in his pocket. When he died on August 2, 2004, he had invested in and operated many family-owned businesses, with over 100 tenants in buildings he owned. In Ow's article, he wrote to his progeny, "If you have big dreams and the willpower to make them come true, you too can make everything you touch a mountain of gold."

In 2016, the Ow family honored their dad's legacy. They built a FedEx distribution center in Watsonville and designed the complex so that parking lot runoff would recharge the area's water table. They also installed 1,000 solar panels on its roof. Additionally, they rejuvenated the Wrigley Building in Santa Cruz. Once a factory for chewing-gum processing, it is now a center for art galleries, businesses, service companies, and small manufacturers. The Ow family trust has also funded over 1,000 American Dream scholarships for low-income and underserved students, as well as numerous nonprofits. As Henry Tom had said, "It is pleasing to see the progress and achievements of the younger people."

President of the Asian American Press Club

From 1967 to 1968, H.K. was President of the Asian American Press Club, a group of Chinese, Japanese, and Filipino newsmen and editors. He was also good friends with many of the writers and editors at the *San Francisco Chronicle and Examiner*, including Herb Caen. Otherwise known as "Mr. San Francisco," Caen was an immensely popular journalist who wrote with candid humor about life in San Francisco for nearly sixty years. He also included interesting tidbits on my dad or gossip about Chinatown. Though he died in 1997, Caen was such a San Francisco icon that the *San Francisco Chronicle and Examiner* continue to publish his columns to this day. In his column, Caen nicknamed my dad "Mr. Chinatown."

Editor and Author

While President of the Chinese Chamber of Commerce of San Francisco, in 1961 H.K. edited the Chinese Chamber of Commerce guidebook, *San Francisco Chinatown on Parade.* In addition to editing the book, H.K. wrote the chapter, "Introduction to Chinatown." H.K. commissioned watercolor artist Jake Lee to paint a scene of Chinatown with the Chinese dragon on parade for the cover of the guidebook. Lee covertly added the initials "H.K." to one of the building signs, to my dad's delight.

Though he would not have known it at the time because the term "New Journalism" was yet to be invented, my dad wrote in that style, personally and directly in such a way that readers were put right into the scene with him. My dad's colorful style can be seen in a retrospective article he wrote in 1955 about the 1939 Golden Gate International Exposition, a San Francisco-based World's Fair. The event celebrated completion of the Bay Bridge and Golden Gate Bridge. Though some people in San Francisco's Chinese community felt that the Fair's Chinese Village did not authentically or fully represent Chinese tradition and culture, H.K. was inspired by newsman Art Linkletter's description of it. Linkletter also acknowledged Lew Dun Quan and his musicians; guest speaker C.C. Huang, the Chinese Consul General of San Francisco; and the Fair's Royal Princess Der Ling.

H.K.'s Corner by H.K. Wong –
"Nostalgic Memories of the Fair" – the *Chinese World*

"The Golden Gate Exposition, the World's Fair on San Francisco Bay at Treasure Island lives on in the memory of men. On February 18th, at 10:30 AM, it will be exactly sixteen years since then Governor Culbert L.

Olsen officially opened the Exposition. He gingerly inserted and turned the $35,000 jeweled key in a replica of the Golden Gate Bridge under the Arch of Triumph. Millions of visitors, with a one-day high record of 183,876, clicked the turnstiles. They wandered and raved over the wonders and pageantry of the place. One of the 'must see' spots of the Fair was the Chinese Village. It was a walled city which cost more than $2,000,000 to build, occupying more than three acres, with many shops, buildings, exhibits, and pavilions. In the center was a colorful seven-story pagoda, the third highest point on the island.

"But, let Art Linkletter tell you about it. He was the roving reporter for the Mutual Broadcasting System on Dedication Day, a three-day preview before the official opening. Here is what Art Linkletter's yellowed script sheets which I retained revealed:

'Well folks, let's you and I set out this last number, or rather, let's walk it out, because right now I'm standing outdoors in the sun-flooded main courtyard of the Chinese Village on Treasure Island. I am carrying a portable microphone and there is a long cord on it, so I can walk among the vividly colored attractions and describe them to you. Let us go down this narrow, winding street of old Peking or Canton. On February 18th, or anytime during 1939, you will see native Chinese craftsmen in bright stores along this street carving ivory, jade, and silver into unbelievably intricate and beautiful shapes. As I walk along these flowered pathways, I'm approaching the home of the Chinese apple peelers, the men with the magic hands, who take two knives and rotate an apple between their blades, peeling it and then throwing it high into the air – and cutting it into three slices as it falls. But now for that magnificent pagoda in the center of the village. Let us be careful to walk around these delicate gardens of lotus, jasmine, and azalea...and more plum trees, too. They are a symbol of romance, you know. And there is romance here! We will look up now to the skies, getting a sweeping glance of this magnificent pagoda...two, four, seven stories high, each roof a different color – Peking blue, the ever-present Imperial Gold, red and green. The curled tip of each of the seven roofs ends in fiery dragons and huge lions. In this pagoda will rest China's art treasures – a priceless five-foot pagoda of solid jade – as well as rare silks, jewels of the Han, Ming, Sung, and other dynasties, going back 4,000 years. Over my left, snuggled against the great wall which encloses the village with an oriental air of mystery, is a real Chinese temple...the Temple of Kuan Yin, Goddess of Beauty. You may come here during the fair and see native Chinese at worship.

'But let us move along toward the main entrance which faces the East shore of Treasure Island. The blessing of Kuan Yin has evidently been invoked again and again, for the main entrance, crowned with a massive arch, is the most intricate and beautiful handiwork I have ever seen. Festoons of oriental flowers, minute carvings and scrollwork, with insets of ancient warriors astride gold lions! Rickshaws piloted by natives will meet us at this gate during the 238 days of the World's Fair of the West. And before we finish our quick tour around the walled village, let us take a last sweeping look at it overall, for we cannot see it again until February 18th. Chinese cafes, cocktail lounges with native furniture, that lofty pagoda again, its dragons looking down at us, tea gardens, flower gardens, a rainbow turned into a city, theatres, a place of Good Fortune, and scores of little shops filled with good things to tickle your appetite and stir your imagination. But our date with the East draws to a close, so let us go back to the dedication festivities.'

"And that was Linkletter's 'East Meets West' description of the famed Chinese Village. He went on to other features of the Fair – he pointed out the Fair's loveliness and beauty, the pageantry and color, the matchless array of exhibits and concessions, and the wonders of the exhibition halls – and excellent symbol of progress, culture, and democracy."

REFELECTIONS ON A RIDE IN AN AIR FORCE JET

On May 25, 1955, my dad took readers for a ride in an Air Force jet.

H.K.'s Corner by H.K. Wong –

"Noble Order of Jet Jockeys" - the *Chinese World*

"'How does it feel to ride in a jet?' That is the universal question everyone asks. Last week I was invited to ride in a U.S. Air Force jet plane for a preview of Armed Forces Day at Hamilton Field. Flashing above the sunny California countryside in a jet at more than 500 mph was an experience and privilege that I will long remember and which I will try to share with you readers through this Corner.

"A jet plane is a tremendously fast aircraft. It is the star of the Air Force and rightfully so. They whiz through the air with ease beyond the speed of sound and often above sight. Latest models can go at supersonic speed and climb to unbelievable heights in safety. On Armed Forces Day, an F-86 Sabre Jet set a new speed record for the Los Angeles to New York and return run on the same day in 11 hours and 26½ minutes. It flew 5,085 miles at an average speed of 445 mph. Planes such as these can fly to Los Angeles in less than 30 minutes and to Sacramento in six minutes. My 50-minute flight was made in a comparatively sedate 600 mph, T-33 jet fighter, 2-place trainer. This type, a development of the 'Star Fire,' is the plane which 9 out of 10 of the worlds' jet-rated fliers are trained.

"Step by step, my excitement mounted as Major Howard Price, Lt. Lew Raines, and Lt. Thomas Davies of the 84th Fighter Interceptor Squadron gave me a lecture on jet-propelled aircraft. In the ready-room, Sgt. Chas. Haig assisted me in the dressing rituals: first, a flight suit, then a Mae West, next a one-man life raft, and then a parachute. Lt. Arthur Roth carefully selected a crash helmet, an oxygen face mask, and intercom unit, and tested the whole affair. He spent 45 minutes briefing me as to their proper procedure and use. He patiently explained to this bewildered groundling what to do in all emergencies, including how to fly the plane in case the pilot is rendered hors de combat. He went over this three times, and I remembered what to do in a vague sort of way – in case. I staggered under the weight of the equipment and walked with the life raft slapping at my backside to the plane. I watched Capt. Irwin check out the plane with his crew staff. When he stuck his head into the cavernous tailpipe, he cracked to me, 'Dark, isn't it?' I numbly nodded.

"I climbed into the cockpit and was tightly strapped to the seat – and was again reviewed on all the emergency requirements, with additional instructions in case of a bail out on how to actuate the explosive charge in the canopy; detonate the ejector seat, pull the chute cord in the air; inflate the Mae West and life raft in the water; how to watch the multitude of dials and gauges, control the plane if necessary; regulate the oxygen if required; and what to do in case of a flame out. With beads of perspiration forming on my brow, I resigned myself to my fate – and to Capt. Irwin.

"We streaked down the long runway at over 250 mph and were airborne in seconds. My pilot, Capt. Walter Irwin of Tacoma, Washington, a fourteen-year veteran of the Air Force, handled the ship with skill and went into a breathtaking climb. I settled down to take notes of my first jet flight.

"The impression of speed is terrific at takeoff and can be visualized when close to the ground as hangers, grounded planes, vehicles, and the scenery blur by. At low altitudes, landmarks are approached and recede at a blink of the eyes. You can feel the sensation of tremendous speed when you climb, dive, or bank by the changing pressure and force of gravity on your body. As you continue up, there is none of that incessant pounding of piston-driven planes, no annoying throbbing of engines, no noisy roar of exhaust, no nerve-wracking vibration. A jet ride is quiet, a sort of sssshhh-ing vibrant silence of swift passage through the atmosphere. It is a wonderful feeling to roam through the sky lanes. It is thrilling and altogether out-of-this-world. When you look down to earth, this is also a wondrous, peaceful feeling – though my peacefulness was mixed with intense excitement and great curiosity.

"In 50 minutes, we swept through the California skies, thrice over the Bay Area, twice over San Francisco, touched Yosemite, came back to Vallejo, Mare Island, on to Sacramento, circled Lake Tahoe and the rugged Sierra Nevada mountains at 18,000 feet. On the way back, the captain did a 'roll-over' and I observed the Fairfield-Suisun Highway, head dangling down. The pinnacle of my excitement came when Capt. Irwin murmured over the inter-com, 'Okay, it's all yours, take it over!' 'Me?'

"I squeaked and grasped the stick. Under the pilot's calm coaching, I was soon diving, climbing, and banking the jet. Five minutes of this and my day was done. The Capt. took the controls and we headed for home at 500 knots an hour (that is over 600 mph). One dive, and we will be there! And that is when I had my uncomfortable moment, but a generous whiff of 100% oxygen took care of me. When we landed, Capt. Irwin and the crew presented me with a signed certificate – the 8th civilian ever to ride a jet at Hamilton, making me a member of the Noble Order of the Jet Jockeys."

IMPRESSIONS FROM A COCKPIT OF
A RACING SPORTS CAR

**On January 24, 1956, my dad also
brought readers into a Jaguar roadster during
a sports car race.**

H.K.'s Corner by H.K. Wong – "My Impressions from
the Cockpit" – the *Chinese World*

"How does it feel to go two or more miles per minute in a sports car race? That question has been fired at me many times when I started writing about sports car races as a member of the Publicity Committee of the San Francisco Region of the Sports Car Club of America. The sports car racing season has ended, and this is the moment to answer that question with 'my impressions from the cockpit,' as it happened.

"<u>On the Grid</u>: A surprised murmur rippled through the crowd of spectators at the Start-Finish line of the Salinas Races. 'There's two fellows in one of the competing cars!' 'It's okay, it's okay,' reassured the announcer. 'He's been cleared with the Course Marshal.' Safety regulations do not allow a rider in any sports car races, but by special permission, the second helmet in Greg Teaby's black, shiny Jaguar XK Roadster was mine. I was riding with Teaby, the Fire Chief of Monterey, to record a cockpit impression of a sport car race in the practice session at the Salinas airport for our Press and Publicity Committee.

"The Start: We line up with 40 other sports cars on the starting grid as an intense excitement and bedlam of noise prevailed. Officials are busy with the many important details that make a smoothly run race. They work efficiently through the terrific turmoil to insure 'Safety First' for machines, competitors, and spectators. Drivers fidget restlessly in the seats of their cars. They nervously pat their helmets, adjust their goggles, and tighten their seat belts, while their pit crew fusses with last minute chores. I glance around, take a deep breath – start the engine, get set, the moment is here, and let 'er roll!

"The Pace Lap: A pace car leads our group for the opening practice lap at moderate speed. Drivers give quick appraisal of the opposition and scrutinize the roadway at close range. Let us look at the course – it is a 2.8-mile circuit with eleven deceptive corners, bands, and high-speed curves. The pace lap is nearly finished now, and we are approaching the Start-Finish line.

"The First Lap: The lead car pulls aside, and the Starter is flagging us on. The landscape instantly becomes a blur as Teaby puts all his mechanical horses to work in one hand-snapping surge, pinning my back deep into the cushion. A thick cloud of acrid exhaust fumes and the smell of hot peeling rubber assails my nostrils. My ears are resounding with the shrill whining of high revving engines. A tremendous rush of air blasts my face on the exposed side of the cockpit as the ground, seemingly inches away, whizzes by. In one spine-tingling burst of speed, we take the center lane, accelerate through a phalanx of jockeying cars, and settle down for the ride.

"At Speed: We maneuver, pass, and corner through the field at high speed. Gas and oil fumes blow by, dust and pebbles stinging our faces as we chalk up two more laps. Another time around the raceway and we are going faster, as Greg, one of Northern California's top Jaguar racers, finds his groove on the smooth macadam. This is it! Lap 5 – we rocket by the Start-Finish line to pass the pits at 110 m.p.h. At the first marker, Teaby gears the snarling Jaguar down to 3rd, and staying close to the pylons, powers through the reverse camber 75 degrees. Turn number one at 80. We 'whoo – oomph' by 60 degree Turn no. 2, with wheels protesting and our safety belts straining tautly against their anchorage but holding us firmly in our seats. There's Turn 3 coming up fast. Teaby brakes hard, downshifts into second, and makes the 90-degree turn at 60 m.p.h., with tires screaming. Quickly working his shift-stick to high, he redlines the RPM counter and streaks down the 2,217 foot straightway to Turn 4 at 124 m.p.h. A deft downshift to 3rd, and we feel the severe pull of gravity and the wind of gale velocity as we storm tensely through Turn 5 and 6 with the last ounce of adhesion on the pavement from our screeching Pirellis at well over 90 m.p.h. Turn 7 with its 90-degree angle is zooming at us. Teaby brakes and throttles hard and sweeps on to equally tricky Turn 7A. He eases into top gear at dog leg Turn 8 and flashes down the back straightaway at 120 m.p.h. The wind buffets us. It is difficult to breathe - we are taking a pummeling from the elements, and the roar of the engine is deafening, but it is exciting. Flogging all his 210 horses, Greg grimly hangs on to the wheel and power-drifts through 45 degree Turn 9 at 95, slithers within inches of the protective hay bales at sharp right Turn 10, downshifts for 3rd for tight Turn 11. He tops his tachometer through the tough, skill-demanding turn, snaps back into high gear – his red-hot engine howling like a banshee and charges eagerly for the Start-Finish line at 110 plus m.p.h. His next lap is faster – at optimum speed. A few more of these breathtaking high-speed circlings and we finish the practice. That is how it all feels.

"By Air: Later we covered the races from the turns and, also from the air in Ed Brady's (KNBC) plane. The sylvan scene, the green pasture, the bustling crowd, the long white runways, make a pleasant picture from the sky, but it is more thrilling from the cockpit of a fast, low-slung, but safely driven sports car! See you at the next race?"

H.K. with his
Underwood typewriter
in the early years of
his journalism career,
circa 1939;
photo by Kem Lee.

Rice Bowl Football
committee ribbons and
press badges, 1938-1941.

H.K. wrote for a variety of newspapers, magazines, and journals. He did his most prolific writing with the *Chinese World* newspaper from 1954 to 1968, in his column "H.K.'s Corner."

Close friend and fellow journalist/columnist Herb Caen of the *San Francisco Chronicle*, with his Royal typewriter. Photo given to H.K. by Herb Caen.

Pre-flight briefing with Capt. Walter Irwin of the 84th Fighter Interceptor Squadron at Hamilton Air Force Base before H.K.'s flight in the T-33 fighter jet trainer, May 19, 1955.

Photo montage of H.K. on top of the T-33 fighter jet trainer. H.K. was the 8th civilian to ride the jet at Hamilton Air Base, and was certified into the Noble Order of Jet Jockeys. May 19, 1955.

H.K. with fellow journalist/ columnist Herb Caen at the Empress of China, circa 1981.

12

PUBLIC RELATIONS/ PROMOTER

My dad believed wholeheartedly in the value of San Francisco Chinatown and the Greater Chinese community. He also had a wide spectrum of personal contacts, both in the media and with influencers in San Francisco city politics, businesses, civic organizations, sports and restaurant associations, festivals, and much more. This wealth of relationships made him a natural to serve as the public relations/community outreach promoter and press agent for countless events and organizations. From his desk at his home on Bernard Street, San Francisco, as H.K. Wong and Associates Public Relations, he represented San Francisco Chinatown and the Chinese community as a one-man press bureau.

Underlying my dad's zest for building and promoting Chinatown was also his irresistibly positive personality, bubbly spirit, engaging smile, sprightly stride, and spirited laugh. Though it is true that he did work tirelessly to promote Chinatown in every way possible, people also just enjoyed being around him. He made friends instantly and could talk comfortably with anyone. His wide smile was warm and welcoming. They wanted him to be a part of their life, their committee, their talk show, their fundraising, and their community outreach and promotion. His personality was infectious. He simply had an uplifting effect on people. In fact, his engaging manner drew them in so much that they often ended up volunteering in whatever cause, event, or political candidate he was championing.

H.K.Wong

Media Liaison

Visitors to today's San Francisco strolling around Stow Lake in Golden Gate Park will likely see a beautiful Chinese pavilion nestled amid the trees, a gift to San Francisco from the City of Taipei in 1970. The sister-city alliance between San Francisco and Taipei was established in 1969. On January 26, 1970, as Public Relations Committee Chair for the Citizen's Committee for the San Francisco – Taipei Sister City affiliation, H.K. wrote a press release that highlighted the visit of Taipei's mayor to San Francisco:

FOR IMMEDIATE RELEASE
January 26, 1970

Henry Kao, Mayor of Taipei, capital city of Taiwan, will be honored at a special Sister City banquet at the Empress of China Restaurant on February 2nd, at 8:00 P.M. The dinner is being given by the San Francisco-Taipei Sister City Committee. The Co-Chairmen are Attorney Zeppelin W. Wong and M. Justin Herman, Executive Director of the San Francisco Redevelopment Agency. The main speakers at the banquet will be Mayor Alioto, Mayor Henry Kao and General Ben Chow, President of China Airlines, Ltd. Also participating in the event will be the honorable T.H. Chou, Consul General of the Republic of China, Mrs. Dianne Feinstein, President of the San Francisco Board of Supervisors and Mr. John A. Ertola, past President of the San Francisco Board of Supervisors, honorary chairman of the banquet. Assemblywoman March Fong will represent Governor Ronald Reagan. Mayor Henry Kao and General Ben Chow will be aboard the China Airlines' Inaugural

Flight, scheduled to arrive at 9:20 A.M. on February 2nd at the San Francisco International Airport to begin "China Week" February 2-7. The airline, flag carrier of the Republic of China, will begin its Trans-Pacific service as of February 2, 1970.

Publicist

On January 29, 1970, H.K. publicized the San Francisco-Taipei Sister City event. Held February 2 to 7, 1970, my dad outlined the program for China Week, the city of San Francisco and the Chinese community's salute to the San Francisco – Taipei Sister City affiliation. The program was distributed to a variety of press agencies.

> **China Week**: The city of San Francisco and the Chinese community's salute to the San Francisco – Taipei Sister City affiliation will be an exciting prelude to the annual Chinese New Year Celebration. Zeppelin W. Wong and M. Justin Herman, co-chairman of the Citizen's Committee, announced a six-day program spotlighting the art, culture, and entertainment of Old China in San Francisco. Taipei was designated as a Sister City by the San Francisco Board of Supervisors and honored as the representative capital of all the Chinese people in the free world with closer relations in friendship and business, commerce between these two cities.

> **Inaugural Flight**: China Airlines transpacific inaugural flight on Monday, February 2nd will bear a full complement of dignitaries from Taipei, for the festivities, headed by Mayor Henry Kao. Among the dignitaries are Chiang Futsung, director of the Palace Museum, and Dr. Paul Wang, director of the Bureau of Cultural Affairs for the Republic

of China. The distinguished visitors will be welcomed by Mayor Joseph Alioto and the Consul General of the Republic of China, T.H. Chou, and a citizen's committee.

My dad also wrote of many other ceremonies associated with the Sister City event. Mayor Kao presented a Tang Dynasty bronze horse to Mayor Alioto and San Francisco for the Chinese Culture Center, the first of a series of valuable art works from China. The 42-member Foo Hsing Opera and Acrobatic Troupe, whose twirls and death-defying acrobatics had captivated Western audiences in their first North American tours in 1963, were also flown in especially for the event. The Palace Theater, 1741 Powell Street, opened its doors to performances of century-old classics, most notably *Lady White Snake*, performed by Catherine Wang of the Foo Hsing players, with Lee Chin Ton as the leading man. The U.S. premiere of the widescreen, full-color movie, *His Shih* (Beauty of Beauties), a historical pageant of love and war in ancient China, also showed there. Starring Cleo C. Chiang as one of China's most famously beautiful women and Chao Lei as Emperor Kou Chien, the film was made in Taiwan by the Grand Motion Picture Company. Also showing at the Palace Theater was the U.S. Premiere of *Sons and Daughters*, a love story set in Taiwan by the Taiwan Film Studio, and a rollicking full-color Chinese Western, *Duel in the Plain*. Nightly, a documentary about Taiwan's World Series Little League Champion was shown as well. Special arts and culture exhibits included classical and modern Chinese paintings from Taipei, relics and artifacts of Chinese '49ers in California from the Chinese Historical Society Museum, and an exhibit of Ming and Ching Dynasty paintings (the Brundage Collection). The Chinese Six Companies, the Chinese Chamber of Commerce, the Chinese Anti-Communist League, and the Kuo Min Tang hosted an official dinner for Mayor Kao and other dignitaries.

Press Agent

In February of 1970, China Airlines inaugurated service to the United

States between San Francisco and the Orient. On March 2, 1970, my dad was thrilled to receive a letter from Carl C.H. Ma, Vice President of China Airlines, LTD. He wrote: "In celebration of the inauguration of our Dynasty Service, we wish to respectfully invite you to be our guest on our inaugural flight from Taipei to Hong Kong, scheduled to take place on March 14, 1970. We will have your ticket traveling on that flight, as well as a supplemental Trans-Pacific ticket ready for your pick-up at the China Airlines traffic counter at the San Francisco International Airport prior to your departure for the Orient." H.K. wrote about the experience:

A ride with China Air – by H.K. Wong

"Dignitaries, civic leaders, and members of the Fourth Estate were on board China Airlines flight #002 for the transpacific San Francisco-Taipei inaugural run last month. They are now straggling home in separate groups, filled with pleasant memories, and loaded with gifts, souvenirs, treasures, and bargains from Hong Kong and Taiwan. They expressed appreciation of the warm treatment and receptions accorded them by airline executives and officials of Taiwan. They extolled the superb skill of the pilots and flight crew, the safety measures of the ground crew, the excellent cuisine and service by the hardworking stewardesses and stewards – and unanimously agreed that China Airlines runs a world caliber operation.

"The China Airlines route to Taipei is via Tokyo by way of Anchorage, so when the sleek new Boeing 707 Jetliner took off, it headed for Alaska. A leisurely cocktail and continental dinner followed by a two-hour movie, and we were over the rugged snow-capped Alaskan mountain ranges with Mt. Whitney on the horizon. An hour to stop for fuel offered some tax-free shopping (American and Canadian whiskey at half price but no Eskimo pies for sale) and we were on our way, racing the sun toward Japan. 8:00 P.M., 10:00 P.M. (by our San Francisco time) and we were still bathed in brilliant sunshine, so bright that most passengers donned sunglasses and only took them off after the sun disappeared.

"The 707 landed at the Tokyo Airport for a brief spell (good wristwatch at $14.00 but American coffee at 50 cents) and then off again. A nap, and we landed at the Taipei International Airport and quickly were expedited through immigration and customs service. Cars transported all to the hotel and after a rest, a series of official functions, civic, social, and sightseeing activities were the order of the day. After these grand events, many stayed over for personal visits and others went on to Hong Kong.

"Our own Hong Kong visit was a hop-skip-and-jump holiday of only four days. In this period, we sampled the cuisine of China at plush restaurants, at popular 10-table eating places, at sidewalk stalls and at swanky night clubs. We enjoyed Szechuan, Swatow, Canton, Shanghai, Peking, American and French food. The Hong Kong breakfast of Hong Kong congee with hot deep-fried Chinese crullers was especially tasty to us. A visual treat – watching the chef slice the skin and meat off a golden-brown Peking duck at our table. The carcass was returned in a few moments as a soup with vegetables. Boneless eel, raw shrimp, fresh seafood, venison steaks, or lamb chops – all were served with a grand flourish and colorful manner, to our delight and enjoyment.

"Kowloon, Hong Kong's sister city on a peninsula that juts out from Mainland China, is opposite Victoria, or Hong Kong Island. The Tsim Sha Tsui district, on the extreme tip of Kowloon, is a bustling tourist haven with world-famed hotels and myriad shops dealing in goods, from cameras and wristwatches to jade. Down Nathan Road, intersected by Jordan Road, is the native shopping area – same merchandise, but if you bargain in Cantonese with shopkeepers, the prices are lower for extraordinary bargains.

"San Miguel advertising executive Benson Lam took us for a tour of the Hong Kong Brewery, home of MON-LEI, the premium Chinese beer now exported to the western market. Water for this beer comes from their own wells in the valley adjacent to the brewery. This water is filtered, conditioned, mixed with malt and hops, ground, cooked in a giant copper kettle, and converted into a sweet liquor called "Wort." This is left to settle, yeast culture added, fermented, tested, stored, aged, filtered, tested again, and finally bottled. Industry surveys shows beer to be the biggest volume beverage used in Hong Kong and Asia.

"We spent a day with members of the press in Hong Kong, and met with our old friend, Mr. Fred Aw, a Stanford University journalism major who is now managing director, editor and publisher of the English language daily, *Hong Kong Standard*. Mr. Aw instigated many new features in his publication and made it one of the leading English language newspapers in Hong Kong. For a complete change of menus, he took us to a foreign restaurant, French food cooked by the Chinese, served by Chinese (and eaten by Chinese!)

"Alan Castro, the former columnist for *Hong Kong Standard*, is now the Associate Editor of *Asia Magazine*. His magazine is distributed as a weekly supplement to the leading newspapers in Asia, with a circulation of 617,000 per issue. He invited us to join him in a dim sum luncheon and press conference with a pair of lovely Chinese songstresses, Sandra and Amina. Mr. Castro, who speaks fluent Cantonese, interviewed the young women both in English and Chinese during the lively season. Known professionally as "The Chopsticks," the young women work night clubs and television. They are the big hit today on Hong Kong T.V. and have captivated audiences by their songs and showmanship. They record hits for Crown Records of Hong Kong.

"We returned to Taipei after four days in Hong Kong. The one-hour mid-morning flight from Hong Kong was pleasantly devoted to the enjoyment of fine food – dim sum served steaming hot on Dynasty china dishes, tea in covered china tea bowls and a hot towel. Jovial repartee with the hostesses seemingly shortened our ride to the capital of Free China.

"The ride into the heart of Taipei City was a revelation. (Our only previous visit was nine years ago.) People are friendly, happy, helpful, and welcome visitors with courtesy, warmth, and Chinese charm. A construction boom is on full blast, even on Sundays. There were tremendous changes – acres of first-class hotels, new buildings, factories, restaurants, streets, parks, roads, schools, and housing in all sectors of the city of 1.6 million population. New capital brings new enterprises from overseas. Agriculture reflects a good harvest year. Imports and exports reach a height in dollar volume. Education is expanding and industries are zooming to record productions. Myriad motorcycles serve as family and commercial cargo transportation. Taxis are abundant and inexpensive, safely driven by ex-soldiers unlike the suicidal driving of Tokyo's cabbies. Streets and buildings are not as brightly illuminated as in America which does not deter people from walking on the street after dark in safety without fear.

"We visited the National Palace Museum accompanied by our friend, art expert MaSa Chuang. The imposing pagoda-roofed building contained a fabulous collection of 300,000 items representing 4,000 years of Chinese culture – masterpieces from all periods of Chinese history. Rotating exhibits showcase the world's rarest treasures, from Shang-Yin to Ch'ing Dynasty (1766 BC to AD 1911) – jade, painting, calligraphy, porcelain, pottery, enamels, tapestry, embroidery, bronze, lacquer, and documents. During our visit, 8,000 items from the collection of Emperor Chien Lung were displayed, along with a thousand rare bronze vessels and hundreds of one-of-a-kind paintings from the dynasties. The visit to the Museum is a fascinating seminar of Chinee culture.

"Sun Moon Lake and the Taroko Gorge are two of the country's major attractions. Because of our limited schedule, we selected the Gorge for our next visit. Miss Grace Yuan accompanied us on CAL's Rolls-Royce powered YS11 for the hour flight. Our pilot skirted the Pacific coast side of the island for a bird's eye view of the cliff-hanging public highway before we landed at Hualien and started off for the 245-mile tour of the Gorge by car.

"The Takoro Gorge, in a canyon of tremendous depth only 30 feet wide, cut through rugged mountain ranges, waterfalls cascading from great heights, swift rapid flows into slow-moving shallows and often emerging around a lower bend with an earth-shattering roar. Our leisure ride on the twisting narrow highway, which snakes through tunnels and hangs on cliffs over the Gorge, kept us on the alert. The road was carved out of solid marble by thousands of ex-soldiers who worked for three years on the task. Craggy cliffs towered above us when we stop at the many marble pavilions and rest areas located at strategic points for visual enjoyment. A visit to Eternal Spring Shrine, a fortune telling session with the cheerful nun at the nearby Grotto, the show at the Ami village, and a quiet lunch at secluded Tien Hsiang Lodge concluded our visit to the Gorge, one of the greatest natural spectacles in the Orient.

"There are countless places to visit but we must reserve them for the future. And in parting, we repeat Miss Yuan's invitation to all – 'Visit Taiwan whenever you can, it is a beautiful country.'"

On that flight and tour of Taiwan, H.K. befriended the head flight attendant, Grace Yuan. My dad had been playing tennis every week in the East Bay with tennis enthusiast Jim Chan. H.K. loved bringing people together and thoroughly enjoyed any chance to do matchmaking. He introduced Jim to Grace, and later, the two married.

On March 31, 1970, H.K. wrote a thankful letter to Carl Ma, Vice-President of China Airlines, expressing his appreciation for being included with other press agents on the flight.

On February 11, 1971, a press release was submitted by H.K. Wong and Associates Public Relations to the *China Times*, *China Tribune*, and *United Journal* in New York City; *American Chinese News*, and *New Kwong Tai*, in Los Angeles, CA; and *Tsing Tao*, *East/West Journal*, *Chinese Pacific Weekly*, *Chinese Times*, *Truth Weekly*, and *Young China* in San Francisco. The press release announced that General Ben Y.C. Chow, president of the Taipei-headquartered China Airlines, said that the company planned to extend its transpacific schedules to include Los Angeles and Hawaii, beginning its new mid-Pacific service on April 26, 1971.

Promoting Tennis

As Director of the Northern California Tennis Association, my dad always looked for ways to promote tennis. He was also astute in his understanding of the power of television advertising and sponsorships. As early as the mid-1950s, he arranged with the manager of Wilson Sporting Goods to have two Wilson tennis rackets, two cans of Wilson tennis balls, and 25 sports booklets appear on the Captain Fortune show for 15 weeks. As one of the show's highlights each week, Captain Fortune gave a girl and a boy from his show's audience a tennis racquet and a can of tennis balls, and spotlighted "the wholesome outdoor sport" of tennis. The quality of Wilson products was also featured, along with tennis films provided by the company. My dad's intent was to promote interest in Wilson tennis equipment, but also to promote tennis in general.

Marketing Director

In 1969-70, my dad was hired to introduce the premium imported Chinese beer, MON-LEI, to the U.S. (San Francisco, Hawaii, New York, Seattle, Portland, and Southern California) and Canada (Vancouver and Toronto). The tour he had taken through the MON-LEI Hong Kong Brewery while traveling with the China Airlines press agents' trip had impressed him. He was eager to introduce the beer to U.S. restaurants. As Marketing and Public Relations Director for the Wan Li Corporation, which imported the Hong Kong-based beer, H.K. marketed the beer to restaurant owners in New York, Seattle, Toronto, Portland, and Southern California. He wrote and distributed press releases, designed press kits, and placed ads in numerous publications. He even traveled to the Ilikai Hotel in Honolulu, Hawaii. Representing the Wan Li Corporation in November 1970 at the discotheque, Hong Kong Junk, H.K. presented MON-LEI beer to the Hawaiian market.

MON-LEI, marketed as "the Infinitely Better Beer," promised a beer that "did the job of a fine wine." ("Mon-Lei" means 10,000 miles or infinity.) To launch the beer, Alan Sand York's venerable Chinese junk, also named Mon-Lei, which was moored in New York City, made a coastal junket to East Coast ports of call. These included Newport, Rhode Island; Boston; New York; Pleasure Point, Ashbury Park; Philadelphia; Baltimore; Washington; Norfolk; and other points south. The Mon Lei wintered from Palm Beach to Miami, Florida. Wholesalers and retailers were introduced to MON-LEI BEER, imported by All Brand Importers, Inc. of Smithtown, New York.

My dad, a fond appreciator of the grace and beauty of Chinese women, posed Miss Grace Poon, a nicely dressed woman, standing next to boxes of MON-LEI for the beer's World Premiere press kit. His first release about the beer exuberantly read, "First United States shipment of MON-LEI Hong Kong Beer Arrives Via Northwest Airlines! Northwest Airlines have carried many exotic cargoes...this time it is a shipment of MON-LEI Hong Kong Beer, which had to be here in time for a Chinese New Year introduction. Northwest's own exotic Miss Grace Poon meets Flight #002 to welcome in the New Year's cheer!" By that description, I would have certainly wanted to try MON-LEI beer.

In a second press release, H.K. wrote, "We have been accustomed to German beer in German restaurants, Danish beer in Danish restaurants, Japanese beer in Japanese restaurants, etc., and now you can expect to try Hong Kong's premium beer, MON-LEI, in Chinese restaurants in the United States. MON-LEI BEER is named after the famous 116-year-old Chinese junk, now in New York. Translated, *Mon-Lei* means '10,000 miles or Infinity.' The Great Wall of China is also called *Mon-Lei*. While some people are under the misconception that only tea is consumed with Chinese food, the truth is that beer or rice wine are the most popular beverages, with beer consumption far out in front. MON-LEI BEER is imported by All Brand Importers, Inc., Smithtown, New York."

My dad noted that the shipment of MON-LEI BEER arrived in time, welcoming in year 4668 (1970), the Year of the Gold Dog, whose traits are warm-heartedness and a willingness to help others – a good trait in social situations while drinking beer. A traditional New Year's banquet ushered in both the Year of the Dog and MON-LEI Beer. At the Port Arthur Restaurant on Chinatown's Mott Street, Chinese dignitaries, beer importers and distributors, celebrities, and friends gathered to welcome in the Chinese New Year.

On April 4, 1970, the *San Diego Union* newspaper reported that MON-LEI beer was introduced to more than 600 California beer wholesalers at their 23rd annual convention. Bottled in Hong Kong and distributed through New York, the new product was the talk of the evening. The newspaper article read, "According to H.K. Wong of the Wan-Li Trading

Corporation, which imports the beer, MON-LEI initially will be distributed through Chinese restaurants. Wong traveled to Hong Kong and after several years of research, came up with MON-LEI. 'It is a premium beer,' he said. 'We're sure it will be a big hit.'"

MON-LEI beer was a private label produced from the San Miguel Hong Kong Brewery. It was a hit for a few years until Tsingtao Beer was introduced to the U.S. from China in 1972 and squeezed the market share. MON-LEI beer is no longer available. My dad saved a few bottles of beer in the storage area of our garage. The 50-year-old bottles of beer are now more suitable as museum artifacts than for drinking.

Producer

"Gung Hay Fat Choy" (Happy New Year) was the cheer amidst 100,000 firecrackers bursting at Caesar's Palace, Las Vegas, in February of 1976 – and H.K. was the promotional and organizational energy behind it. The Chinese New Year festival at Caesar's Palace was well attended, producing enormous goodwill between Caesar's Palace and the Chinese community. In fact, the event was so well publicized that in a post-event letter that Charles J. Monahan, Vice-President of Sales and Marketing, wrote to my dad, he noted: "The public relations aspect of this event will continue to be far-reaching. There are still articles in the Hong Kong newspapers."

An ancient Chinese tradition says that a symbolic dragon passes by your house on Chinese New Year to protect your home against evil spirits and bring you good fortune. Since the time of the Han Dynasty (206 B.C. to 220 A.D), twelve animals have ruled over the years in the Chinese lunar calendar. Those born in the year of a Fire Dragon are allegedly smart, imaginative, easygoing, and loved by others. Powerful, strong, and willing to take risks and welcome challenges, when given an ability to grab opportunity, Fire Dragons do it with aplomb. As such, they tend to be quite successful in life. It is no surprise, then, that 1976 was a Fire Dragon year, nor that my dad chose to produce the Chinese New Year Celebration that year at Caesar's Palace in Las Vegas. The flashy, exuberant, showy atmosphere of Las Vegas made the perfect backdrop for a Fire-Dragon-year celebration and the gold-and-red glittering dragon dancing unfettered on the stage. My dad coordinated everything, down to finding a truck to haul the massive dragon head and other equipment to Las Vegas. "There were anxious and nerve-wracking moments," H.K. wrote, "but it all ended up in a great big, wonderful event."

H.K. and Honey's niece, Sue Fawn Chung, remembers the event vividly. "In the 1970s, Caesar's Palace realized they were attracting Chinese visitors to their casino. January and February were downtimes for Caesar's Palace, so they got the idea to have a Chinese New Year celebration in February. They contacted H.K. to organize it. He hauled a massive dragon all the way to Las Vegas. He also invited me to the opening night banquet. Much to our surprise (and to the dismay of some), they served us Uncle Ben's wild rice with our dinner. H.K. politely let them know that was not appropriate for a Chinese meal. In a big way, he influenced the celebration of Chinese New Year in Las Vegas. H.K.'s event at Caesar's Palace was the first, but today numerous casinos in Las Vegas celebrate Chinese New Year."

Philanthropic Promoter

Due to his deep commitment to bettering conditions in Chinatown, my dad often donated time and energy to raising money for nonprofit organizations. One lighthearted evening, he consented to helping the Chinese Hospital Auxiliary raise funds by running in an election for the "Emperor of the August Moon," to reign over an evening of dinner, dancing, and a festival of lion dancers and drum performances on September 24, 1977 at the Marriott's Great America, a 112-acre amusement park in Santa Clara, California. Mrs. Ronald Ong managed his "campaign." Dinner at the Empress of China Restaurant was also part of the invitation, of course. My dad gave Ong a mailing list of people he thought might enjoy the evening. On August 31, 1977, as "Manager for the Candidacy of H.K. Wong," she sent out a request for "campaign funding." A new Chinese Hospital facility was desperately needed.

To sweeten the fundraising, the Committee to "elect" H.K. Wong as Emperor of the August Moon also offered a limited supply of my dad's watercolors from his travels in Mainland China for a specified donation. My dad sold 132 paintings. He also convinced 113 people to donate to his "campaign." Included on the list was Bud Lenox, father of my co-author, Catherine. H.K. won second place that night and was named "Crown Prince of the August Moon," a nickname that joined his already well-established monikers, "Mr. Chinatown" and "Mayor of Grant Avenue."

The following year, in September 1978, H.K. organized and promoted a weekend Chinese Moon Festival at the Marriott's Great America theme park. The two-day festival included a dragon parade, lion dances, Chinese arts and crafts, a martial arts display, and offerings of moon cake. The Moon Festival promoted Chinese heritage, culture, and traditions. It was so successful that Marriott planned to stage a yearly event to promote Chinese heritage. For his efforts in organizing the Moon Festival celebration, Marriott named H.K. an honorary mayor of the theme park for that weekend.

Public Relations Director

When tourists visit San Francisco, one of the experiences many enjoy most is an open-air ride on the city's famed cable cars. Unique to San Francisco, there is nothing quite like riding on the Powell-Hyde cable car line as it reaches up over Russian Hill and drops down on the north side to a breathtaking view of San Francisco Bay and Alcatraz Island. Climbing into a cable car at the intersection of Powell and Market Street, sitting on its vintage wooden seats, feeling the car sway and grab the track, and enjoying a slight breeze ruffling your hair as you roll down the hill is nothing short of exhilarating.

But in 1979, this unique, century-old San Francisco experience was very nearly lost to time. Muni, the transportation system for the city of San Francisco, decided that its cable car system was in dire need of complete renovation. Changes to improve safety and operability of the lines were critical. However, it was a job estimated to cost in the millions. Senator Dianne Feinstein, then Mayor of the City and County of San Francisco, took the lead in accomplishing this monumental effort. Initially, she recruited Chevron USA executive Ken Derr to raise local matching funds from San Francisco businesses, spearheading the campaign, "Save the Cable Cars." She also appealed to the federal government for the millions of dollars that would be needed and reached out to regional businesses and tourists to raise matching funds. A kick-off luncheon was held at the St. Francis Hotel on Wednesday, October 29, 1980, to launch the campaign.

As the Public Relations representative of the Empress of China Restaurant and Roof Garden, my dad was among the first business and civic leaders invited to attend the luncheon. H.K. was quite pleased to receive a letter from the Office of the Mayor, signed personally by Mayor Dianne Feinstein. In the letter, dated October 2, 1980, Mayor Feinstein wrote:

Office of the Mayor

Dear Mr. Wong:

San Franciscans reacted predictably when they learned that their City was in danger of losing its beloved cable cars. As with other crises, our local citizenry was quickly galvanized into action and formed a broad-based "Save the Cable Car Committee."

In concert with the Mayor's office, it was decided to appeal to the Federal Government for the millions of dollars necessary to keep our cable car system on track, and at the same time, appeal to both the local community and visitors to San Francisco to raise matching funds to ensure that our cable cars have a future to match their past.

I am sure that you are already apprised of the fact that a minimum of $10 million is needed from the private sector, and that Chevron U.S.A. got our campaign off to a superb start by donating $1 million.

Since this generous donation, other companies have come forward to ask what they might do, how much can they contribute, where do we go from here?

Our campaign to Save the Cable Cars is now ready to get started in earnest. We are going to tell you where we stand, where we plan to go, and how you can participate fully at a mammoth kick-off luncheon which will be held at the St. Francis Hotel on Wednesday, October 29th. Please note this is not a fundraising event!

You will find enclosed an invitation to attend, and hopefully you – or your company – will purchase a table of 10. I personally hope to see you, your friends, and your associates there.

We simply cannot – and will not – let our cable cars go, and only involved cooperation and participation by our community leaders such as yourself will ensure the success in our campaign.

Sincerely,

Dianne Feinstein
Mayor, City and County
of San Francisco.

As anticipated, H.K. not only attended the kickoff luncheon for the Save the Cable Cars campaign and filled a table of 10, he became an outspoken advocate for it. By 1981, my dad was actively serving as the public relations manager for the newly organized Chinese Community Cable Car Restoration committee. P.Q. Chin, partner of the structural engineering company, Chin and Hensolt, and husband of June Gong Chin, the first Miss Chinatown USA, oversaw the cable-car renovation. At the launch event for the newly renovated cable cars, in the tradition of christening the hull of a new sailboat, Mayor Dianne Feinstein broke a bottle of champagne across one of them. My dad arranged for a lion dance as part of the festivities. Saved from extinction, the San Francisco cable car system remained the world's last operating cable-car system. If there was a way to be at the forefront of any cause to build a stronger, more vital San Francisco community, my dad would always be there.

Chinatown's first television coverage on KPIX-TV's "Man-on-the-street" interview in cooperation with the *Chinese Press*, June 1949. Interviewer William Winters was talking to little Raymond Der. Behind them was H.K., one of seven participants for the segment. Photo by Kem Lee.

San Francisco Mayor Joseph Alioto welcomed Mayor of Taipei Henry Kao at the San Francisco International Airport to kick off the San Francisco – Taipei Sister City relationship and the China Airlines transpacific inaugural flight. January 1970. Top and bottom photo.

Promotional flyer for
MON-LEI Beer, circa 1970.

Aboard Alan York's Chinese junk the *Mon Lei* ("Ten Thousand Miles"), the namesake of
the Chinese beer MON-LEI, May 1970.

MON-LEI beer promotion with Grace Poon at the Empress of China, in conjunction with the Year of the Golden Dog celebration, February 1970.

Los Angeles Mayor Sam Yorty presented a commendation to representatives of the Wan Li Trading Corporation on the introduction of MON-LEI beer to the Southern California market. Left to right: Mayor Yorty, Linda Lau, H.K. Wong; Lawrence Chow, importer. August 1970, photo by John Gaines.

H.K. organized and promoted the Chinese New Year celebration at Caesar's Palace in February 1976, the first one held in Las Vegas.

H.K. and
Bugs Bunny
conducted a
press conference
at the Empress of
China promoting
the Chinese
Moon Festival
at the Marriott's
Great America
theme park,
August 1978.

H.K. organized and promoted the Chinese Moon Festival at the Marriott's Great America theme park in Santa Clara, CA., in September 1978. Marriott named H.K. an honorary mayor of the theme park for the weekend of the festival.

13

COMMUNITY SERVICE

> "Only a life lived for others
> is a life worthwhile."
>
> – Albert Einstein

My dad was driven by public engagement and community service, and frequently involved in local politics affecting San Francisco Chinatown. He took his civic responsibility very seriously. A staunch Democrat, H.K. worked on numerous projects alongside many San Francisco mayors, including George Christopher, Joseph Alioto, and Dianne Feinstein. H.K. was appointed Publicity Chairman of the Harold Dobbs for Mayor Chinese American Citizens' Committee in September of 1963. My dad even recruited me as a 5-year-old to pose in a sweater plastered with "Dobbs for Mayor" stickers for Harold Dobb's campaign for S.F. Mayor. It was his first of Dobb's three runs for Mayor. He lost first to Congressman Jack Shelley, and then twice to Joseph Alioto. Dobbs served on the S.F. Board of Supervisors from 1951 to 1963. H.K. was also on the San Francisco Chinese Committee to elect Hubert Humphrey for President in 1968 and hosted a reception for Jimmy Carter at the Empress of China Restaurant during Carter's campaign visit for President in 1976. My dad was also a good friend of Dianne Feinstein and served on several of her committees while she was the Mayor of San Francisco.

Constantly advocating for the needs of Chinatown youth, in 1954, H.K. served as the San Francisco Chinatown coordinator for the Guardsman, a nonprofit, volunteer-run San Francisco business group that supported summer camps for underprivileged and at-risk youth. The organization

H.K.Wong

raised money for higher education scholarships and outdoor sports. In 1955, my dad was also Chairman of a Citizen's Committee for Proposition C, a $7M bond issue to provide expansion and renovation of the City of San Francisco's recreational and park facilities.

On September 14, 1959, President Dwight D. Eisenhower released Proclamation 3313, announcing his endorsement of an event to be held in San Francisco between September 18 and 27, the City of San Francisco Pacific Festival Days. The festival's aim was to foster understanding among cities, states, and foreign nations that bordered the Pacific Ocean, and to focus on growth and development of these regions. Always keenly interested in promoting San Francisco Chinatown, H.K. was deeply involved with the festival. From 1959 to 1960, my dad served as its San Francisco Chinatown Festival Coordinator. A strong advocate of developing prosperous development and positive relationships in local San Francisco neighborhoods, H.K. also became an active member of the North Beach – Chinatown Cultural Advisory Committee in 1970.

Working with round-the-clock energy, it could be said that H.K.'s extraordinary community service contribution laid the foundation for lasting, sustainable change in San Francisco Chinatown. Many of the organizations he was actively involved in thrive there to this day. Chinatown, which continues to retain its cultural heritage due in no small part to my dad's enormous efforts, is now one of San Francisco's most popular tourist destinations, second only to the Golden Gate Bridge.

Chinese Consolidated Benevolent Association
(The Chinese Six Companies)

In the 1940s, my dad served as the Executive Secretary of the Chinese Consolidated Benevolent Association (Chinese Six Companies and the Official Representative Association of the Chinese in America). Founded in 1882 by a group of six important Chinese organizations and known by the Chinese as Chung Wa Woey Koon, the organization was the most publicized, powerful Chinese organization in America. The Ning Young,

Kung Chow, Yeong Wo, Sue Hing, Hop Wo, and Yan Wo Associations were its original members; the Sam Yup District Association joined later. Its Board of Directors were influential Chinese businessmen who negotiated with local, state, and national governments on behalf of the Chinese community in America. Headquartered in San Francisco Chinatown, it was established as a general board of arbitration to speak and act for the Chinese nationwide in all matters of general welfare; political, social, and civic. In many ways, the Association functioned as a Chinese Embassy, an official body that voiced opinions on legislation affecting Chinese people in America. Located on Stockton Street in San Francisco, the Chinese Six Companies identified twenty-five laws, statutes, and regulations aimed specifically at the Chinese.

The organization also founded a community native-language school to teach Chinese children basic Chinese history, language, and philosophy – and in 1924, established the Chinese Hospital. Later, they built a shelter for impoverished men. When notables from China arrived in Chinatown, they met first with the Chinese Six Companies to show respect. When charity organizations requested funding, Chinese Six Companies elders were consulted for their approval. To this day, whenever San Francisco Chinatown participates in civic and cultural affairs, the Chinese Six Companies are involved.

Public Perception of San Francisco Chinatown

In the fall of 1967, a series of newspaper articles appeared in the *San Francisco Chronicle* about labor unions and the garment factories located in San Francisco Chinatown. The articles were largely unfavorable profiles of the garment factories in Chinatown, and criticized the San Francisco Chinese community. Though the writers claimed their intent was to stimulate action on behalf of the Chinese factory owners and not condemn them, the Chinese community felt differently. They were hurt. As an active member of the Chinese Six Companies, H.K. took the lead in communicating Chinese sentiment about the articles to the public.

In a press release, he noted that the Presidents of the Six Companies, representing the voice of all Chinese people in the Western United States, felt that the articles were a blanket indictment of Chinese people in San Francisco. He noted that many benevolent associations in Chinatown were supportive of residents. My dad was intent on preserving cultural pride and knew as early as November 1940 that an informational booklet had been written to counteract misconceptions about San Francisco Chinatown. The booklet's conclusion was "In a society closely bound by ties of kinship, and with a tradition that makes the rights of the individual secondary to the honor of the group, the vicious elements of the community are fairly well controlled. The Tong wars, murders, and other crimes of violence are largely the work of overzealous newspapermen...organized gambling, prostitution and trafficking in narcotics are unknown in this community."

In his press release, H.K. also encouraged the San Francisco Planning Commission to aid in preserving the cultural heritage of Chinatown's architecture, listing Chinatown's virtues.

In response to the unfavorable articles, select leaders in San Francisco Chinatown decided to unify and form a committee that would not only reflect the Chinese community's thinking but also support a study of its needs and problems. Along with Dr. Alfred D. Lum and Charles L. Leong, my dad was endorsed by San Francisco Mayor Joseph Alioto to serve as Co-Chairman of the newly formed Chinese Citizens Survey and Fact-Finding Committee.

From 1968 to 1969, with administrative support from Mayor Alioto, H.K., Dr. Lum, and Leong conducted extensive research in Chinatown. Mayor Alioto also assigned Alessandro Baccari to serve as the City's liaison and Committee Project Coordinator. Lim P. Lee, H.K., and Albert Lim served as co-chairmen of the committee.

Lee was the first Chinese American postmaster in the United States, serving in that post from 1966 to 1980. He was also a close friend of our family. When I was working on the Stamp Collecting merit badge as a Boy Scout, he helped me build my stamp collection. He also generously provided many first day covers of U.S. stamps throughout his tenure as Postmaster.

When their research was completed, their report included input from more than 300 people serving as members of the Committee, on its Subcommittees, or as its advisors. The result of this research ultimately became a comprehensive 227-page book, the *San Francisco Chinese Community Citizen's Survey & Fact-Finding Committee Report*. The book outlined the findings and recommendations of the Committee's fourteen subcommittees. Its chapters covered Chinatown demographics, the impacts of immigration on its population, and surveys of its land and building use. It also explored Chinatown's housing, employment and business development, social services, health, and senior-citizen needs, as well as its youth, recreation, education, culture, landmarks preservation, traffic and parking, and police relations.

When my dad's press release was distributed, an abridged 37-page version of the Committee report, entitled *Chinatown U.S.A. in Transition*, was attached to it. The report was distributed to all news media to foster better understanding of the importance of the Chinese community in America and to educate the public about the strengths and needs in San Francisco Chinatown. The abridged version that H.K. wrote began:

"Since the magic word 'gold' in 1849, the Chinese have become a part of the life and history of America, and in particular, San Francisco. Always the Chinese have made good news copy, be it exotic or sociological – the Chinese are woven firmly into the American folklore and literacy, from Bret Harte's *Heathen Chinese*, written in 1870 to C.Y. Lee's own Chinatown opus, *Flower Drum Song*. In today's changing social scene, the Chinese Six Companies, as an official key organization of the Chinese community, feels that it has a duty to the public and its news media, which needs updated information on the Chinese community. This is, in effect, an FYI sheet, the first of occasional informational reports which is planned to be issued to the public."

Dispelling common beliefs about the Chinese community in America, the report cited numerous achievements by the Chinese community, noting that Chinatown had been a vibrant part of San Francisco in its founding years, located where the heart of the city began – at Portsmouth Square. It observed that young Chinese Americans were comparatively less delinquent than non-Chinese youth - the rate of delinquency in Chinatown was one of the lowest in the city. Crime rates in Chinatown overall also represented, on average, less than one percent of all complaints in San Francisco. As H.K. wrote, "The reputation of the Chinese community as being law-abiding citizens is a long and honorable one."

Enthusiastically praising Chinatown, H.K. also said, "Chinatown, even now, is still San Francisco's most different district. As a state of mind, to the tourist, Chinatown is an exotic, fascinating place to visit; to the immigrant, Chinatown is (as it was a century ago) the stepping stone to a new world, with Chinese undertones; to the real estate man, Chinatown footage is among the most valuable in the city; to the gourmet, Chinatown's food is among the greatest in America; to businessmen and suppliers, Chinatown is one of the heaviest wholesale and retail consumer groups; to social workers, Chinatown's complex problems are a challenge to be met; to the San Francisco Chinese, it is his hometown where he does his job and conducts his business, and preserves a social structure which is satisfying to his needs; to the Chinese throughout the United States, Chinatown is the Chinese Capitol of America."

Though the discovery of gold in California did bring most of the Chinese into the U.S. rather than other parts of the world, H.K. noted, "The first Chinese immigrants who came to America were not gold hunters. Their migration to the United States, Australia, Hawaii, and Southeast Asia was greatly accelerated by the hardship which they suffered from the Taiping Rebellion in China of 1850 to 1864. Likewise, the coming of so many Chinese to the United States in recent years (the 1960s) is due to the occupation of the mainland of China by the Communists and to American humanitarianism for allowing them to enter the United States."

During the gold rush, H.K. pointed out, "The Chinese were so law-abiding, hardworking, faithful, and industrious that they were encouraged to come to America to work in the mines and farms and construction of the Central Pacific and other railways. From 1848 to 1882, it was a period of free Chinese immigration into the United States, and the Chinese contributed their full share to the spectacular growth of San Francisco and California."

H.K. also referenced the perception many had that Chinatown was the only place Chinese residents lived in San Francisco. He wrote, "Because of the distinctive visual identity of Chinatown itself, an oft-time casual conclusion is that the Chinese of San Francisco live only in the 24-block confines of official Chinatown, in buildings which (though remodeled) are of the immediate post-earthquake vintage of 1907. The fact is that since the restrictions on Chinese being allowed to buy property were removed, Chinese are scattered all over San Francisco."

Before World War II, Powell and Mason Streets were the westernmost boundaries of Chinatown. In 1967, there were distinctly two types of Chinese-occupied dwellings. In Chinatown proper it was mostly rental apartments. Most of the occupants were from lower-income groups and newcomers from Hong Kong. World War II halted a major community project in Chinatown. Instead, the Ping Yuen housing project was built, completed in 1952. At the time, Chinese citizens were not allowed to live anywhere else in the city. In 1967, Ping Yuen was still noted for having a feature no other housing development in San Francisco offered: quarters for the San Francisco Department of Public Health's Northeast Health Center. The site included a fully staffed medical center, with payment based on patients' ability to pay. Ping Yuen also boasted low maintenance costs. Home life and the social environment could be summed up by the Chinese characters inscribed at its Palou Gate, "Peace and prosperity prevail among virtuous neighbors." A marble tower at the front of Ping Yuen North had another saying etched across it, "Within the four seas, all men are brothers." The site, H.K. admitted, had the "appearance of a ghetto," but millions of dollars in remodeling and improvements were actively in process on Chinatown properties. Most buildings were owned by Chinese associations spending private capital. This proved, H.K. argued, that the belief that Chinese associations had a "do-nothing attitude" was incorrect.

H.K. went on to write, "For those Chinese Americans with established roots in San Francisco, it may be a surprising fact to many that they own homes in almost every district in San Francisco: modest homes in the Mission; middle-class in the Sunset and Richmond, where there are even Chinese school classes; swarming the Polk area; a scattering on Nob Hill and Russian Hill; some on Pacific Heights; many in Bayview; solid new homes on Twin Peaks and the new Diamond Heights area; and the formerly predominantly Italian North Beach now has a Chinese theater to cater to the heavy Chinese population. Many executives and business and professional people rent in high-rise apartments on Russian Hill and the new Golden Gateway."

As for health, my dad wrote glowingly of the Chinese Hospital in Chinatown. Commended by the California Medical Association for its high medical practice standards, the hospital passed all state inspections with flying colors. H.K. wrote, "During the Chinese New Year Festival, colorful teams of 'lions' dance on the streets of Chinatown. They leap and gobble the money offerings hung over doorsteps. At wedding parties and other happy occasions, the principals usually donate a certain sum to the Chinatown's favorite charity. Donations from the Lion Dance and weddings all go toward the maintenance of the Chinese Hospital. This is the only institution of its kind in America. It is self-sustaining. It has not asked for outside help, although it is open to all races and creeds. Its patients have ranged from millionaires to paupers. It is truly a democratic institution."

Communism, Democracy, and the Chinese people

In 1951, San Francisco's Consolidated Benevolent Association (the Chinese Six Companies) staged a New Year parade in San Francisco to "support the anticommunism policy of the U.S. government." That same year, the Immigration and Naturalization Service (INS) and the Federal Bureau of Investigation (FBI) harassed many Chinese American citizens to determine if they were communist sympathizers. Despite the fact that no Communists were ever found in the process, anyone with connections to communist regimes, even if they were naturalized citizens, was deported. Agents regularly and randomly stopped Chinese Americans in Chinatown and even questioned children on playgrounds. Members of the Chinese American Democratic Youth League were questioned and some deported simply because their organization's vast library included a few works written by communist Chinese. Even *Chinese World*, the publication my dad wrote for, fell under hysterical anticommunist scrutiny.

To emphasize that the Chinese people were strong advocates of democracy, no doubt in response to this recent history, a section of the Committee's report was emphatic in its assurance that the Chinese people of 1967 were not communists. America was in the middle of the Cold War at the time, and because of the relatively recent Korean War, Chinese Americans were subject to scrutiny. He wrote: "The Chinese people are not communists and will never accept Communism in spite of the fact that they are now ruled by the Communist Regime in the mainland of China because Chinese civilization is unique, family-oriented, and democratic. The Chinese people believe in freedom and democracy. Although China was ruled by absolute monarchs in early history, the Chinese people enjoyed freedom and democracy long before democracy was known to the Western world. As early as the fifth century B.C., the great Chinese philosopher, Confucius, said that 'the eyes and ears of Heaven are the people.' And, another hundred years later, Mencius, another great Chinese philosopher, said, 'the people are the most precious element in a state and the ruler is the least important,' which means the people are at the top and the ruler is at the bottom. This certainly means democracy.

"The teachings of Confucius and Mencius were known to the Chinese people long before democracy was known to the Western world. Democracy was not even known to the Western world until the English writer, John Locke, in the 18th century, said that 'the voice of the people is the voice of God.' Although the interpretations of Confucius, Mencius, and John Locke were different, their meaning is the same – democracy -

the Chinese in San Francisco are a democratic and peace-loving people."

My dad, in cooperation with the Community Design Center of the University of California Extension, also became a central figure in a Chinese Six Companies citizen's committee's feasibility study of several sites in Chinatown. The committee determined the practicality of developing low- and moderately-priced housing, and whether commercial and residential uses could be developed on the same site. They also identified what zoning regulations would be most suitable to achieve that end. He observed that while casual observers might think that Chinatown's residents were poverty-stricken, in fact their lack of visible affluence and a self-imposed frugality was a way of life, not a lack of money. In fact, those living in Chinatown had millions of dollars in savings, representing broad-based ownership of land.

On January 27, 1970, San Francisco Mayor Joseph Alioto wrote in a letter to Alessandro Baccari, coordinator of the 12-month Chinatown study, and to the Co-Chairmen, "Progress is being made on a number of fronts." Mayor Alioto lauded their report as being "among the best... an extremely in-depth and accurate accounting of the condition of San Francisco's Chinatown Community." Mayor Alioto reported the following progress:

1. A medical center over Broadway Street that would serve the entire Chinatown North Beach area was nearing completion.
2. New public housing in Chinatown was being planned.
3. Assurances were made from the Department of Education and Recreation and Parks Department that all playgrounds and schoolyards would be utilized to their fullest extent.
4. Plans were being drawn for new Chinatown Branch of the San Francisco Public Library.
5. The Central Station of the San Francisco Police Department,

which would serve Chinatown, would soon be completed on Vallejo Street.

6. Assistance would be given to ad hoc committees in Chinatown to acquire funding for increased medical needs and bilingual education services.

7. The Mayor's office would work with the North Beach Youth Council to secure equipment and supplies for the Council's headquarters.

8. The San Francisco Police Department Police Athletic League would establish a recreation center for Chinese boys and girls near St. Mary's school on Stockton Street.

9. Mayor Alioto would work with the Department of City Planning on a meaningful program of development and social reform for the greater Chinatown community.

10. Mayor Alioto's office would closely follow negotiations between unions and management to improve the working conditions of Chinatown's labor force.

In concluding his letter to Alessandro Baccari and the three Chinese Community Committee Co-Chairmen, Mayor Alioto cited their work as a "truly significant step in improving the working relationship between City government and the Chinese Community." I imagine that was an exceedingly proud moment for my dad.

The On Lok organization was founded in 1971 as a direct result of the Chinatown study. On Lok started as a senior day healthcare center providing older adults in the Chinatown, North Beach and Lower Nob Hill neighborhoods with hot meals, health, and social services. On Lok has expanded over the years to include complete senior health services and long-term care in San Francisco, Fremont, San Jose, Gilroy, Morgan Hill, and San Martin.

Chinatown Parking Garage Projects

My dad knew that attracting visitors to San Francisco Chinatown would bolster the community's economy. He also realized that tourism would overload an already burdened, crowded parking situation. To that end, from 1957 to 1982 H.K. was Co-Founder and Director of the Portsmouth Parking Corporation. In 1958, he was instrumental in constructing the Portsmouth Square Garage, and in 1966 he became a project coordinator for the San Francisco Waverly Place Parking Project.

Portsmouth Parking Corporation

My dad and Mr. Paul H. Louie had been friends for many years when they both served on the $3.2 million Portsmouth Plaza Parking Garage project. As President of the Portsmouth Plaza Parking Group, Louie worked alongside my dad. H.K. was a Co-Founder and Director of the Corporation.

Opposition to the Portsmouth Square Garage project was organized by the California Heritage Council in November of 1957 on the premise that the garage would demolish San Francisco's most historic spot. Posters were distributed throughout the city to announce a protest rally. Chinatown civic leaders prevailed, however, as a new, improved park above the garage was included in the project plans.

In 1958, the group began construction on the Portsmouth Square Garage. Its Grand Opening Ceremony was held on Friday, August 24, 1962. With H.K. as the Program Chairman, the garage officially opened with the cutting of a red scroll-papered door. Mayor George Christopher rode first into the 500-space garage aboard a rickshaw with Mrs. Chinn Lee Shee Wing, a 91-year-old great-great-grandmother. The older, rough-hewn square was replaced with pristine walking paths, gathering areas, green space, benches, sculptures, restrooms, and a children's playground. Portsmouth Square Garage, with its entrance at 733 Kearny Street, provided parking and easy access to Chinatown or North Beach. Throngs gathered to celebrate the historic occasion. Public officials, including James H. Loo, then President of the Chinese Chamber of Commerce; Y.C. Lee, President of the Chinese Six Companies; and the Honorable Yin – Shou Che, Consul General of the Republic of China, attended. Albert C. Lim, Director of the Portsmouth Plaza Parking Corporation, was the master of ceremonies.

Of the Portsmouth Garage, on Friday August 24, 1962, Louie wrote in the *Young China* Chinese American Section, "The completion of the garage, in my opinion, will herald a new page in the economic development of our community. I wish that our businessmen take heart and use this facility as a spark plug to improve their properties as well as to upgrade our ways of doing business. I do not see how it is possible for any of our people to ignore a three and a quarter-million-dollar improvement in their own backyards. Here is a wonderful chance for our people to continue the work that has been started on this project five years ago. There remains so much to be done. We should not wait for a government program to come in and tell us what should be done. Our people are known for their love of their properties. We can, with a concerted effort, make San Francisco Chinatown really a jewel on this side of the Pacific. We have the resources. We have the natural setting. And we certainly have many, many talented people to carry out our goals."

In his column, "H.K.'s Corner," my dad wrote, "Portsmouth Square, nestled between Clay and Washington, Kearny and Brenham Place, a few steps off Grant Avenue, is the birthplace of San Francisco. Four flags – Mexican, Spanish, California Bear, and American--have flown over the Plaza. Once the center of the city's population and business, it is where the citizenry gathered for every important event and fled to as a haven in times of disaster. The first Custom House under Mexican rule was located here in 1844. The stars and stripes were raised here by Capt. John B. Montgomery of the USS Portsmouth to make Yerba Buena an American city on July 9, 1846. The first public school was built in 1847. It was the site of the first Post Office and first City Hall in San Francisco. On its sunny slope, Sam

Brannan first shouted the discovery of gold in California on May 11, 1848. The admission of California into the union was celebrated here in 1850. Also, the presence of Chinese in the city was first recognized in a public ceremony here. Portsmouth Square was Robert Louis Stevenson's favorite park, and for Rudyard Kipling and Jack London too. A plaque in honor of Andrew S. Hallidie, the inventor of the cable car, marks the Square as the eastern terminus of the first streetcar in the world propelled by cable. What was once a potato field between sand dunes and chaparral thickets will be a beautiful, functional park – a link between the stirring past and the great, glowing future of San Francisco."

Waverly Place Parking Project

Due to the tremendous success of the Portsmouth Square garage and the continued need for more parking in Chinatown, in February of 1966, H.K. encouraged a group of Chinese businesspeople and professionals to form a nonprofit corporation. Its purpose would be to finance and erect a public garage under the Chinese Playground, to be located west of Grant Avenue on Sacramento Street between Waverly Place and Pagoda Alley. A detailed study of parking demand was drafted, based on daily use, location of available off-street parking, new and proposed construction, existing businesses, and pending residential developments. The City of San Francisco Planning Commission was notified of the Committee's proposal.

In early 1967, H.K. resigned from his position as vice-president of the Portsmouth Square Parking Plaza Corporation to act as the project coordinator for the Waverly Place Parking Project. After 3½ years of work, the nonprofit corporation presented its feasibility report to the Chinese community and the City of San Francisco. The new recreational location for the Chinese community would include a clubhouse, sports facilities for adolescents, and (under the direction of the Recreation and Parks Department) tennis, basketball, volleyball, ping pong, touch football, and water sports facilities. The nonprofit organization would provide all funding and technical engineering to improve recreational facilities at the location. They would also hire the construction firm (Williams and Burrows, Inc.) to build a 500-car parking garage underneath the Children's Playground. They had already hired Frank E. Carroll, Jr., a parking consultant, who determined that the proposed garage would not affect revenue from the existing garage under Portsmouth Square.

On March 16, 1968, the City Attorney's office issued a statement that once land is designated for park purposes, it falls under the jurisdiction of the Recreation and Parks Department and that it can be used only for park purposes. On February 5, 1969 in the *East/West* English Chinese weekly, Asian Studies professor Ling-Chi Wang of U.C. Berkeley misconstrued the good intentions of the nonprofit San Francisco Waverly Place Parking Project and wrote an article, "Future of Chinese Playground at Stake." In the article, Wang claimed that "the San Francisco Waverly Park Plaza Corporation was a business enterprise only interested in the profits from an underground garage." The only problem, he wrote, was that "the new garage would benefit the rich and leave the needs of the community unattended."

The nonprofit group wrote a press release in response, stating that this was not their goal, that their intention was to turn the Chinese Playground into a "mini-park." However, some groups opposed the corporation's efforts, including conservationists, Historical Society members, and the San Francisco Bay Area Planning and Urban Research Association (SPUR), arguing that parking facilities should be located outside Chinatown rather than in already congested, overcrowded districts and that public land should remain undisturbed. Due to a Charter provision, lease negotiations for the garage could not begin until the Chinese Playground was re-designated as a park or plaza. SPUR opposed this re-designation, claiming that increased traffic generated by the garage would be hazardous to children in the area and would "only benefit special interest groups." An ad hoc committee against the building of the garage at the Chinese Playground attracted 4,500 supporters. An article in the *San Francisco Chronicle* on Wednesday,

June 11, 1969, claiming the Children's Playground would be moved to the top of a 9-story garage, neglected to mention that the garage would be underground. Another journalist posed the question, "where would children play during construction?" A nonprofit corporation with good intentions received heavy pushback. Ultimately, after years of work, the project did not go through.

In the final analysis, the nonprofit corporation determined that the only way recreational facilities could be built for Chinatown on the site of the Chinese Playground would be to allow building of an underground garage with new recreational facilities on the top, funded by a nonprofit corporation bond with no cost to the City of San Francisco. On January 10, 1969, my dad, Thomas Hsieh, and Zeppelin Wong met with Deputy City Attorney Robert A. Kenealey. Ultimately, the naysayers halted the project. The underground parking lot was never built.

However, my dad's dream of a renovated Chinese Children's Playground park did come to fruition. Renamed the Willie "Woo Woo" Wong Playground in 2006, and located at 830 Sacramento Street between Waverly Place and Pagoda Place in Chinatown, it is a half-acre park with two sand-floor playgrounds, tennis and volleyball courts, and a clubhouse with a rooftop basketball court - all located on a verdant, terraced hillside. The site is named for Willie Wong, a Chinese American USF basketball star of the 1940s, who grew up across the street from the Chinese Children's Playground, where he learned to play basketball. He was nicknamed "Woo Woo" by a San Francisco sportswriter because whenever he scored, his fans would shout out, "Woo Woo." I like to think if my dad saw the Chinese Children's Park with its improvements today, he would shout out his own enthusiastic "Woo Woo." I know the park would make him smile.

Civic Involvement

My dad's belief in the importance of cultural tourism in San Francisco Chinatown also led to his serving as a Director of the San Francisco Convention and Visitors Bureau from 1981 to 1984. He was also Co-

Chairman of the Chinatown Committee for the City of San Francisco 200 Year Celebration and U.S. Bicentennial in 1976. In 1979, he became a member of San Francisco Mayor Feinstein's China Gateway Committee and served on the San Francisco - Shanghai Sister Cities Subcommittee.

San Francisco Visitors and Convention Bureau

On July 9, 1981, Peter Goldman, President of the San Francisco Convention and Visitors Bureau, welcomed my dad to its Board of Directors. During H.K.'s time as a member of the Board of Directors, membership doubled. H.K. actively promoted the Empress of China and Chinatown as destination spots and kept the Board abreast of all cultural events in Chinatown.

China Gateway and the San Francisco – Shanghai Sister Cities Subcommittee

Based on the countless times it has been photographed, a palatial ceremonial gate at the intersection of Bush Street and Grant Avenue has impressed many visitors to San Francisco Chinatown. Marking the southern entrance of Chinatown, it was built in the style of a traditional Chinese *pailou* in 1969 and was given as a gift to the City of San Francisco from the Republic of China (Taiwan). Chinese lions flank each side of the portal. Four Chinese characters read, "All under heaven is for the good of the people," "respect," "love," and "peace." This gift represented the beginning of friendly relations between the City of San Francisco and China.

Mayor Dianne Feinstein made her first trip to Shanghai in June of 1979. During that visit, she gave a key to the City and a piece of San Francisco Golden Gate Bridge cable wire to Shanghai, symbolizing that San Francisco's door was open to them, and that the two cities' friendship was as solid as steel.

In 1979, my dad was a member of Mayor Feinstein's China Gateway

Committee, a group selected to continue fostering communication between the two countries. On January 28, 1980, a year after China and the United States had established formal diplomatic relations, Shanghai and San Francisco became sister cities. On December 3, 1980, H.K. received a letter from San Francisco Mayor Dianne Feinstein notifying him that she had changed the name of the China Gateway Committee to the San Francisco-Shanghai Friendship Sister City Committee. Her letter informed him of his appointment to the new Committee. She wrote:

"It is an honor for me to appoint you to the Mayor's San Francisco – Shanghai Friendship Sister City Committee. As you know, the City's new 'sister city' association with Shanghai was the first approved between a U.S. and Chinese City and was made at the very highest level of government in China. Since the final signing of this agreement last January, the number of opportunities for friendly association has increased dramatically. To meet this challenge, I have acted to broaden and strengthen the China Gateway Committee and have renamed it the San Francisco – Shanghai Friendship Sister City Committee. Because of your background and interest, I would like you to consider an appointment to the Host Subcommittee. I look forward to a long association with you in this exciting opportunity for economic, cultural, and people-to-people exchanges with a nation and city that has so many ties to San Francisco. Warmest personal regards, Cordially, Dianne Feinstein, Mayor."

On June 5, 1981, Mayor Dianne Feinstein hosted a luncheon for Shanghai Mayor Wang Doahan at the Empress of China Restaurant.

Since that time, the two cities have shared more than 200 projects in the areas of economy, international trade, finance, medicine, hotel management, technology, culture, and sports. Most of Shanghai's mayors have visited San Francisco, and most San Francisco mayors have reciprocated with trips to Shanghai.

In July 1995, the *Los Angeles Times* reported that Senator Dianne Feinstein openly objected to Beijing's treatment of Tibet. However, as Mayor Xu Kuangdi of Shanghai pointed out when he decided to visit San Francisco despite political unrest, "This is not a political question. It is a city-to-city relationship, not a state-to-state one."

On February 18, 2020, at the Bay Area Council's annual Chinese New Year celebration, Senator Dianne Feinstein was honored for her outstanding leadership and commitment to San Francisco. She said that when she was Mayor of San Francisco, she thought developing a sister-city relationship with the city of Shanghai was a good way to bring both cities closer. Since that time, the sister-city partnership has fostered numerous mutual exchanges between China and the United States. Cultural ties between the two cities remain strong, as has Senator Feinstein's admiration of my dad and his legacy.

The Chinese Consolidated Benevolent Association (Chinese Six Companies) welcomed Madam Chang Kai-Shek to San Francisco, March 1943. H.K. (in the tan suit) was Executive Secretary of the Association.

My dad dressed me in a sweater plastered with "Dobbs for Mayor" stickers to campaign for Harold Dobbs (left), September 1963. Photo by Edward Lee.

H.K. was on the S.F. Chinese Committee for Hubert Humphrey's campaign for President in 1968. The committee was discussing strategy with VP Humphrey in Congressman Philip Burton's (third from right) office.

H.K., Lim P. Lee, and Albert Lim, co-chairmen of the Chinese Citizens Survey and Fact-Finding Committee, presented the committee's report to S.F. Mayor Joseph Alioto in August 1969. Photo by Kem Lee.

Portsmouth Square, circa 1938.

Portsmouth Square (at the corner of Clay St. and Kearny St.) before construction of the Portsmouth Square Garage, circa 1957. Photo by Kem Lee.

Harold Dobbs (center left), and Paul Louie (center right) prepared to light the firecrackers on the opening day of the Portsmouth Square Garage, August 24, 1962. Photo by Chang's Studio.

Portsmouth Plaza

AT

PROTEST MEETING

**Wednesday, November 4th
12:15 Noon**

Join in the Public Protest Against **BUILDING AN UNDERGROUND GARAGE ON PORTSMOUTH PLAZA** San Francisco's Most Historic Spot!

Costumes! Bands! Speakers!

Write your personal protest to the Board of Supervisors, the Mayor and your S.F. Newspapers TODAY!!

USE OTHER SITES FOR PARKING NEEDS

Sponsored by the CALIFORNIA HERITAGE COUNCIL
Please do not throw this handbill on the street – Thank You

Portsmouth Square Garage protest rally poster. November, 1957.

Commissioning ceremony in 1971 with S.F. Mayor Joseph Alioto, in which "gold dust" was poured into the foundation for construction of the Chinese Culture Center building.

14

THE CHINESE NEW YEAR FESTIVAL

"The Miss Chinatown USA 1958 title blessed, expanded, and enriched me in the vast, valuable Chinese cultural experiences, beyond my imagination!"

– June Gong Chin (first Miss Chinatown USA)

From 1953 to 1954, 1956 to 1957, and 1959 to 1960, H.K. served as Director of the San Francisco Chinese Chamber of Commerce. Since he could serve only two consecutive years as Director, in 1955 and 1958, my dad stepped down from this position to serve as the organization's Publicity Chairman. During these years, his most public and long-lasting achievement was most certainly co-founding the annual Chinese New Year Festival and Golden Dragon Parade in 1953. As Co-Founder of the event, H.K. was instrumental in convincing San Francisco government officials and businesses to support funding and promotion of the Chinese New Year festival in Chinatown.

My dad wanted to elevate the image of Chinatown and its residents by opening San Francisco Chinatown and its New Year Festival to non-Chinese tourists. He envisioned an event that would rival Mardi Gras in New Orleans and the Rose Bowl Parade in Pasadena, California. The Chinese New Year Golden Dragon Parade was organized with the intent of changing the impression that non-Chinese visitors tended to have at the time about San Francisco Chinatown and de-mystify attitudes they had about its Chinese residents being "esoteric and exotic." As the parade had before in 1951, the festival H.K. envisioned would demonstrate to McCarthy advocates that Chinatown was not a bastion of Chinese Communists, but rather a community of loyal Chinese Americans open to sharing their community with other loyal Americans. Chinese American veterans of World War I, World War II, and the Korean War marched alongside Air Force, Army, Navy, and Marine bands. A blocklong colorful dragon wove its way through the bands. Intent on also introducing the non-Chinese public to Chinese culture, H.K. promoted "cultural tourism," presenting an authentic view of Chinese art, music, costume, and dance.

Until 1953, Chinese New Year had been a private affair, celebrated only in family homes among friends and relatives. Chinese families from smaller Chinatowns across America converged in San Francisco to meet with relatives and friends. The banquets and celebrations were strictly private observances. In 1953, however, H.K. approached the Chinese Chamber of Commerce with a proposal to open the festival to non-Chinese spectators. The first three days of Chinese New Year would remain a private, family gathering, but the private gatherings would be followed by a huge public celebration, displaying Chinese heritage and culture to a wider audience.

With approval from the Chinese Chamber of Commerce but no money to promote or present the festival, my dad and his friend, Paul H. Louie, tirelessly searched through the streets of Chinatown to find community residents who might want to contribute their talent or money to developing the event. They found lot owners who were willing to contribute space to the event, an electrician to hook up lighting, police officers who were willing to donate time after work, carpenters to donate wood and build a stage, and a man who worked in radio and had access to a wonderful PA system. As owner of the Ti Sun Company, my dad donated all the nails needed for the construction. The first parade, led by the blind Korean War veteran Grand Marshall Joe Wong, featured a blocklong twisting, gyrating, colorful dragon and "Miss Firecracker," Chinatown's festival queen.

In his February 1953 column, "H.K.'s Corner," my dad wrote: "His eyes will not see the glory of it all, but he will hear the sounds of gongs and drums, and sniff the exotic fragrance of an old China on Sunday, February 15th, when the 1st Annual Chinese New Year Festival invites all San Franciscans to a gala round-the-clock free public celebration and program of the 4651st Chinese New Year. His name is Corporal Joe Wong, and he will be the Grand Marshal of the colorful parade leading the snappy 6th Army Band and its guard of honor, veterans and civic organizations, dancing lions, and a bevy of Chinese beauties and flower floats depicting ancient Chinese legends. Corporal Wong, now running a business of his own – a candy store at the Veteran's Administration – will feel the grandeur of it all, but he cannot see. He lost his sight as a U.S. Army infantryman in the first bitter fighting against communists in Korea. But Joe Wong, like the rest of the citizens of San Francisco's world-famous Chinatown, is thankful that in the democratic atmosphere of the United States, people are free to celebrate and worship in complete freedom. In this America of ours, with so many diverse cultural strains, perhaps one day the Chinese New Year, almost 5,000 years old, will be celebrated as another colorful holiday such as St. Patrick's Day."

Free and open to the public, from 10:00 AM to midnight, the festival included a championship tennis exhibition and other sports, and a three-hour Grand Opening celebration from 2:00 PM to 5:00 PM with Chinese music, lion and sword dances, brush painting, silkscreen demonstrations, and exhibits of lively arts, priceless relics, and art treasures. That first year, a crowd of 140,000 people thronged the streets. In an interview with Harvey Wong of the Chinese Historical Society, archived by the San Francisco History Center, San Francisco Public Library, H.K. related the story of that first Chinese New Year Golden Dragon Parade and Festival.

"It was 100 percent a community effort. All this done for nothing for San Francisco and Chinatown. We had a young girl as our festival queen named Pat Kan who we named 'Miss Firecracker of 1953.' We asked a car salesman friend of ours to loan us 30 convertibles. Miss Firecracker rode in her own convertible. We had a parade that went through Stockton Street in Chinatown, not only for our own community but for people outside Chinatown. We had school bands. We had a short program but announced a more elaborate show. When Mr. Louie and I looked up Stockton Street to see every block filled with humanity, I thought to myself, 'this is a good start.' That evening, we showcased young women in costumes and music. We put on a two-hour show. We asked a friend in Shanghai to lend us some costumes, and the next thing we knew, we had

Emperor's and Empress' robes on loan to us. Eighteen different young women from our community and some from other towns modeled the costumes – they put on a marvelous show. Then we asked the Chinese Musical Society if they would play the background music and perform after the show. Later they had singers from the Canton and Peking Opera. The boys from the Kung Fu group put on a wonderful fast-paced show in good taste. It was probably the first time a demonstration of Kung Fu had ever been seen in public. Mr. Louie gave a speech and said that one day he hoped it would one day become a national festival."

When asked if they had problems that first year, my dad laughed, replying, "Oh, yes. We had no public relations contact from Chinatown, so I talked to all the media, contacted them, and learned what they wanted to know - I started writing stories. I became their public relations contact in Chinatown. I learned about the flavor of Chinese New Year from my mother. As a child, when I asked her why we celebrated it, she replied, 'I feel I should meditate on all good wishes to my family, my people, and also to my friends.' So, I sent a release to all the media and they used it. I thought to myself, 'this festival is something different for them and this way they will know more about our people from this public affair.' I was able to get several thousand clippings per season, so I felt it was very well received."

As for challenges H.K. faced in that first festival, he said, "We ran out of nails that first time. They delivered 4-inch nails rather than 2-inch nails. I was also given the job of wrapping firecrackers around Miss Kan and I did not know I was going to do it. She was topless, and there was no dress under the firecrackers, which is why I was having difficulty. I asked Pat to close her eyes. The photographer was laughing. Everyone was laughing, except me. I was blushing. But I finally got it done and Miss Kan wore that string of firecrackers in the parade. It was a very pretty sight. She was untouched, and she was fine."

Three years later, on February 29, 1956, H.K. wrote, "Thirty to forty million people saw the colorful New Year celebration in San Francisco via the *Wide Wide World* show broadcast over 92 television stations stretched across the country. The pelting rain kept many would-be spectators at home glued to their T.V. set." Jake Wong, who had enthusiastically watched the show from Duluth, Minnesota wrote, "I could recognize the scenes and every one of the faces on the screen. I saw Queen Estelle's dimple, Angie Wong's smile, Barbara Yee's graceful gestures, and even knew the fellow who lit the string of firecrackers for the Chinese Hospital Lion Dance." Jake Wong's 80-year-old mother had added, "I had never seen such a wonderful Chinese New Year show."

A news release H.K. wrote dated January 3, 1957, entitled "Chinese New Year Festival," read, "A grand night parade will introduce the new block-long (150 ft.) Golden Dragon, made in Hong Kong especially for this occasion." With its enormous head, bulbous eyes, jagged teeth, and lengthy sparkling tail, the Dragon became an icon of the festival.

Staged by the Chinese Chamber of Commerce and New Year Festival Committee in 1957, the festival parade swelled to more than 200,000 spectators. A living floral plaque with a Chinese character was also placed by the main drive in Golden Gate Park.

For weeks before the event, H.K. promoted the festival. Queen Estelle Dong appeared twice on NBC TV's national network, followed by daily festival personnel appearances on Bay Area television stations. Captain Fortune of KPIX did a four-hour salute to the festival, and it was featured on the nationwide *Queen for a Day* program on national television and radio. During the *Queen for a Day* broadcast on January 25, 1957, scenes of the New Year Festival, the coronation ceremony, and the Golden Dragon were flashed on the screen to an audience of over 40 million people. The contestant chosen as "Queen for a Day" that day was honored at the New Year Festival on Friday, February 1st, and was a dinner guest at a Chinese New Year banquet at Kuo Wah Cafe in Chinatown. Other broadcasts covering the event were CBS, Danish, Swedish, and European television networks. Over 4,500 press releases were sent to newspapers, radio and television stations, Associated Press, United Press, National Education Association wire service, railroad and bus public relations offices, airline companies, the Redwood Empire Association, the San Francisco Chamber of Commerce, travel and hotel bureau magazines, club magazines, NBC in New York, Australia and Paris correspondents, freelance writers, and Chinese magazines in Hong Kong, Canada, and New York. All the organization of the event and all the writing and distribution of press releases were managed by my dad, who spent five solid months on the project. He noted that his "valued assistant during that busy time was

Miss Honey Quan."

That year, much to my dad's dismay, City Hall banned firecrackers on Grant Avenue. He wrote: "There is a strong current of deep disappointment that our City authorities see fit to interfere with this district's concept of religion regarding shooting firecrackers. This feeling is in most everyone of the 25,000 people that make up Chinatown and in the minds of hundreds of thousands of friends who see no reason for this stand. Burning of firecrackers was used to exorcise the evil spirit centuries ago. It was used, too, a hundred years ago when the Chinese struggled amidst hardships to construct our state's railroad. After a season of tough work, our forefathers would pause for the year, meditate, pray, and set off fireworks. By this ingrained religious action, they would chase the evil and badness away and hope and wish for happiness for their families, for their friends, and for themselves in the coming year. After this deed, he would return to labor, serene in mind that the Gods were pleased and happy that his wish would be granted.

"To the Chinese, it is the same today and unthinkable that in this free land, one's method of expression of hope and happiness could be throttled. In a state where the Chinese have played a vital role in the building of the railroads, in which the Chinese are among the most law abiding group, in a metropolis which boasts Chinatown as one of its major attractions, in a community in which one district (Chinatown) puts on a public festival at its own expense that is a credit to the city, in a city which has such a proud, historic, and vivid past, it is surprising that such an edict was thought of, much less justified. A Chinese New Year without the roar of its firecrackers and its pungent smell is like bread without butter or mush without cream. Under such conditions, Chinatown leaders and businessmen may well be discouraged from staging another Festival – a festival that adds to the glory and achievement of San Francisco.

"The color and attraction of San Francisco's Chinatown has been flung to the four corners of the land by radio and T.V. on coast-to-coast networks. Reams of dispatches have been filed on the wire services, and theaters throughout the U.S. have flashed the pictures and news of our queen and festival on their screens. A great influx of visitors will come to San Francisco this weekend. They will come to see the picturesque Festival with all its trimmings. Only this year, there are no trimmings –

sorry, no firecrackers."

In 1957, if my dad had known how dramatically he would win the battle over firecrackers in later years, he would have grinned broadly, ear to ear. The February 2020 San Francisco Chinese New Year Festival discharged over 600,000 firecrackers.

The Miss Chinatown USA pageant did not join the Festival until 1958. All the time, H.K. was looking for a way to introduce it to the public. He felt the addition of young women to advertise the Chinese New Year Festival would help publicize the event. Up to that time, the festival selected a San Francisco Chinatown queen, and there were regional beauty pageants in Hawaii, Seattle, and New York. H.K., however, thought the event should be more inclusive of Chinese people nationwide on a larger scale. Because Chinatown was the largest community of Chinese residents outside of China, H.K. decided they should find a young woman from all Chinatowns across the U.S. to reign as Miss Chinatown USA. With that in mind, and because he wanted to interest these young women's families to participate in this public event, Albert Lim and my mom and dad toured the U.S. to encourage parents to send their daughters to the parade because H.K., having researched the standard by which Chinese beauty was measured, wanted the young women who participated to be a showcase of Chinese heritage and beauty. Parents were eager for their daughters to be involved.

Said H.K., "I found out that a scholar said she must have a melon face, a very fair complexion, willowy eyes, arched eyebrows, shapely nose, cherry lips, medium height, and a radiant smile. Contestants should also possess the education, training, and versatility to meet the challenges of the modern world. I sent out a press release that the Chinese community was searching for a beauty to best represent this Chinese concept of beauty to represent not only San Francisco Chinatown, but all Chinatowns in America. When it came about, we had seventeen young women from all over the U.S., including Hawaii. The girl that won the first Miss Chinatown USA was a girl, June Gong, from Miami representing New York City. It did a lot for the young women. It was an opportunity to see what the Chinese culture was about."

Each contestant was sponsored to enter the Miss Chinatown USA Beauty Pageant by a Chinatown merchant or family association. June Gong was a late entrant and did not have a sponsor. H.K. was not able to find a sponsor for Gong, so he decided to sponsor her through his hardware business, the Ti Sun Company. Gong's father was a hardworking grocery-store owner of modest means in Miami. Her parents had immediately trusted my parents, so they allowed their daughter to travel to California to visit with H.K. and Honey during the pageant. Gong performed a modern dance and in addition to being crowned as the first pageant winner, won $500, a portable TV, a transistor radio, and 25 pounds of Chinese Sausage. Of being crowned, Gong said, "H.K. sent me everywhere after I won the title – all over the United States and even to Hawaii. He was such a wonderful, vibrant man."

As the new Miss Chinatown USA Queen representing all U.S. Chinatowns, Gong visited many locations and events, including the Vacaville, California Sports Car Race, Hawaii, Las Vegas, Hong Kong, and the Rose Parade in Pasadena, California. On January 1, 1959, the Chinese Chamber of Commerce sponsored a Chinese New Year float in the Rose Parade, also known as the Tournament of Roses Parade, featuring a Chinese dragon and models of some Chinatown buildings along with Gong and her Miss Chinatown USA court.

In a letter dated March 14, 1958, my dad wrote, "The excitement of the 'Miss Chinatown USA' pageant and the Chinese New Year Festival is still echoing among the Chinese newspapers and magazines. Newspaper clippings of the event are still coming in by the hundreds confirming that this was a grand success. The judges' choice of Miss Gong for queen coincided perfectly with the public's feeling."

In reminiscing on the first national contest in the February 23, 1980 issue of the *San Francisco Chronicle*, H.K. also recalled, "It was the first year [1958] and everything was special, but it was like electricity in the room when June Gong walked on stage."

In the 2017 issue of the *University of New Hampshire Alumni Magazine*, Gong recalls her experiences as a beauty contestant during her time as a student at the university. As a member of the Alpha Chi Omega sorority in 1956, Gong was Homecoming Queen at the University of New Hampshire (UNH). The following year, she was selected to represent the university in the 1957 Miss New Hampshire Beauty Contest. As the first Chinese girl in the Miss New Hampshire contest, Gong placed second and tied for Miss Congeniality. Gong also entered and won the title of Miss

Chinatown New York 1957, but was a reluctant entrant. All she wanted then was a weekend in New York City with her sister Lillian Gong, a medical researcher at NYU. Gong's friends persuaded her to enter the contest, going so far as to buy her a plane ticket when she said she couldn't stay because she had to drive back to UNH to get back to class on time. Upon winning the 1957 Miss Chinatown New York contest, Gong was eligible to enter the Miss Chinatown USA contest in 1958. She was also reluctant to enter that contest because she would again miss classes. But her argument against entering was lost when she learned that the contest was taking place in February 1958, during winter break. At the urging of her sisters and friends, Gong entered the first-ever Miss Chinatown USA Pageant, and won.

As it turned out, Gong also proved a perfect match for P.Q. Chin, a prominent structural engineer. H.K. shared an interest in Jaguar sports cars with Chin. As Gong said to me later, laughing fondly, "H.K. introduced me to my 'rascal husband.' The rest was history."

In the Chinese Historical Society of America video, *Glamour and Grace: The History & Culture of Miss Chinatown USA*, Gong said, "It was a privilege and it was a very surprising crown for me. It was wonderful being crowned and meet the ladies from all over the United States and to have this one desire to represent this Chinese community all over the United States and in the Far East. It was an honor."

Now in her eighties, June Gong Chin, lives in San Francisco. On February 11, 2017, to celebrate the 60th anniversary of the Miss Chinatown USA pageant, she lit a ceremonial string of 30,000 firecrackers (which she did not have to wear) and rode in the Chinese New Year procession. She said the parade still celebrates the joy of being Chinese American and brings attention to the community's rich heritage.

Following the success of the first Miss Chinatown USA pageant, H.K. and Honey were invited as official observers to the Miss America pageant at the convention hall in Atlantic City, New Jersey in September 1959. They were special guests of Mr. Nesbitt, Chairman of the pageant, and were invited to attend the TV show rehearsal, the dress rehearsal, and the finals. H.K. observed that the Miss Chinatown USA pageant compared favorably with the Miss America pageant. My dad extended the East Coast trip to search for candidates for the 1960 Miss Chinatown USA pageant. He met with Chinese civic leaders in New York City, New Orleans, Houston, and Denver to promote the San Francisco Chinese New Year Festival and to sponsor and recruit young Chinese women for the national contest. Chinese leaders in each of the cities were very receptive and eager to participate.

My dad, who left the pageant in 1961, noted that as time went on, the concept of Chinese beauty changed. Chinese young women in the 1950s were very modest, so the committee had designed a playsuit for them. After H.K. left, the pageant changed to a more Western style of bathing suit. By the late 1960s, radical Chinese feminists in San Francisco disparaged both the parade and the beauty pageant. They claimed that white tourists showed disrespect for Chinatown, which had more than its share of overcrowded housing, inadequate medical supplies, tuberculosis, and suicide, the very issues H.K. tackled while working with the City of San Francisco and Mayor Alioto on the year-long Chinese Six Companies study. Activists also protested building a Holiday Inn in Chinatown instead of government-subsidized low-cost housing. Low-cost housing feasibility was a feature of the Chinese Six Companies study H.K. later co-chaired.

In 1966, the festival also came under scrutiny. That year, City Hall decided that the parade would bypass Chinatown's crowded Grant Avenue, which was unthinkable to longtime spectators. Even more upsetting to them was the fact that Chinese year 4664 was a year of the Dragon. The parade was to hold even more significance that year.

On January 26, 1966, my dad wrote a press release pleading for a change to this plan entitled, "Wanted: A New Year's Parade on Grant Avenue, Chinatown." He wrote:

"It is an ancient Chinese tradition that a symbolic dragon passes your doorway each year to ward away evil spirits and to bless the household in the coming year with good fortune. In San Francisco's Chinese community, this tradition is carried on by the lion dances during the week-long celebration. All along Grant Avenue, the family associations are alive with people paying their respects to the elders and greeting each other with '*Gung Hay Fat Choy.*' This is the time of their biggest family gatherings, for there is nothing to rival the warmth and tradition of a Chinese New Year, the height of which is the Chinese New Year parade. In San Francisco, the parade has always come through Grant Avenue. In years past, the parade was a local affair, and many a proud parent and aunt or uncle, head bobbing from second-story windows, could recognize their children were proudly showing off their Chinese heritage and their community spirit.

"A few years ago, Chinatown invited their friends and neighbors to share in this exciting celebration. Through the efforts of many people, Chinese New Year in San Francisco has become of national interest. Next to the Cable Car, Chinatown and her New Year celebration is the symbol of the City by the Golden Gate. Along with New Orleans' Mardi Gras, it is one of the most important metropolitan celebrations in the United States, for it draws interest of visitors from all over the state, across the country, and all over the world. The Grant Avenue Parade has been an annual tradition since 1953. Last year it was changed so only the 'Chinese' contingent of the parade could proceed through Chinatown, while the remaining portion of the parade was shunted down Kearny Street. This year, no part of the parade can go through Chinatown's Grant Avenue. It has been shanghaied to Kearny Street.

"In the past, the Chinese Chamber of Commerce has always wanted the parade through Chinatown. Then there was a meeting held in City Hall and it was announced that the parade would be diverted from Grant Avenue at Bush to Kearny, because of the police and fire control problem. Suddenly, San Francisco's Chinatown, her friends, and neighbors cannot celebrate this Chinese New Year, 4664, with their beloved Dragon. And without the symbolic Dragon in the heart of Chinatown, a great tradition is destroyed. In another sense, it is as if Christmas trees will not be allowed during the Christmas season because of fire hazard.

"Is San Francisco really 'the City that knows how?' Because of practical expediency not thoroughly studied, the Grant Avenue parade is no more. We ask only that City Hall and Chinatown come together and give the problem every consideration to preserve the heart and soul of the celebration, to make this parade possible. On Thursday, January 27, 1966, at 12 noon on the Polk Street side of City Hall, we are rallying to ask the City Fathers 'Don't take the parade away from the people!' The Chinese New Year parade must go through Chinatown."

On Tuesday, February 8, 1966, local Don Bowman also wrote a scathing letter to the *San Francisco Chronicle* editor, "I did not attend the Chinese New Year parade this year. Something had rained on my parade and it was not Jupe Pluvius. Prior to 1966, the Chinese New Year parade up Grant Avenue was unique in America. No other city could boast such a spectacle – the packed crowds on the sidewalks, the Chinese children spilling off the curbs and into the narrow streets, the exotic shops, the crowded bars and family association halls, the glaring neon calligraphy, the TV trucks, the photographers. The intimacy of the entire production generated an excitement and atmosphere unmatched anywhere. To be a part of the crowd on Grant Avenue was to be a participant in this celebration and the evening was a sheer delight. Then came 1966. The parade was routed up Market Street and was completely lost in the vastness of that thoroughfare. The parade was a big nothing. If the parade is not returned to Chinatown and Grant Avenue next year, I suggest the Chinese Association withdraw completely from its participation, leave a couple of floats from gambling clubs in Nevada, armed service bands, and about 15 open convertibles loaded with grinning, glad-handing Irish and Italian office seekers. Should be quite a show. Gung Hay Fat Choy!"

By 1981, nearly 250,000 people watched the parade. My co-author, Catherine, remembers joyfully running through the crowds that year, following the tail of the Golden Dragon as it twisted and turned its way through San Francisco Chinatown. In 1994, the Travel Channel broadcast the parade. That year, the Gay Asian Pacific Alliance joined the parade, receiving boisterous support. In 1996, the *San Francisco Chronicle* bought rights to the name, renaming the event "The *San Francisco Chronicle* Chinese New Year Festival and Parade."

National television coverage now tends to focus more on San Francisco than Chinatown. Though critics have called it stereotypical and inauthentic, the festival is popular in San Francisco, with two fairs, the Chinese New Year Festival Flower Fair and Chinatown Community Street Fair, and the Miss Chinatown USA pageant. The annual Chinese New Year 5K and 10K runs, which start in the heart of Chinatown, attract 1,700 runners each year. Proceeds from the runs support a variety of community programs.

A week before Chinese New Year, San Francisco Chinatown hosts a Lunar New Year Fair, with flowers, tangerines (symbolizing relationships and family), craft vendors, magic shows, acrobatics, folk dancing, and opera. Free admission is available to the Chinese Historical Society of America, which presents dragon dancing, arts, crafts, and other traditions of Chinese New Year. The San Francisco Symphony presents a festival reception with arts and crafts, lion dancing, calligraphy, tea, and food before their concert of Asian, Eastern, and Western music in Davies Symphony Hall. A Chinese Dragon dances before the concert. Proceeds from the evening benefit the Orchestra's music education program for children.

Today the San Francisco Chinese New Year Festival and Parade is the oldest and largest Asian cultural event in North America and considered one of the world's top ten parades. Over 100 groups join the parade. The 2020 Chinese New Year Parade, held February 8th, was sponsored by Southwest Airlines. At its conclusion, a stunning 288-foot Dragon, operated by over 100 puppeteers, wove through the heart of Chinatown. My dad's wish that Chinese New Year in San Francisco Chinatown, complete with firecrackers, would be celebrated as a notable, colorful holiday came true tenfold. Chinese New Year parades to celebrate the Lunar New Year, in addition to San Francisco, are now also held annually in New York City, Chicago, Boston, and London. He left quite a legacy.

H.K.'s sister Phoebe (center right) and mother on Grant Avenue during the first Chinese New Year Festival, February 1953. Photo by Wayne Miller for *Life Magazine*.

Frank Yipp and H.K. lit firecrackers to celebrate the first Chinese New Year Festival, February 1953. Photo by Wayne Miller for *Life Magazine*.

The Scottish Bagpipe band marched in the first Chinese New Year parade on Grant Avenue, February 1953. Photo by Wayne Miller for *Life Magazine*.

Chinese New Year parade on Grant Avenue, circa 1954. Photo by *San Francisco Chronicle*/Polaris.

The golden dragon snaked its way down Grant Avenue in the Chinese New Year parade. Close to one block long, the dragon was guided by over 100 dancers. Circa 1954.

A lion dancer moved through the fireworks' haze in San Francisco's Chinatown on Feb. 16, 1964. Photo by Gordon Peters / *San Francisco Chronicle* / Polaris.

Newly crowned 1958 Miss Chinatown USA Winners: Flavia Hsu (2nd runner-up), June Gong (Queen), Mabel Wing (1st runner-up). Photo by China Newspicture Service.

First Miss Chinatown USA, June Gong, with H.K. in the background, February 1958. Photo by Ed Lee.

Miss Chinatown USA, June Gong, with the Chinese New Year Float at the Tournament of Roses Parade in Pasadena, CA., January 1, 1959.

15

CULTURAL LIAISON

Holiday On Ice

On November 25, 1957, while still serving as Director of the Chinese Chamber of Commerce, H.K. was contacted by the national Holiday on Ice show. The producer of this major ice-skating show, one that traveled throughout the U.S., was requesting information about the pageantry and costumes surrounding the Chinese New Year celebration. In addition to the well-known fireworks and fire dragon already associated with the Chinese New Year celebration, Executive Producer George D. Tyson wanted to know what types of costumes were used in the festival. The show reached 2.5 million people in the U.S., with other shows in Europe, South America, and South Africa. San Francisco Chinatown's Chinese New Year celebration would receive worldwide publicity. This notion excited my dad. On December 2, 1957, he responded, "Your idea of paying tribute to the annual Chinese New Year celebration in your production of 'Holiday on Ice' is a wonderful one. The Chinese New Year celebration in this city has attained nationwide fame and draws tremendous crowds to Chinatown each year for the 3-day public fete. Having the New Year celebration incorporated in 'Holiday on Ice', which plays in the U.S. for 45 weeks each year and to approximately 2½ million people, will be terrific publicity for San Francisco and Chinatown."

As one of the original founders of the Chinese New Year celebration in San Francisco's Chinatown, in 1953 my dad had been a driving force behind opening the festival to people outside of Chinatown. At the time, H.K. had said, "this was such a happy event and marvelous occasion, why not invite friends to it?" Friendship had been the initial reason behind inviting people from outside Chinatown to attend, and now that spirit of friendship had grown to include thousands. By 1975, the celebration was drawing attendees from all over the country. Since the festival was "near and dear to my heart," H.K. was thrilled to see how much it had grown. He felt that when people arrived in Chinatown and "gathered round the family table," they were creating an important, lasting memory that they would take back to their hometowns. He thought the festival would become a fine showcase for Chinatown and that people would be fascinated to see Chinese heritage and culture demonstrations; Tai Chi, Gung Fu, and dances from Tibet, Mongolia, and all over China. He had been right. Countless visitors were now enjoying the Chinese New Year celebration, and their positive impressions were bolstering the Chinatown Chamber's goal of bettering Chinatown's image. H.K.'s tireless work to elevate Chinatown had also been noticed by civic leaders in San Francisco, notably Mayor Joseph Alioto and Supervisor Dianne Feinstein. They admired H.K.'s motivation to heal what had been a silent divide between San Francisco and its Chinatown.

George D. Tyson, producer of Holiday on Ice, had been among those who had heard about the celebration that H.K. had launched in Chinatown. Holiday on Ice was considering paying tribute to the Chinese New Year celebration in one of their production numbers in July 1959. They were seeking authenticity in their show. On January 24, 1958, H.K. received a letter affirming that the Holiday on Ice production team wanted to salute the Chinese New Year Festival in its 1959 performance season. My dad sent 75 large, colorful parasols and 80 Chinese lanterns to Mr. Meza, the production's Prop Designer. In his letter to George D. Tyson, my dad also mentioned that the Chinese New Year Festival included sword dancing, shadow boxing, and blessing of the New Year Lion, a smaller parade puppet than the giant Dragon. The Golden Dragon, he noted, was nearly a block long and, if used, would need many people to handle its twists and turns. The Oriental Lantern Dance would be performed by a bevy of "Holiday

Glamour Icers" skating in a circle, dipping and turning with a lighted lantern on a light bamboo rod, shifting the lantern from one side to the other as they gracefully twirled around. In the final performance, nearly 40 skaters dressed in scanty Chinese-style attire with gilded, tasseled headdresses performed on ice. Unfortunately, a snowstorm barred my mom and dad from seeing the performance in Salt Lake City.

Boy Scout Advisor

On June 6, 1959, the San Francisco Scout Council hosted the National Annual Meeting of the Boy Scouts of America. My dad served as an advisor to the Boy Scouts to arrange a dragon dance ceremony that day at the Scout-O-Rama at Kezar Stadium. Ordinarily only snaking its way through Chinatown at the Chinese New Year parade, the dragon dance ceremony was staged at the stadium as a tribute to honor Troop 3, founded in 1914, the oldest Chinese Scout troop in the world. The ceremony was also a way to introduce this colorful Chinese tradition to the greater Scouting community. Handled by 40 dancers, the famed dragon entered the stadium escorted by drum and bugle corps, and Troop 3 Scouts dressed in traditional Chinese costume carrying Chinese battle weapons and flags. The Scout-O-Rama was a huge event that year, featuring 12,000 of San Francisco's scouts. It coincided with the National Annual Meeting of the Boy Scouts of America, with over 2,500 delegates in attendance.

In a letter dated June 11, 1959 following the event, Glen Rice, Executive Producer of the 1959 Scout-O-Rama, wrote: "Dear Mr. Wong: There seems to be no question about the fact that the performance of the Dragon was the highlight of the 1959 Scout-O-Rama, and directly responsible for the show's success."

Chinese Exhibition of Archeological Finds

On Saturday, June 28, 1975, I am guessing that my dad's happy, buoyant spirit was bubbling over with even more enthusiasm than usual. Confident, excited, and leaning his slim body into a long stride, his broad smile must have beamed as he breathed the moment in deeply and reflected on the past year. He had worked tirelessly alongside Mayor Alioto to promote Chinatown. The work had paid off. With financial support from private donors, local foundations, corporations, and a National Endowment for the Humanities grant, H.K.'s dream of seeing his hometown celebrate Chinese culture was reaching new heights.

Now, in addition to his success with the Chinese New Year Festival, as Coordination Chairman of the Chinese American Committee, H.K. worked hard to have the first exhibition of the Archeological Finds of the People's Republic of China seen in San Francisco rather than just in Washington D.C. and Kansas City, Missouri. Through his efforts, the exhibition made a stop in San Francisco before returning to China. It was the first time that an exhibition of artifacts from the People's Republic of China had ever been seen outside China. In 1966, San Francisco's Asian Art Museum had opened as a wing of the M.H. De Young Memorial Museum in Golden Gate Park. The exhibition opened that day at the Asian Art Museum.

The previous year, returning to San Francisco from the East Coast on the plane, my mom read that an Archeological Finds of the People's Republic of China exhibit was coming to America. At the time, it was scheduled to be exhibited only in New York City and Kansas City. My mom mentioned to my dad that they should find influential people to arrange for the ancient artifacts to come to San Francisco. Negotiation, she mentioned, would be required between Tom Hsieh of the Chinese Six Companies and Cyril Magnin, a patron of the arts in San Francisco and head of the California Museums Foundation. Without my mom's suggestion and my dad's efforts, the exhibit could have easily come to the U.S. without ever stopping on the West Coast.

My dad agreed fully with my mom that bringing artifacts from the People's Republic of China to San Francisco's Asian Art Museum was a resoundingly good idea – and, once something appealed to my dad, there was no stopping his enthusiasm to make it happen. He immediately contacted Hsieh and Magnin. Hsieh and Judge Harry Low were the co-chairmen of the Chinese American committee in support of the exhibition. H.K. served as Marketing Director. Before negotiations were even finalized, H.K. had already fired up interest for the committee to have a special preview night at the Asian Art Museum.

On Saturday, June 28, 1975, for the first time, visitors to the M.H. De Young Memorial Museum's Asian Art Museum wing saw 385 Chinese art and archeological artifacts. Among the displays were an iconic bronze flying horse and a 2,000-year-old Han Dynasty jade burial suit. Princess Tou Wan and her husband's jade burial suits, the first ever found by archaeologists, had only just been discovered in 1968 in Mancheng County, Hebei Province. In her journal, my mom noted that unprecedented crowds created record attendance at the exhibition, unequaled by any previous event at the De Young. During the two-month show, nearly 900,000 people visited the free exhibition at the Asian Art Museum. The attendance was the largest turnout for any traveling exhibition in the world at the time and exceeded all previous showings of the exhibition. The importance of Chinatown's contribution to the City of San Francisco was now sealed internationally.

My dad befriended two curators from the Peking Museum, Mr. Kang and Mr. Huang, in charge of coordinating the Exhibition of Archaeological Finds. After the exhibition ended, the curators extended a personal invitation to our family to visit the Peking Museum. President Richard Nixon had opened U.S. relationships with mainland China in 1972 with his ping-pong diplomacy, and China was starting to allow foreign visitors. However, it was difficult to obtain a tourist visa to China in 1975. The visit to the Peking Museum was part of a 33-day tour of China that also included stops to the Great Wall, Shanghai, and my dad's ancestral village of Foo Shan in Kwangtung province.

Han Tang Murals

In January of 1977, as coordinator of the Chinese American Committee, my dad was approached to organize another exhibition from the People's

Republic of China. In cooperation with the U.S. State Department, the People's Republic of China, the Chinese Culture Foundation, and in support of the Exhibition of the Archeological Finds of the People's Republic of China, H.K. proudly promoted "Murals from the Han to Tang Dynasty." A magnificent collection of tomb paintings and murals from the Han to Tang Dynasty, the exhibition was held at the Chinese Culture Center, 750 Kearny Street, San Francisco. It was open from January 29, 1977 through March 13, 1977, with a special sponsors' premiere viewing held on opening night.

Marco Polo Festival

H.K.'s community engagement and civic pride extended beyond Chinatown into the neighboring North Beach area. In 1978, H.K. joined with his dear friend Alessandro Baccari to develop the Marco Polo Festival, the first of its kind in the U.S. celebrating Chinese American and Italian American heritage. Together they formed a joint committee of Chinatown and North Beach civic leaders to stage the event at Washington Square; it included a street fair, music, and lion dancers. The North Beach Museum was also formed in an upstairs loft at the Eureka Bank on Columbus Avenue to showcase Italian artifacts from the area plus rotating exhibits from Chinatown. The goal of the Marco Polo Festival was to strengthen community bonds between Chinatown and North Beach and to provide another attraction for the city of San Francisco.

CHINESE NEW YEAR
Festival
SAN FRANCISCO

FRANKIE SAWERS

RAY BALMER

H.K. supplied the props for the elaborate dance number celebrating the Chinese New Year Festival that was introduced in the Holiday on Ice Show of 1959. It included a Chinese dragon and over 30 dancers.

Program from the 1959 Scout-O-Rama at the Kezar Stadium. H.K. staged a dragon dance ceremony to honor Troop 3 of San Francisco, the oldest Chinese scout troop in the world.

Poster for the Chinese Exhibition of Archeological Finds, held at the Asian Art Museum in June-August 1975. H.K. was the Coordination Chairman of the Chinese American Committee that brought the exhibition to San Francisco.

The flying horse of Gansu was H.K.'s favorite piece from the Chinese Exhibition of Archeological Finds. Also known as the Bronze Running Horse, the bronze sculpture (from the 2nd century AD) depicts a galloping horse perfectly balanced on one leg atop a flying bird.

H.K. was the Coordination Chairman of the Murals from the Han to Tang Dynasty Exhibit, held at the Chinese Culture Center, January-March 1977.

16

HISTORIAN

"History is not a burden on the memory
but an illumination of the soul."

– Lord Acton

My dad and his friend, William "Bill" Hoy, were friends long before World War II. Meandering through the streets of San Francisco, Chinatown, they often met friends for coffee and conversation at the Fong Fong Café. Hoy never tired of conversing with old-timers and hearing tales of the early migrants. He told H.K. that after the war ended, he planned to live in the Mother Lode Country and attach true names to stories the old-timers told. He planned to research their countless family histories and document their ancestral names, rather than "Ah Lee" or "Ah Sam," as history had recorded them. Hoy died in 1949 and was never able to live in the Mother Lode. However, in the early 1930s, he traveled through California to interview Chinese families about their histories. His documentation of their stories became the foundation of the Chinese Pioneer Historical Society, which he founded in 1935 and which existed until his death.

Travels with Bill Hoy

In the early 1930s, my dad was the only person Hoy knew who had a car that could navigate the rugged country roads in the Gold Country of Northern California. Roaming in H.K.'s car, the two men went on numerous road trips together. With a pen and notebook in hand, Hoy combed the Mother Lode for old-timers, collecting facts, figures, and tales as he sipped tea or *ng ka py* (a 96 proof Chinese liqueur) with them and they willingly talked about their memories. Hoy's tales covered a variety of subjects, from the early history of the Chinese Six Companies and the Chinese in Bakersfield to five versions of the origin of chop suey. My dad, who often enjoyed collecting unusual finds, also picked up abandoned artifacts from Chinatown backyards and junk piles. He did not realize their historic value until years later.

Until 1963, Hoy's interviews were all but forgotten, stored in a box in my dad's basement. H.K. had been inspired by Hoy's work and wanted to continue it, but his home and civic responsibilities took precedence during those years. However, Hoy's vision was never far from H.K.'s mind.

The Chinese Historical Society of America

The idea of a Chinese Historical Society originated in the mid-1930s when Chingwah Lee and historian Thomas Chinn, its founding president, started the first English-language news magazine for Chinese Americans in San Francisco, the *Chinese Digest*. Beginning as a weekly on November 15, 1935, and changing to a quarterly in 1937, it ceased publication in 1940. With Hoy as its editor, the *Chinese Digest* encouraged the publishing of Chinese historical articles. H.K. was also a major contributor to the publication. During that time, Hoy formed the California Chinese Pioneer Historical Society. When Hoy died suddenly in 1949, the Society dissolved, but not before he had interested my dad in the organization.

In 1962, H.K. took the artifacts he had collected, gathered Hoy's interviews, and with the help of Thomas W. Chinn, C.H. Kwock, Chingwah Lee, and Thomas W.S. Wu, DDS, reenergized the Chinese Pioneer Historical Society. In addition to my dad's contribution to the museum, the Society was given relics from the last of the Chinese stores in Chinatown that had served as headquarters for the Chinese arriving and departing from San Francisco. An entire basement of personal belongings and papers that were never claimed, dated shortly before and after the 1906 fire and earthquake, were retrieved for the museum. To be inclusive of all Chinese Americans, the five founders renamed the organization the Chinese Historical Society of America (CHSA).

This group, incorporated on March 16, 1963, held its first general meeting on April 17, 1963 at Chinn's house. Founded to preserve the history of the Chinese in America, it was the first organization of its kind.

An article in the *Young China* two days later noted: "With the formation of the Chinese Historical Society of America, a dream cherished by many Americans of Chinese ancestry and their friends became reality." Temporary headquarters and general meetings were held at the Ti Sun Company. Permanent headquarters and a museum came three years later.

Emphatic that Chinese American history should be preserved through living accounts, H.K. continued Hoy's work and expanded it. Soon after the CHSA was established, field trips were made to areas of significance to Chinese American and California history: Hanford and Armona's ghost Chinatown, Weaverville, Marysville, and Mendocino. Religious temples in these towns had served as important centers for Chinese immigrants. Napa Valley's noted limestone wine-aging tunnels, the 750-mile rock wall on the Silverado Trail, and over 100 bridges had also been built through the diligence, patience, and creativity of the Chinese.

Applying countless hours of determination, dedication, conversations, and personal time, H.K. established a library of documents, the bulk of which were the materials collected by Hoy, who had willed his work to H.K. The building was also a museum of art and artifacts, stocked largely by the artifacts collected by my dad on his California trips with Hoy.

The Society also created exhibitions, participated in historical programs, organized field trips, started its own oral history department through recordings of old-timers, and gathered and authenticated relics and manuscripts for display in its museum. H.K. even embarked on two 240-mile roundtrip drives to Marysville, California to interview a 94-year-old man. Due to the man's rigorous medication schedule, it took an hour to prepare him for H.K.'s interviews. Each of the two interviews was only five to seven minutes long, but to my dad, they were treasures and well worth the 500 miles he had driven to get them. In a *JADE Magazine* article, writer Phyllis Quan wrote, "H.K. Wong, a writer, author, painter, and speaker on radio and television, is directing one of the Society's largest and most exciting projects – 'Oral History of Chinese Americans in America.'"

"The true record of the Chinese in America," H.K. wrote, "is meager and often slanted. The Society hopes to convey an honest impression and add true facts and information to the still unwritten history of our Chinese pioneers. I have been working on the Society's new series, which are being transcribed and authenticated by historians and humanities scholars. The oral history project is a continuing challenge and satisfaction. Although still raw in form, the material gathered thus far is truly nuggets of gold and will be transformed into papers for the public. The finished material will add dynamic chapters to the history of the Chinese in America."

Seeking a permanent headquarters and a museum space for the CHSA, H.K. approached the Shoong Foundation. Milton Shoong, the president of the foundation, presented the building at 17 Adler Place, off Grant Avenue in Chinatown, and a $25,000 grant to transform the building's interior and exterior. The new headquarters and museum were officially dedicated on October 2, 1966 to a large crowd that filled the entire alleyway.

The Early Years of the CHSA

Sue Fawn Chung, Professor Emerita of History, University of Nevada, Las Vegas, and H.K. first became friends when H.K. was courting Sue's aunt, Honey. Sue said, "H.K. was always introducing people to each other. He had a great community spirit and a mind for public relations. He knew I was interested in journalism during junior high school and high school. At the time, he was close friends with *San Francisco Chronicle* columnist Herb Caen. So, H.K. arranged for me to do stories for the Vancouver *Chinatown Press* and to go on the radio in San Francisco."

Chung's interest in sharing stories of the Chinese in America did not stop with high school, though. While a senior at the University of California, Los Angeles (UCLA) majoring in history, she noticed there was a dearth of history about the Chinese in America. In fact, there was none. She shared her concern with Roger Daniels, who also had an interest in Asian American history and immigration and was working toward his Ph.D. at UCLA. Sue also contacted H.K., who asked Daniels, "What can we do to heighten awareness for Chinese history in America? How do we build the Chinese Historical Society of America?"

Daniels laid out numerous ideas, but one idea particularly caught my dad's attention. With his gregarious spirit and love of people and their stories, H.K. liked the idea of creating an oral history of the Chinese in America. Thomas Chinn joined my dad and wrote up their observations. These early history interviews and subsequent recordings were invaluable and formed the core of the CHSA. The organization blossomed from that early effort and spurred the Chinese American history movement in the U.S. The interviews also served to dispel early writings about the Chinese in America that contained stereotypes and racism.

Chung noted, "When the Society moved to their current YWCA location, the larger community could see glimpses of Chinese history that they had not known before. It takes a long time to make an impact on culture, but H.K. had a big part in starting it."

Oral History of Chinese Americans in America

The stories my dad captured are too numerous to share here, but they were posthumously published in October 1987 in his book, *Gum Sahn Yun* (Gold Mountain Men). Dedicated to the many early Guangdong men who came to Gum Sahn (California), the book is a collection of seventeen stories of early Chinese life in California. Below are four of the shorter ones, as written by H.K.:

- "Wong On, later known as Ah Louis, came to America at age 21 in 1860. He walked from Oregon to the end of Southern California in search of gold and health. He found both at the mid-point in San Luis Obispo, on the coast halfway between San Francisco and Los Angeles. The weather was favorable and the gold from the many business ventures he established was constant. He went on to become the most important Chinese pioneer of the region. His children, the youngest at 71 and the oldest at 88, combined their memory bank for recollection of their father's life.

    "Wong Young, Ah Louis' number one son, is now 88 and in his 67th year as a chief motion picture projectionist. A busy civic leader, he is strong and active in the historical organizations of the county. He scrambled up the steep Cuesta Mountain with me recently to point out roads built by the Chinese a hundred years ago. It was 92 degrees.

    "Stella, Young's wife, age 85, recalled their experiences when they drove a new 'Death Valley' Dodge touring car to San Francisco in 1915. The twisty mountain road was a gamble, and after many tire changes, two fordings of the Salinas River and frequent outings into the roadside bushes...they made it! She recounted the days when she drove Ah Louis to his many farms and ranches in the county...and told her how he exchanged rice for game meat from the Indians."

• "Quan Chin came to San Francisco when he was 17 in 1898 from Ngou-am-sui village in Hoy Ping. By a strange quirk, he did not suffer any of the problems of the early immigrants. He was immediately questioned and, when he complained that he was hungry, was promptly fed and released the same day. Quan worked for a wealthy family as a cook, but when the 1906 earthquake and fire hit San Francisco, the whole family was left penniless on the streets. Quan dug up his tobacco can of money that he had saved and gave it to his employer, which provided food for the tough days of the disaster. By 1910, Quan had saved enough money to return to China and come back with his lovely bride. His grateful employer had granted him a leave of absence to return to China."

• "Seventy-two-year-old Freddie Wing, now in his 43rd year as the head chef of a Sonoma hotel, reminisces how he learned to cook Italian meals from the Italian grandmother of the hotel owner. She spoke no English and Wing, then 16 and newly arrived in the country, spoke only Chinese. Their avenue of communication was their love for cooking. Today Wing is the top chef in town. He recalled his adventures in North Africa with the U.S. Army – how he boosted the morale of the combat team by baking pies and cakes as special treats and cooked Chinese meals for them on the battlefront."

• "Mr. Woo, a 104-year-old Chinese man, was honored

by the Nevada Centennial Committee in 1964 at Sparks, Nevada. Our Society came up with the intention of taping his story, but we could not communicate – he was deaf! I returned to Sparks the next weekend with a recorder, camera, and list of questions written in Chinese. A burglar broke into our hotel room and disappeared with everything. I borrowed equipment and came home with the story of his trials and hardships in Nevada. Mr. Woo read the written Chinese characters, answered the questions in Chinese, all the while clutching a box of fat cigars to his chest. I had learned previously that Mr. Woo needed no money, was well fed, and loved cigars – big, fat Otimos always sharpened his memory!"

On January 14, 1967, over a dinner of Birds Nest Soup, Manchurian Beef, Chicken Filet, and Peking Duck at the Empress of China Restaurant, H.K. became president of the Chinese Historical Society of America. He served in many positions until 1985. In 1981, during his tenure as President of the CHSA, my dad was also an advisor to the North Beach Museum and the Pacific Heritage Museum. Additionally, he served on the San Francisco History Museum Board of Trustees, a position that he was recommended for by Mayor Dianne Feinstein.

Oral History Program

In the 1970s, Phyllis Quan, an active writer about ethnic communities in America, wrote in an article for *JADE Magazine* about the CHSA:

"Like many of the small alleyways and side streets in San Francisco's Chinatown, Adler Place begins and ends in less than one city block and is flanked on the side by two bustling streets – Columbus and Grant Avenues. Nevertheless, since 1966, thousands of visitors, including school children and tourists, have purposely found their way here. They have come to see the small Chinese Buddhist altar built in the 1860s, the three-pronged fighting spear made in Weaverville, California by town blacksmiths as a weapon for a local 'war,' and the redwood sampan built by Chinese craftsmen in Marin County for their fishing activities. They are all part of the fascinating collection of artifacts of the Chinese Historical Society of America. The Society sees its charge as an important one:

To establish, maintain, and operate a scientific, literary, and education organization; to study, record, acquire and preserve all suitable artifacts and such cultural items as have a bearing on the history of the Chinese living in the United States of America; to establish a headquarters to enable the display of such items as are acquired; to issue publicity and papers pertaining to the findings of the Society; and to promote the contributions of Chinese Americans, both past and present, to the public.

The task is a monumental one. But, as a nonprofit, membership-supported educational organization, the Chinese Historical Society of America, with its membership, has dedicated itself to researching and promoting the history and contributions of the Chinese in America."

As Project Director of the Oral History Program of the Chinese Historical Society of America, in an article for the *Chinatown News* dated November 3, 1980, H.K. explained the importance of such a vast undertaking:

"Chinese Americans were and still are an important constituency in the fabric of American life. During the 19th century, they were a significant element in the gold mining areas. Chinese labor was indispensable in the construction of the railway network. They were important in speeding the growth of light industries such as the production of cigars, shoes, and garments. Chinese were prominent in agriculture as farmers, truck drivers, gardeners, harvest laborers, and so on. Their horticultural skills contributed to the new varieties of produce such as the Bing cherry and the Lue Gim Gong orange. Others were pioneers in developing the shrimp industry and abalone fisheries. Many served Americans as domestics and laundrymen. The one thing they had in common was they all worked hard. Victimized by years of prejudice and racial discrimination, the full story of the Chinese has yet to be told.

"Today, the role of the Chinese has changed greatly. They are part of the mainstream of America. Many have become professionals and white-collar workers and have left the fields and factories. It is only through the elderly who are still living that we can get more information on the past achievements and activities of the Chinese Americans. The Society's initiation of the 'Oral History' Project, consisting of the taping of the experiences and recollections for transcription, was its top priority. Many of the interviewees represent a living cultural heritage who are getting old and whose stories must be recorded for posterity. Today the Society has hours of tapes of interviews with many persons, representing firsthand information of the elderly Chinese. This is an important element in the multi-ethnic heritage of America that should be recorded and made available for the edification of future generations, Chinese and non-Chinese alike."

Dignitaries in San Francisco and across the country took notice of the Society. In August 1964, H.K. and C.H. Kwock were invited along with 150 foreign-language editors and publishers to the first foreign press association conference at the White House. During that gathering on Monday, August 3, 1964, President Lyndon B. Johnson was made an Honorary Member of the Chinese Historical Society of America. H.K. and the Society's secretary, C.H. Kwock, announced the proclamation, and my dad presented a Chinese scroll to the president. In making President Johnson an Honorary Member, the five founders of the Society sent the following letter to him:

July 28, 1964

Dear Mr. President:

The Chinese Historical Society of America is privileged to make you an Honorary Member. Like similar historical societies throughout the country, our organization is dedicated to the preservation of early-day records, stories, and artifacts that led toward the growth and progress of America – with one difference: we specialize in the field of the Chinese pioneers. In this endeavor, the first organization of its kind in America, we have as members many persons of varied business, religious, social, and racial backgrounds. Organized and incorporated as a non-profit, non-political, non-sectarian group, we have the good will and support of community and civic leaders and nationally and internationally known persons.

As our first Honorary Member, Mr. President your duty will be to continue to lead our great country in the best traditions of good government, ever mindful of the precepts contained in the Constitution conceived by our founding fathers.

Most sincerely yours,

The five founders of the Chinese Historical Society of America

Thomas W. Chinn, C.H. Kwock, Chingwah Lee, H.K. Wong, and Dr. Thomas W.S. Wu

After the White House visit, my dad received the following letter from Jack Valenti, Special Assistant to the President.

The White House
Washington

August 10, 1964

Dear Mr. Wong and Mr. Kwock:

I am enclosing photographs which were taken during your presentation of the Chinese scroll to the President.

The President has asked me to express his appreciation for the high honor you bestowed upon him. He wants you to know that he is very much aware of his responsibilities and duties toward our country and is confident that as long as citizens take an active interest in the welfare of our country, our nation will continue to lead the world in preserving democracy so that all may enjoy our great heritage of freedom.

With Kindest Regards,

Sincerely,

Jack Valenti
Special Assistant to the President

A History of the Chinese in California: A Syllabus

In April 1969, due to the scarcity of historical information about the Chinese in California, and in response to requests from a California school-district representative, regional teachers, and historians to provide classroom materials on the subject, the Chinese Historical Society of America compiled and published a syllabus about the history of the Chinese in California. Noting that the fishing industry often drew Chinese residents of California to Alaska to work in the canneries, the Society also included the history of Chinese Californians in Alaska. Complied by Thomas W. Chinn, editor, and Him Mark Lai and Philip P. Choy, associate editors, with contributions from H.K., the Society published *A History of the Chinese in California: A Syllabus*. The book, designed and printed by Lawton and Alfred Kennedy, was also used as the text for the seminar, "A History of the Chinese in California," held April 19, 1969 at the Chinese American Citizens Alliance Auditorium, San Francisco. My dad worked with the CHSA to present the seminar. Registrants from academic and community groups were the first to make use of the syllabus.

In a letter dated June 30, 1973, three of the founders of the CHSA wrote to the Peoples' Republic of China Premier Chou En-lai in Peking, China:

> "Greetings. On the occasion of the first air mail service to the Peoples' Republic, we thought this would be an appropriate time to observe the event with the enclosure of two copies of a syllabus: *A History of the Chinese in California*. On this occasion, it is our pleasure as individuals to present the syllabus as a token of our appreciation for the bond of friendship that exists between the peoples of the United States and China."

By 1975, the Syllabus was in its fifth printing, with a readership that extended throughout the U.S.

San Francisco 200 Year Celebration
and U.S. Bicentennial

On July 4, 1976, the San Francisco 200 Year Celebration commemorated the arrival of Spanish settlers to San Francisco (which they named Yerba Buena) for the first time. Some 6,000 people enjoyed dancing and watching reenactments of the settlers' arrival. That same day, San Francisco joined the nation in celebrating the U.S. Bicentennial. The highly popular "people's mayor," George Moscone, was Mayor of San Francisco at the time. A crowd of 14,000 came to a bicentennial performance of the play 1776 at Stern Grove, San Francisco. The spirit of the Bicentennial was active everywhere in the United States, from the post office where you could buy postage stamps commemorating the event, to artists printing revolutionary broadsides on antique presses. Collectors bought 1776 souvenir coins in a frenzy. Celebrations sprang up in cities nationwide. From historical reenactments to 4th of July events, San Francisco was no exception. Following an hourlong music program by the Golden Gate Park Band and opera baritone Walter Hinton, on July 4, 1976, sparkling firework rockets lit up the sky at Candlestick Park.

My dad, always energized by the opportunity to be part of anything of note happening in San Francisco, wanted to be sure that Chinatown was represented in the events. He served as Co-Chairman of the Chinatown Committee for the City of San Francisco 200 Year Celebration and of the U.S. Bicentennial. Highlighting his contribution was serving on the executive committee for the Chinese Historical Society National Conference on Life, Influence, and Role of Chinese in the U.S, 1776-1960. In 1975, as part of the Twin Bicentennial Celebration of the United States and San Francisco, CHSA assembled the conference at the University of San Francisco. It was the first national conference on the history of the Chinese in America. The Society's objective was to discuss the influence and contribution of the Chinese who were in the United States between 1776 and 1960 in a national forum, and to encourage further research and development of papers on the subject. Many lectures and papers were presented by academic scholars and historians My dad contributed to a follow-up 338-page book about the conference, *Proceedings/Papers of the National Conference*. The book was published in 1978 and is still used today by educators and historians.

The First Transcontinental Railroad Centennial

On May 4, 1969, H.K. also organized a gathering of more than 200 people in San Francisco to recognize the role of the Chinese in building the First Transcontinental Railroad in America. Called the Central Pacific Railroad until it joined with the Union Pacific Railroad in Promontory, Utah on May 10, 1869, that section of the First Transcontinental Railroad took the longest to build because workers had to span the Sierra Nevada mountains. Ninety percent of those workers were Chinese because they were able to endure the hard labor and dangers of the steep and treacherous mountains, which involved blasting multiple rocky tunnels. To commemorate the railroad's Centennial, CHSA presented two bronze plaques to Sacramento, California, and Promontory, Utah in honor of the important role Chinese pioneers played in the construction of the railroad.

Tommy Tong's Golden Star Radio "Chinese Hour"

From 1939 to 1979, Tommy Tong's Golden Star Radio, the first Chinese-language radio station in North America, was broadcast from the basement of Tong's appliance shop. His show, "Chinese Hour," covered news, music, opera, public events, and community announcements. In 1940, Tong introduced an English-language segment that centered on historian Bill Hoy narrating the "Tales of the Early California Chinese." In *Chinatown News*, on March 3, 1982, H.K. wrote about Tong's radio broadcast:

> "Tommy Tong's fascination with radio dates to the mid-1920s when he built his first tiny crystal receiving set and picked up KPO on the first try. He studied the subject to become an expert and made radio and communications his lifetime work. In 1930, he operated the largest sales and service radio outlet in Chinatown. The shop turned out to be the springboard to launching his 'Chinese Hour' Chinese-language broadcast over KSAN. As a one-man production crew, Tong was the producer, director, and technician, but never took to the airwaves himself. His wife, May, was the familiar personality and voice heard on the 'Chinese Hour.' Listeners throughout Northern California, whether in homes, stores, restaurants, or

farms, instantly recognized her voice whenever she was on air. May had a distinctive style of delivery in Cantonese, with perfect enunciation, and her tonal quality always drew plaudits from appreciative listeners. To this day, no one has matched or surpassed her in popularity as a Chinese language broadcaster in the San Francisco Bay Area. The 'Chinese Hour,' after 39 continuous years of public service to the community, finally succumbed to the passage of time."

Hoy's radio shows covered a variety of topics, such as the first Chinese in California, social organizations of the Chinese, why the Chinese came to America, the Chinese Six Companies, the Chinese theaters, Chinese laundries, the Chinese in Bakersfield, and the Ghost of Hornitos.

H.K. documented excerpts from one of those programs:

"Throughout the length and breadth of California, on the coast from San Diego to San Francisco, and in the interior from Bakersfield in the south to Yreka in the north, there exist today numerous Chinatowns, big and small. Some, like the one in San Francisco, date their beginnings way back to the 1850s, to the time of the Gold Rush. The list of California cities that have Chinatowns over half a century old today is quite long – places such as San Francisco, Newcastle, Sacramento, Marysville, Oroville, Chico, Red Bluff, Weaverville, Yreka – all names which are intimately associated with the pioneering era of this state. Some of the earliest and liveliest Chinatowns in California were in the romantic Mother Lode Country, but all of these have since vanished from the map, leaving practically no traces. Some of these Mother Lode towns where once Chinatowns flourished include the famous Chinese Camp, Sonora, Jamestown, Columbia, Angels Camp, Jackson, Plymouth, Placerville, Coloma, Michigan

Bluff, Gold Run, Auburn, Dutch Flat, Grass Valley, Nevada City, Washington, San Juan, Camptonville, Downieville, and many more.

"These are colorful names for equally colorful places, and not a little of their color came from the fact that there were Chinatowns in their midst. These were famous towns, too, in this golden empire's frontier days, for from their mines, riverbeds and diggings have come billions of the shining gold metal which helped to change the course of California's history.

"The Franciscan padres brought Christianity to the Western shores through its twenty-one California missions. There is a Chinese parallel to these missions. Through more than half the length of the state, from Los Angeles to Weaverville, is a string of Chinese temples, commonly called joss houses, and there are more than twenty-one. Many of these temples are in ruins, some have been abandoned years ago, but a few are still splendidly preserved and looked after by a few pious souls. What is the significance of these temples? Simply this: they are the outward evidences of a way of life lived by the particular group of Chinese who, by a strange accident of history, came to California in the wake of the Gold Rush and brought with them many of the traditions, customs, and social and religious practices of their own land."

Today, the Chinese Historical Society of America is the oldest and largest organization dedicated to the cultural, social, and political contributions of the Chinese in America. The CHSA museum is currently located at 965 Clay Street, in the former Chinatown YWCA building, designed by the renowned American architect, Julia Morgan, best known for her work on Hearst Castle. The CHSA energetically continues the work that H.K. and the four other founders started. The work the Society does is a large part of my dad's enduring legacy.

C.H. Kwock and H.K. presented a Chinese scroll to President Lyndon Johnson at the White House and proclaimed him an honorary member of the Chinese Historical Society of America, August 3, 1964.

Milton Shoong and H.K. dedicated the opening of the new Chinese Historical Society of America (CSHA) museum at 17 Adler Place, October 2, 1966. Photo by Kem Lee.

H.K. commented to a reporter about the Chinese Buddhist temple altar display at the opening of the CHSA museum, October 2, 1966.

My dad and I tested the water pump in the Armona, California Chinatown during a field trip with the CHSA. The trip also included stops in Hanford and Weaverville. June 1964. Photo by Kem Lee.

A CHSA field trip to Weaverville, California on September 26, 1964. Thomas Chinn presented a CHSA plaque to Moon Lee for the Joss House. Photo by Kem Lee.

17

ARTIST AND TRAVELER

"Paintings have a life of their own that derives from the painter's soul."

- Vincent Van Gogh

My dad enjoyed traveling for business and to visit his friends. He made numerous trips to the Eastern U.S., Hawaii, Canada, and the Far East. By the late 1960s, he had accumulated enough airline miles to become a member of the United Airlines 100,000-mile club. He was proud of this unique distinction and treasured the brass membership card. This long predated the Frequent Flyer programs that are commonplace today with most airlines.

My parents always had a desire to travel to mainland China to visit their ancestral villages. While coordinating the Exhibition of Archaeological Finds in San Francisco in 1975, two curators from the Peking Museum had extended a personal invitation to H.K. to visit the Peking Museum. Little was known about China at that time because travel to the country was severely restricted, so my dad readily accepted the invitation. Though my grandfather had never returned to Fu-Shan village after he moved to America in 1877, it was always his hope that his children might return there someday. So, when H.K. applied for permission to visit the People's Republic of China, he specified that he wanted to visit Tiger Hill Village. It had always been H.K.'s dream to visit his ancestral home. His application was approved shortly after the opening of the Exhibition of Archaeological Finds. The Chinese ambassador to Washington D.C. helped arrange all the necessary visas for our journey.

Our 33-day trip through China sparked my dad's interest in watercolor painting. While visiting the Kweilin Mountains, he became entranced with their beautiful formations. With his felt pen, he created a stack full of sketches of the scenery. My dad's artistic talent had been evident at an early age in two pencil sketches of farmworkers he drew in grade school. He received high marks for those drawings. He also created much of the artwork for the marketing materials for the Empress of China and the Ti Sun Company and won many awards for his window displays. He liked to doodle on scrap paper or cardboard and make sketches or drawings with a ballpoint pen or felt marker. To get a watercolor effect, he would wet the marker or dab the drawing with water or tea.

In a letter dated April 3, 1978, Dr. LaVay Lau, who had stayed in touch with H.K. and Honey since my adoption, wrote to my dad: "Your drawings reflect your aliveness and humor and deep appreciation of life and its richness."

Journey through China

Traipsing through China on trains, buses, taxis, and a rented Toyota minibus, our trip was such a wonderful and eye-opening experience that my dad was inspired to write an article about it. The November 1978 issue of *Travel Holiday* magazine's feature story, "China" was written by my dad. The magazine's cover, a watercolor painting of the tiered-roof Imperial Palace in Peking, was also painted by him.

We visited Taipei, Hong Kong, Peking, Canton City, Nanking, Shanghai, Hangchow, Sian, Kweilin, Soochow, and villages along the way. Highlights of the trip were the vistas of Kweilin peaks and Li River, an area which inspired early artists to make treks to Southwestern China to paint scrolls of its beauty; Beijing, where we visited the Summer Palace, noted for being the best-preserved, imperial garden in the world, and the largest in China; and the Temple of Heaven.

While in China, H.K. was given the unique opportunity to visit the ancestral village and house where his father was born. Before visiting, my dad had known that his father's birthplace was Fu-Shan village (Tiger Hill village) in Canton (Kwangtung) Province in mainland China. But in the 1930s, shortly before his father's death, when H.K. had inquired about the house where his father was born, all my dad could remember his father saying was "it had two big wells." To make the search even more challenging, the last name of all 800 inhabitants in Fu-Shan village was Wong.

But my dad was lucky. Stopping en route to Fu-Shan village in a town called Sam-Fow, he was informed that the chairman of the Hoy San District where my father's hometown was located had been told that 40 years prior, a Chinese American who was the sixth son of a Wong had migrated to America and then come back to Fu-Shan village for a visit. While in Fu-Shan, he had married a girl from the Lee family who lived in a nearby non-Wong village. Amazingly, the man the chairman had been talking about was H.K.'s brother, David, who had wed Mary Lee when he'd been sent by my grandfather to study in China.

In an article written for the *San Francisco Sunday Examiner* by H.K., as told to journalist Donald Canter, my dad talked about our trip:

"Two of the Chinese curators who were in San Francisco during the exhibit met me, my wife Honey, and son Wesley in front of the old Imperial Palace as we arrived in Peking (Beijing). The palace is now a museum. They greeted us like long-lost brothers. We were treated to an official tea out of priceless Imperial yellow cups in an elaborately furnished room where an empress of China once entertained her guests. My hosts drew my attention to a small stage at one side of the room where the dancing girls would perform for the empress. The thought occurred to me that we do not have such a feature in San Francisco's Empress of China Restaurant.

"In the Chinese Historical Museum in Peking's famed Tien An-Men Square, we had a reunion with an old friend – the bronze Galloping Horse admired by thousands when on exhibit in San Francisco last year. When we were planning our trip, my wife was determined to do 'something typically American' while in China. She decided to bring a Frisbee. Honey, Wesley, and I let it fly in the middle of Tien Ah-Men Square as many Chinese watched in amazement. Honey presented the Frisbee to a young Chinese boy. His parents made him give it back – with profuse thanks for the gesture. On mainland China, they do not accept anything from foreigners.

"In Tiger Hill Village, things were different. Youngsters could keep the candy we had brought. But then, over there, we were not foreigners. Like everybody else, we were Wongs. It was all in the family."

Fu-Shan (Tiger Hill) Village

"En route to Fu-Shan, our minibus passed several caravans of bicycle riders. Each bike had two baskets, one on each side of the back carrier. The baskets were filled with building materials, mostly white rocks. In China, everyone works.

"The entrance to Tiger Hill Village was marked by a pagoda-roofed pavilion. My guide told me how the village got its name. The hill at whose foot it is cradled is shaped like a tiger. We got out of the car and walked down the same road on which my father walked out of his hometown on the day he went to America – 99 years ago. Many of the villagers thronged around us. Others remained respectfully distant. They appeared both surprised and delighted that I, a Chinese dressed in American clothes, spoke the dialect of their town and district.

"And so, the word went around: 'Someone from Gum Sahn has returned to the village!' Gum Sahn means 'Golden Mountain,' the name the Chinese gold rushers used to describe California. A village official, a fellow Wong, of course, greeted us and asked me where I wanted to go first. 'To the house of my father,' I said.

"Past rice paddies, bamboo sticks, and stands of banana trees, we walked through the farming village with its bunched-up houses. Every inch of land appeared to be cultivated. I shouted a greeting to a man thrashing rice with a passion. All seemed to have an intense pride in what they were doing. Nowhere did I see fat people. My father's house was only partially intact. The present occupants of the house, a young Wong couple, explained that they had recently torn down the front of the house as part of a do-it-yourself modernization project.

"Two large wells stood on the property, just as my dad's father had remembered. H.K.'s relatives welcomed us warmly with fresh roasted peanuts and piles of sweet potatoes.

"Another meaningful visit was to my mom's village in South China, a place called 'Ngou-am-sui,' translated literally as 'buffalo carrying water.' Honey's ancestral home, famous for its garlic, was on the other side of the river from Fu-Shan. We found her relatives living in a clean, well-kept three-story house with a courtyard that was overrun with rabbits and chickens."

H.K. was impressed with the artistic ability of workers in an arts and crafts factory in Peking. He said, "There, they have old masters teaching the young so that the traditions can be kept alive."

From Peking, we flew to Nanking for two days, and then took a train to Soochow and Hangchow. Being in the restaurant business, my dad was intrigued by the food. He said the best meal he had was in Hangchow, a soup of fish heads cooked with bean curd and lake fish, steamed Hangchow style with hairy crabs. Our entire meal cost us only $4.50.

After visiting Hangchow, we took a 26-hour train ride to Kweilin, where we boarded a boat to ride along the Li Jiang River, a place of indescribable beauty often depicted in Chinese scroll paintings. The river and its soluble rock caves were breathtaking. We then flew to Canton and were there just in time for an Autumn Fair.

In Shanghai, where we spent five days, my dad tried acupuncture for the first time. He claimed that after two visits, the arthritic pain he suffered in his little finger disappeared, as did the pain in his knees. Once home, he presented a slide show of our journey to many public groups in Northern California and the San Francisco Bay Area.

I have included excerpts from the lengthy *Travel Holiday* magazine article my dad wrote about our trip. The original article also included photos. I was the family photographer for the trip and took over 1,000 color slides.

From the *Travel Holiday*, November, 1978 "China" article by H.K. Wong

"The Bronze Flying Horse of Kansu was a major attraction at the Exhibition of Archeological Finds of the People's Republic of China. This fabulous collection of 385 artifacts uncovered in China since 1949 drew record audiences in its United States tour. We first admired this magnificent horse at the Asian Art Museum in San Francisco and for our second look, it was at its home in the Museum of Chinese History off Tien An-Men Square in Peking. I served as coordinating chairman of the Chinese American Committee for the Exhibition in San Francisco. This facilitated our visa for a visit to China. Applications for Mrs. Wong, Wesley, our 18-year-old son, and myself were approved at the Liaison Office in Washington D. C. Thus, our journey to China, closed to outsiders for more than a quarter century, became a reality. We saw many people during our 33 days inside the People's Republic of China but still only an infinitesimal percentage of the 800 million population. We selected major cities, scenic attractions, historic locales, agricultural areas and our ancestral villages for our itinerary on the eastern and southern coastal regions where 90 percent of the population live."

Arrival

"We flew to Hong Kong where China Travel Service, the official tourist organization known as Luxingshe, verified our itinerary and completed arrangements for our entry. We traveled as individuals rather than with any groups. English or Cantonese speaking guides were designated to greet us at each designation.

"Early the next morning, with travel documents, badges, train, and plane tickets supplied by Luxingshe, we took the train from Hong Kong to Lo Wu, the gateway between Hong Kong and Kwangtung. We were assisted through customs clearance and scrutinized by border guards who verified our faces matched those of our passports. Then we crossed the Shum Chun Bridge into China – a world totally different from anything we had experienced before.

"We were immediately aware of the hospitality of the people, as courteous personnel directed us to the various rooms for clearance. Sessions with health and immigration officers and baggage inspection were speedily accomplished. Visitors changed their money at the station's government bank into Renminbi or People's money.

"A Luxingshe guide escorted us across the track to a large hotel surrounded by a tropical garden with a huge fishpond. Lunch in the spacious dining hall for $1.00 U.S. per person was scrumptious. After lunch, we boarded the train for Canton City, one hour and 45 minutes away. The train was immaculate. Young women swept and wet mopped the aisle at intervals. Covered teacups were kept full and boiling hot. The 'soft' seat section allotted to visitors was comfortable. Vendors walked by with broiled chicken, goose, and other foods. Passengers sipped tea and gazed out of the windows at South China's richest agricultural district, the Pearl River delta area. Here, rice is harvested three times a year. Every bit of land is used, up to within a foot of the track. People were working in the fields planting, cultivating, or harvesting a variety of crops."

Canton

"We arrived in Canton, pronounced Kwangchow, a metropolis of three million people. This principal city of South China is the home of the National Commodities Fair (Canton Fair) held every spring and autumn for sales of Chinese products. A China travel guide (*tung gee*) welcomed us at the station and we were bussed to our hotel. After a briefing on the facilities and tours available, we were on our own. We walked the busy streets along the Pearl River bridge. The sights and sounds were like San Francisco's Chinatown – a medley of Cantonese mingling with the soft-spoken Mandarin dialect. It was from this city, inhabited for more than 2,800 years, that Chinese in the Gold Rush days transferred from tiny river boats to larger crafts for Hong Kong, and eventually the long trip across the ocean to Gum Sahn (California). Excellent restaurants, historical pagodas, and temples are noteworthy sights of Canton. Early the next morning, were driven to the White Cloud Airport."

Peking

"In Peking (Beijing), capital of China, almost continuously since 1207 A.D., emperors of the past built palaces, gardens, and parks for their personal enjoyment. The progress of today's administration is visible in the new construction, huge government buildings, factories, and medical facilities. During strolls in the older section of the city, we passed single-story homes with central courtyards and uniformly gray tile roofs. The unhurried atmosphere, the same as in past centuries, was disturbed by the roar of the buses, the honk of automobile horns, and the tinkling of bicycle bells. In this city of eight million people, there are five million bicycles, all plain, heavy-duty models which are work horses of the people and their chief mode of transportation. We expanded our knowledge of new China at museums, libraries, arts, crafts, and cultural centers, factories, industrial exhibitions, schools, nurseries, plants, medical facilities, communes, farms, workers' homes, sports stadiums, restaurants, and shops – all State owned. These visits included greetings and tea parties with briefings on the statistics and progress since the Liberation. My family speaks Cantonese, but not Mandarin, the national tongue. Cantonese-speaking guides assigned to us were of great help whenever we needed them.

"People's Road, formerly Wang Foo Ching, is the main commercial street in Peking. There we browsed in Pai Huo Ta Low, the largest department store in the city. The Tung-feng Commercial Center is a bustling bazaar with hundreds of small stalls and shops, all piled with merchandise. Foreigners are a center of attention in the shops and on the streets. We were objects of continual intense staring, which was disturbing at first. But we soon learned to ignore this as the stares were not unfriendly but merely curious.

"The irresistible sights and scenes of China are everywhere in Peking. The visit to the Imperial Palace alone was worth the ten thousand miles (16, 000 km) of travel from America. The complex of magnificent palaces and pavilions is the largest and most complete group of ancient buildings which China has preserved. This complex of 9,000 rooms, formerly known as the Forbidden City, was once reserved only for royalty. It is now open to the public as Gu-Gong, the Palace Museum. Mr. Kang and Mr. Huang, two curator friends we met while they were in San Francisco for the Archaeological exhibition, met us at the Main Gate. They guided us through the vast collections of artifacts and treasures. For a rest, they escorted us to the former residence of the Empresses, a palace in the Inner City. We wished that the gnarled cypress in the 500-year-old Imperial Garden could speak and tell us stories of love, intrigue, and romance.

"Tien An-Men Square, 'Gate of Heavenly Peace,' is in the center of the city. The Monument to Heroes of the People is located here, flanked by the quarter-mile-long Great Hall of the People on one side and the equally large Museum of Chinese History and Revolution on the opposite side. The peaceful courtyards and gardens of the Summer Palace afforded a pleasant place to relax. This 700-acre (280 ha) retreat of Tz'u Hsi, the last of China's imperial rulers, is now a public park and museum. A Sunday brings out the crowd – young adults for boat rides on Kunming Lake, and families with picnic lunches. Visitors can dine and sample some of the 132 varieties of delicacies that were concocted here for the Empress Dowager."

The Great Wall

"The Great Wall, or Wan Li Chang Chen ('the Wall of 10,000 *li*'--a *li* is 1/3 mile), is a marvel of construction, 2,500 years old. It snakes up steep mountains and rough terrain for nearly 3,500 miles (5,600 km). The wall, 22 feet (6.6.m) high, 18 feet (5.4 m) wide at the top and 22 feet (6.6 m) thick at the base, is built of granite blocks and gray stone bricks. We walked up the steep incline of the restored section at the Chu Yung Pass to the top of the guard house for our breathtaking view into Mongolia. Huge stones and rocks are still piled high at many defense points at the base of the wall, which were at one time used against invaders from the North."

Dining in Peking

"China abounds with restaurants, which serve a variety of regional food. Peking has them all, from tiny stalls to international dining places. In our childhood, we heard of a shop in Peking that had kept a huge iron pot of meat cooking day and night, continually since the Ming Dynasty, 1420 A.D.! Fresh meat and ingredients were added daily. We searched in vain for this shop and for a restaurant which served tiger meat; both no longer exist. Menus of restaurants today may offer camel's hump stew, fish lips with duck gravy, shark's fin in a broth of gravy, spicy Szechuan eggplant, hot Hunan pork, Mongolian lamb, fresh fish, poultry and vegetables cooked in a bewildering variety of ways. Tientsin snow pears, persimmons, glazed apples, and stewed dates are favorite fall desserts. We selected Peking duck for our first dinner in the Capital City at the 132-year old restaurant of the same name. Nine kinds of hors d'oeuvres and plates of sweetmeats awaited our arrival. The dinner commenced with a round of hot tea. But first, the chef's helper, a demure young lady in a white coat, brought from the oven a whole freshly barbecued duck for our inspection. Upon our approval, dish after dish was carried in; finely sliced heart, gizzard, liver, tongue, webs, and crisp skin were served on beds of vegetables, artfully arranged. Each dish was decorated with carrots, beets, and turnips carved into delicate flowers and animals.

"Foods are equally enticing in other parts of China outside Peking. Duck kidney in specially prepared vegetables is a gourmet treat in Nanking. In Shanghai, we warmed to broiled, spiced, boneless eel in sizzling oil and lavishly sprinkled with black pepper. Among Soochow delicacies are sweet dumplings, fashioned into dainty miniature birds, flowers, animals, fruits, and vegetables. One of the highly prized game foods in Kwangsi Province is roasted raccoon. This fruit-eating animal, trapped by farmers in the hills, is prepared like roast pig. The crisp skin and tasty meat are excellent with fiery Mao Tai drinks. A Chinese saying is 'To eat in Kwangchow (Canton) is to eat the best food in China.' Chefs proved this correct as they transformed a variety of fowl, meats, seafood, and vegetables into savory dishes."

Soochow

"Soochow, one of the most celebrated cities south of the Yangtze, is noted for its artistic gardens. Thousands of these showplaces are secluded behind walls, but open to the public. Soochow women in the past were famed as the most beautiful in China. Today, natives deny this, but privately acknowledge that the complexion of their women is clear because of the gentle climate and fresh air. The city is also a center of textile, silk, and cotton industries and the growing of silkworms."

Hangchow

"Hangchow, at the southern extreme of the Grand Canal, with its famous Westlake, is China's 'Paradise on Earth.' A Ch'ing Emperor built a pavilion here, exclusively for moon viewing. It was here that we found a grove of square bamboo and a luxuriant grove of bamboo six to eight inches in diameter and 50 to 75 feet (about 19 m) tall."

Nanking

"Nanking, an ancient city with wide tree-lined streets, 24 city gates, and rust-colored buildings, has a history dating back 2,500 years. The mausoleum of Dr. Sun Yet-Sen, China's first President, is in a setting of grandeur and dignity atop a ridge of Chung Shang Mountain. Thousands of visitors walk up the 395 steps of Soochow marble to the tomb.

"The small shops and eating places are always busy on Nanking Road, the principal street of the city. At a snack place outfitted with wooden tables and stools, soup noodles were served for 5 cents U.S. Visitors may also board at Chinese hotels; the cost for three meals a day per person is $2.50 U.S. Food is wholesome, tasty, and quickly served with plenty of fresh fruit for dessert.

"The boiling water vendor is a unique sight. She sells boiling water for making tea. Her single charcoal-burning stove serves hundreds of families in the neighborhood. With one hand, she dexterously pours water into customers' thermos jugs without spilling a drop and collects pennies with the other.

"The Yangtze River Bridge at Nanking, 7,406 yards (6,772 m) long, double-decked for rail and automobile traffic, is a vital connection between North and South China. It is toll-free and one of the government's proudest construction feats."

Shanghai

"Shanghai, the principal commercial and manufacturing hub, is the largest city in China. The downtown area between the railway station, Soochow Creek, and the Whangpoo River bustles with activities and people. The Shanghai Industrial Exhibit, located in a huge hangar-like building, is the commercial showplace of Shanghai-made products. The Children's Palace, an old mansion converted into a teaching clinic for talented youngsters, serves a thousand children a day. Factory craftsmen, artists, doctors, mechanics, and retired persons conduct classes in arts, crafts, science, math, medicine, and special subjects. A mind-boggling scene – two seven-year-olds practicing acupuncture with sharp needles on each other, all the while giggling with fun."

Kweilin

"Kweilin, in the southwestern section of China, is famed for the scenic beauty of its misty mountains, eroded pinnacles, reflecting waters, and the spectacular stalactites and stalagmites of the Seven Star and the Reed Flute Caves. Painters made the hazardous journey from the capital to record these scenes. Even I was inspired to try my untutored hands at painting on the 7½-hour boat ride down the Li Kong (River) and returned with several sketches. Entertainment is available, but there are no night clubs or floor shows as there are in the West. Concerts, shadow theaters, operas, puppet shows, movies, circuses, athletic competitions, and acrobatic shows are always well attended, not only in the cities, but also in the towns, villages, factories, and communes."

A commune

"More than 500 separate groups of farmers banded together as the 'Long March Commune' in a mutual effort to increase production of their land. This commune, an hour from Shanghai, has its own health clinic, medical staff, school, nurseries, housing, factory, repair shop, irrigation system, and lakes. Growing time is strictly controlled. Certain greens are cut precisely on the 14th day and sent to market immediately. Mushrooms are cultivated in huge sheds and harvested on the 40th day; they are cleaned, processed, and trucked to market by nightfall."

Stone collection

"Collecting rocks is my hobby, and it was easy in China. At the Temple of Heaven, we looked longingly at the beautiful blue tiles atop the structure and reasoned, 'What goes up, must come down' in the 500 years since its construction. So, there we were, squatting in the courtyard, surrounded by curious persons, assisted by our cheerful guide – scraping away at the earth with hands and sticks. Half a foot down, we found a piece of dirt-incrusted but authentic tile. My China rock collection includes portions of Imperial yellow tile from the roof of the Imperial Palace, rocks from the parks of the Ming Tomb, stones hurled from the top of the Great Wall against invaders, and pieces of Ming porcelain from the Soochow gardens and the Purple Hills of Nanking. These artifacts were dug up from old construction piles. Our Gugong curator friends' parting gift was a time-battered, weather-chipped, ceramic animal corner tile from the roof of the Imperial Palace. This historical artifact is a treasured token of their friendship."

Friendships

"Expressions of friendship came at unexpected times and places. I offered to purchase an artist's painting at the Ming Tomb Park. He declined, as he said he painted for his pleasure and for the enjoyment of friends. This observation triggered off a friendly discussion between us and a gathering audience. Later, he completed the painting, brushed my name and words of friendship on the wet watercolor, and presented it to me amidst applause and hurrahs. He accepted nothing in return, but I persuaded him to share an apple with me. We also became friends of a commander of the People's Army on a train ride. Upon arrival at our destination, he personally carried our heavy luggage off the train to the station, and left us with a cheery, *'jaijian'* (see you again). We met children everywhere; they were ebullient, happy, and lovable. On the streets, they waved and looked on with lively interest at us. They sang, danced, and acted with gusto in school and nursery performances. After their shows, they held hands with visitors whom they address as 'Uncle and Auntie.' When visitors applauded them on departure, they returned the applause with even greater vigor."

As I have mentioned before, H.K. made friends easily wherever he went. China was no exception. During the visit to H.K.'s ancestral village, one of the villagers asked my dad if he was rich. My dad replied that in America, he was not considered rich in money but was rich with many friends. His two Rolodex files were completely full, containing over 500 address cards.

Artistic process

After our trip to China, I started my first year of college and took a course in watercolor painting. I passed on the knowledge of techniques for preparing the papers and applying different types of washes I learned in that class to my dad. With these newly acquired watercolor techniques, my dad's painting hobby took off. Describing his artistic process as instinctual, he said, "When I start a painting, I don't know how it's going to come out." He created hundreds of paintings of bamboo trees and landscapes based on the photographs from our trip to China.

Dong Kingman, a Chinese American artist and one of America's leading watercolor masters, was a good friend of my dad's. On one of Kingman's trips to San Francisco in October 1976, H.K. asked him to critique his artwork. Kingman said my dad's paintings were well done and that he was surprised that H.K. had only been painting for a year. Dong told him, "Do what you've been doing. Do not go to any classes. You have good perspective, individualism, and mood. You have a natural skill. Just work at it every day."

My dad took Kingman's advice and continued to paint for the rest of his life, mostly depicting trees, mountains, and sunsets. He diligently rose early every day to paint. On October 7, 1976, my dad presented one of his bamboo paintings to President Jimmy Carter during one of Carter's campaign stops for President at the Sheraton Palace Hotel in San Francisco. On the back of the painting, my dad wrote, "The bamboo is a symbol of growth, strength, and the ability to bend with the wind and not break. That is Governor Jimmy Carter, our next President of the United States." My dad had completed the painting in the morning just before meeting Jimmy Carter that day.

After the visit, my dad received the following letter:

Jimmy Carter Walter Mondale Campaign

October 13, 1976

To H.K. Wong:

The bamboo painting is beautiful! If this is any indication of your talent in this medium, you will be assured of great demand of your artwork.

Please give my regards to the staff of the Empress of China. Rosalynn and I look forward to returning someday for more of your warm and gracious hospitality.

Sincerely,

Jimmy Carter

P. S. I deeply appreciate your words of dedication on the back of the painting. And I will do my best to deserve your confidence.

In 1976, H.K. also presented a one-man art show at the Chinese Culture Center. Throughout his lifetime, he donated countless paintings to nonprofit organizations in Chinatown and their fundraising events. By 1979, he had given nearly 140 paintings to benefit Chinatown's Chinese Hospital.

Carrying H.K.'s Artistic Legacy Forward

From junior high school to this day, like my dad, I have had an interest in art. In the early 1980s, I took a stained glass class and discovered I was drawn to glass art. Since then, I have carried my dad's artistic and journalistic tradition forward by creating stained glass, mosaics, and fused glass art, and by serving as a regular contributing writer and an editorial board member for *Glass Patterns Quarterly Magazine*. Like the old masters did in China, you could say that I am keeping my dad's artistic spirit alive. My glass art is featured at countless exhibitions throughout the U.S. I teach art glass workshops at the annual Glass Craft and Bead Expo in Las Vegas, and at various studios throughout the U.S. I have also traveled twice to Australia to conduct workshops in Melbourne and Brisbane. I create my glass art and develop new techniques through my Glasstastique Studio in San Jose, California.

Riverboats on the Pearl River on the way to H.K.'s ancestral village, circa 1975.

H.K.'s ancestral village of Fu-Shan (Tiger Hill) in Kwangtung province, circa 1975.

H.K. interviewed a Fu-Shan villager near the rice paddies and banana trees, circa 1975.

H.K. proudly displayed a brick from his father's original house. The occupants of the house tore down the front of the house as part of a do-it-yourself remodeling project. Circa 1975.

H.K. received high marks for several pencil sketches drawn in the 4th grade at the Oriental Public School, including this one of a Chinese farmer. Circa 1917.

H.K. presented one of his bamboo paintings to future U.S. President Jimmy Carter during one of his campaign stops at the Sheraton Palace Hotel in San Francisco, October 7, 1976. Photo by Kem Lee.

H.K.'s watercolor painting of Peking at sunrise.

H.K.'s watercolor painting of
a Nanking tree-lined road.

H.K.'s watercolor painting of the Imperial Palace on the cover of *Travel Holiday* magazine, November 1978.

H.K. at work in his office at the Empress of China, surrounded by some of his artwork.
Circa 1978.

KWEILIN, CHINA '75 MK

18

FLOWER DRUM SONG

"A hundred million miracles,
a hundred million miracles are
happening every day."

– **Mei Li**, from *Flower Drum Song*

On February 8, 1963, scriptwriter Joseph Fields submitted his final screenplay for the new musical film, *Flower Drum Song*, to Universal International Pictures, Universal City, California. Based on a novel by C.Y. Lee, the movie featured music and song lyrics by the renowned creative team Richard Rodgers and Oscar Hammerstein. At that time, Rodgers had already written the music for such well-known productions as *Oklahoma*, *Carousel*, *South Pacific*, *The King and I*, and twenty other scores for the theater. Hammerstein, who co-authored the *Flower Drum Song* musical with Joseph Fields, had also written many of the lyrics for Rodgers' films. For their combined work on *South Pacific*, the two had already won a Pulitzer prize for drama.

The Broadway Production of *Flower Drum Song*

The Broadway version of the musical, directed by Gene Kelly, displayed his influence on the dance numbers. With expansive staging, lavish costumes, swirling skirts, and tapping feet, dancers lit up the stage with swing dancing, the Virginia Reel, acrobatics, and traditional dances. The blend of Asian and early-American dance routines was a colorful backdrop to the song lyrics, "you are like the Chinese dish Americans made up – chop suey. Living here is very much like chop suey." Though relatively new to directing at the time, Kelly was already well-known as an actor, from his first role in William Saroyan's *Time of Your Life* to the enduring classics *Brigadoon, On the Town, Singing in the Rain, The Three Musketeers,* and *An American in Paris.*

Lee was born in Hunan Province in China. A former city editor of *Chinese World* and *Young China,* he had also worked as a feature writer for *Radio Free Asia* and contributed articles and a play to *Theatre Arts Magazine.* At 25, when he arrived in the United States, he had graduated from the National Southwest Associated University in Yunnan. He became a U.S. citizen and received a Masters in Drama from Yale University.

Flower Drum Song is a love story set in San Francisco Chinatown against a background of a Chinese immigrant family's strict old-world traditions and the modern westernized attitudes of their American-born Chinese youth. Initially presented as a musical stage play, opening in December of 1958 on Broadway, the play was made into the movie a couple of years later. Central to the story is Wang Chi Yang, a conservative elder gentleman who wants his son, Wang Ta, to marry Mei Li, a delicate Chinese girl who has arrived in the U.S. as a "picture bride." The plot thickens because Wang Ta cannot make up his mind among three women: Linda Low (who is not as innocent as Wang Ta believes); Helen Chao, whose love he cannot return; and the naïve Chinese girl, Mei Lei. In a pull between tradition and modernism, Wang Ta is also conflicted about defying his father. The result is pure Rodgers and Hammerstein kitsch with wonderful compositions about love, life, and the pursuit of happiness.

The original Broadway production of *Flower Drum Song* opened in New York City at the Saint James Theater on December 1, 1958. It ran for 600 performances. Nominated for the 1959 Tony Award for the Best Musical, notable actors included Juanita Hall, most recognizable for her role as Bloody Mary in *South Pacific,* for which she won many awards, and Keye Luke, known for his roles in *Around the World in Eighty Days* and *Love is a Many-Splendored Thing.* Luke, an artist born in Canton, China while his parents, who had become U.S. citizens, were visiting their homeland, also performed as No. 1 son in the Charlie Chan series, as well in numerous television shows. Other actors included Miyoshi Umeki, a Japanese American singer and actress; Jack Soo, a Japanese American actor from San Francisco; Ed Kenney, a theater actor discovered by the author-producers of *Flower Drum Song*; Ely Carrillo, a lead opera soprano, with many credits to her name; Susanne Lake, also an opera soloist; and Bill Sugihara, a radio actor-singer. Talented dancers included Gene Castle, Chao Li, Helen Funai, Denise Quan, Khigh Dhiegh, Harry Shaw Lowe, Lucretia Gould, Jon Lee, the Ribuca Twins, and George Li. Also participating were Carol Haney, dance director; Oliver Smith, designer; Irene Sharaff, costume design; Robert Russell Bennett, orchestration; Peggy Clark, lighting; and Robert Stanley, music director.

In a letter dated January 30, 1959, San Francisco Mayor George Christopher appointed my dad to the *Flower Drum Song* Day Mayor's Committee. To recognize the attention that the book and Broadway hit had brought to San Francisco Chinatown, *Flower Drum Song* Day was held on February 9, 1959 to honor San Franciscan Lee, author of the book.

On August 6, 1959, H.K. received another letter from the Lynn Farnol Group, publicists for the musical in New York City. My dad and mom were personally invited by Rogers and Hammerstein to attend a performance in New York, all expenses paid, including transportation and living expenses, for their three-day stay. Lee joined H.K. and Honey on the trip. While visiting New York City, my dad was interviewed by television, radio, and newspaper reporters. My parents were also hosted by Rogers and Hammerstein at a dinner in New York Chinatown.

The Film Version of *Flower Drum Song*

Three actors in the stage musical, Jack Soo, Miyoshi Umeki, and Juanita Hall, reprised their roles in the film version of *Flower Drum Song*, which premiered on November 9, 1961. In 1958, Umeki had won Best Actress in a Supporting Role for her work in *Sayonara*, becoming the first Asian woman to win an Academy Award. She also garnered a Tony nomination in 1959 and a Golden Globe recognition for her role in *Flower Drum Song*. Other new replacements were director Henry Koster, producer Ross Hunter, James Shigeta, Benson Fong, and Reiko Sato. Nancy Kwan, already known for her debut in *The World of Suzie Wong*, was also new as the nightclub entertainer, Linda Low. Headstrong, she often fitfully objected to her character's wardrobe and hairstyles. "This *cheongsam* is too old-fashioned," she protested. "They'd all laugh at me in Hong Kong if I wore this. No one wears cheongsams like that anymore!"

However, years later, on January 25, 2002, when Nancy Kwan recalled the 1961 version of the film in an interview with the *Los Angeles Times*, she noted that it was a landmark film, the first movie to ever feature an all-Asian cast. She also said that working with choreographer Hermes Pan, who had worked with Fred Astaire on most of the legendary dancer's films, was a big highlight. "He was a terrific man and great to work with. Fred Astaire used to come down once in a while and watch us dance. All the dancers got a big thrill out of it."

However, in the opening credits of the movie, one new name stands out to me more than any of the others. Years later, as I watched the film, my dad's name boldly appears on the screen as the Technical Advisor for the movie. It was his job to make certain that the scenes and settings the filmmakers were portraying in their movie were as close as possible to real life in San Francisco Chinatown. Without compromising the storyline, he was responsible for adding authenticity to the production.

My best guess is that Lee may have been consulted as to who might be a good Technical Advisor for the film. Lee and Mayor Christopher likely both recommended my dad to the filmmakers. As former city editor of *Chinese World*, where my dad was a regular contributor, Lee worked quite closely and creatively with H.K. Mayor Christopher had also worked with H.K. to honor Lee on *Flower Drum Song* Day. The studio executives were made aware of H.K.'s extensive involvement in the San Francisco Chinatown community, and his deep knowledge of all aspects of life there. In a 1978 radio interview, my dad related that the film producer, Ross Hunter, had tracked him down at a Chinatown coffeeshop to interest him in the film. Albert Lim was also recruited for the film as a co-Technical Advisor, along with my dad.

I imagine there was great excitement the day San Francisco Chinatown welcomed the *Flower Drum Song* film crew to Grant Avenue to shoot the first scenes. Watching the movie gives me a smile because I can see my dad's contribution to it. Thumbing through the pages of the final screenplay, I see scenes and dialogues in the film that are missing from the screenplay. These added moments are small and subtle but appear to me to be in there by way of my dad's input. One moment is when a Chinese elder, performed by Juanita Hill, calls an order into a Chinese restaurant in Chinatown. My dad would certainly have known what to order! The character, Madame Le Jong, says, "send me four pounds of seahorse, two pounds of dried snake meat, a dozen thousand-year eggs – and be sure they are fresh." In another scene, the character "Mr. Wong" writes a letter to the editor. In still yet another scene, the Spirit of 1776 parade in Chinatown includes a Miss Chinatown USA float, with Miss Chinatown waving from its decorative throne.

My dad not only made certain that the scenes and settings the filmmakers were portraying in the movie were authentic to San Francisco Chinatown, he also added scenes to promote the aspects of Chinatown that were near and dear to his heart. Since it was determined that Grant Avenue in Chinatown was too narrow for most of the film, the filmmakers rebuilt an exact replica at the Universal Studios in Hollywood, authentic to the last detail. At a cost of $310,000, it covered 51,030 square feet, with 54 buildings, many of them three stories in height. It was considered one of the largest and costliest sets ever built for a movie at that time. As a Technical Advisor, my dad ensured that every detail was correct.

In a letter to Mr. Norman Deming, Unit Production Manager, Universal International Pictures, Universal Studios, dated December 27, 1960, H.K. wrote:

"Dear Mr. Deming:

We had the pleasure of hosting Henry Koster and spent a few days with him to familiarize him with the Chinatown scene. Now we are very pleased to learn from your letter than you will do some actual filming for *Flower Drum Song* in San Francisco Chinatown.

The New Year's Parade is the highlight of the annual Chinese New Year Festival, and we feel it will enhance your picture. In answer to your questions, I have conferred with Mr. T. Kong Lee, President, Chinese Chamber of Commerce and Mr. John Young, Parade Chairman, both of whom like the idea of having their parade in *Flower Drum Song*.

The Festival Committee is very pleased to approve your lighting any spot as necessary and we can assign favorable positions for your camera. When you arrive, we can work out details for lighting, etc.

Your float will be most welcome in our parade. Naturally, the theme is Chinese New Year, and it would be easy for you to work *Flower Drum Song* into this motif. The only limitation would be height (must not exceed 13 feet) and width (cannot be over 9 feet overall), because of the narrowness of Grant Avenue.

At this writing, Mr. Young is working on a parade lineup and he expressed a desire to place you right in the middle of the procession.

Happy New Year and looking forward to seeing you, I am.

Sincerely,

H.K. Wong
Publicity Chairman"

Promotional Tour for
Flower Drum Song in the Far East

In January of 1962, H.K. and Honey had just returned from a two-month tour of the Far East. During that trip, my dad had acted as San Francisco Mayor Christopher's emissary while promoting Universal International's film, *Flower Drum Song*. My dad met with heads of government in Hawaii, Japan, Taiwan, Hong Kong, The Philippines, Thailand, and Singapore. H.K. and Honey played tennis whenever and wherever they could. In Hong Kong, they were invited to play at the Chinese Recreation Club on 18 well-kept clay courts. At the time, Nancy Kwan, star of *The World of Suzie Wong* and *Flower Drum Song*, was visiting her home in Hong Kong. Kwan invited H.K. and Honey for an afternoon of tennis at the famed Kowloon Tong Club on its clay and grass courts. In Honolulu, they played at the Waikiki Club and on public courts.

The Legacy of *Flower Drum Song*

Included in his memorabilia from that time is a photo of my dad, with a broad smile, presenting a Chinese hand-painted scroll to Rogers and Hammerstein. He was clearly thrilled to have been a part of that project. To modern audiences, the 1958 stage production of *Flower Drum Song* may seem outdated, clichéd at best, and perpetrating derogatory stereotypes at worst. In 2002, Kwan herself said that Asians felt the musical and movie portrayed stereotypes and that the Chinese were also upset that Japanese actors played Chinese characters. But at the time, *Flower Drum Song* was a landmark production. It was the first Broadway musical that focused on Asian Americans. After release of the 1961 film version, the musical was rarely produced, due to concerns that Asian Americans might be offended by how they were portrayed. But in 2002, to update the story for modern audiences, Tony Award-winning playwright David Henry Hwang revitalized *Flower Drum Song*, calling the 1961 film version a "guilty pleasure." Using Rodgers and Hammerstein's music, the intergenerational and immigrant themes, and a 1950s San Francisco Chinatown setting, he changed the song order, plot, and tone of the musical. Regional theater companies still perform this version of *Flower Drum Song*.

At the time of this writing, the original 1961 film version of *Flower Drum Song* can still be seen, streaming on Amazon Prime Video, FuboTV, Kanopy, Hoopla, Pluto TV, and VUDU. H.K.'s name will always be associated with the authentic aspects of the film.

Playbill from the Broadway musical of the *Flower Drum Song* at the St. James Theatre. November 30, 1959.

Pat Suzuki, Richard Rodgers, Oscar Hammerstein, Joseph Fields (star and composer-authors of the *Flower Drum Song*) celebrated the first anniversary of the musical on Broadway with Honey and H.K. with a huge anniversary cake, December 1, 1959.

Nancy Kwan as Linda Low, performed a dance sequence in the Chinese New Year parade, during the filming of the *Flower Drum Song* movie, March 1961.

The cast of the *Flower Drum Song* movie, in full costume outside Stage 12 at Universal Studios: Patrick Adiarte (Wang San), Kam Tong (Dr. Han Li), Jack Soo (Sammy Fong), Nancy Kwan (Linda Low), Henry Koster (Director), Miyoshi Umeki (Mei Li), James Shigeta (Wang Ta), Juanita Hall (Madame Li), and Benson Fong (Wang Chi-yang); April 1961.

H.K. presented a Chinese scroll from the Chinese Chamber of Commerce to Richard Rodgers, Oscar Hammerstein, and Joseph Fields for their work on the *Flower Drum Song* movie, November 1961.

The Universal Studios camera crew filmed the Chinese New Year parade on Grant Avenue for the *Flower Drum* Song movie, February 1961.

THE CAST

Linda Low	NANCY KWAN
Wang Ta	JAMES SHIGETA
Auntie (Madame Liang)	JUANITA HALL
Sammy Fong	JACK SOO
Wang	BENSON FONG
Helen Chao	REIKO SATO
Wang San	PATRICK ADIARTE
Dr. Li	KAM TONG
Frankie Wing	VICTOR SEN YUNG
Madame Fong	SOO YONG
Professor	CHING WAH LEE
Headwaiter	JAMES HONG
Dr. Chon	SPENCER CHAN
Dr. Fong	ARTHUR SONG
Policeman	WEAVER LEVY
Holdup Man	HERMAN RUDIN
San's Girl Friend	CHERYLENE LEE
San's Girl Friend	VIRGINIA LEE

and

Mei Li	MIYOSHI UMEKI

Program guide from the premiere of the *Flower Drum Song* movie, November 1961.

THE CREDITS

Produced by **ROSS HUNTER** / Directed by **HENRY KOSTER** / Screenplay by **JOSEPH FIELDS**

Based on the novel "THE FLOWER DRUM SONG" by C. Y. Lee; Photography, RUSSELL METTY, A.S.C.; Art Directors, ALEXANDER GOLITZEN and JOSEPH WRIGHT; Original Title Paintings by DONG KINGMAN; Set Decorations, HOWARD BRISTOL; Costumes, IRENE SHARAFF; Choreography by HERMES PAN; Unit Production Manager, NORMAN DEMING; Film Editor, MILTON CARRUTH; Technical Advisors, H. K. WONG and ALBERT LIM; Sound, WALDON O. WATSON and JOE LAPIS; Make-Up, BUD WESTMORE; Hair Stylist, LARRY GERMAIN; Assistant Director, PHIL BOWLES; Produced in Association with FIELDS PRODUCTIONS.

H.K. and Honey with Nancy Kwan on the clay tennis courts at the Chinese Recreation Club in Hong Kong, during their two-month tour of the Far East promoting the *Flower Drum Song*, January 1962.

19

AWARDS AND RECOGNITIONS

"Nothing great was ever
achieved without enthusiasm."
– Ralph Waldo Emerson

n 1974 and 1981, in recognition of his many achievements, my dad was listed in *Who's Who in America*. Though he sometimes faced opposition to proposed projects, his upbeat attitude did not let that stand in his way. He noted, "If I feel the path is a right one, I do it. I prefer to look at the positive, at our potential as a part of San Francisco."

This philosophy motivated H.K.'s work as a "one-man press bureau" in Chinatown. It also inspired him to become the liaison between Mme. Chiang Kai-Shek and San Francisco City Hall, coordinate two exhibitions from the People's Republic of China, and serve with the Chinese Chamber of Commerce. It also prompted him to become technical advisor for the movie *Flower Drum Song*, co-founder of the Chinese Historical Society of America and the Empress of China, and so much more, as shared earlier in this book. To honor his exemplary service in the Chinese community, H.K.'s contribution was recognized multiple times by the larger community.

Keys to the Island of Maui and City of Honolulu

In recognition of my dad's publicity efforts on behalf of the Chinese community in Hawaii, in 1961, Mayor Eddie Tam presented H.K. a key to the island of Maui. That same year, Mayor Blaisdall also presented H.K. a key to the city of Honolulu.

Jefferson Award

In March 1978, the *San Francisco Examiner* participated in the second annual American Institute of Public Service Jefferson Award Program for community service. Department editors named six San Francisco citizens worthy of the 1977 award. H.K. was one of the six men and women to receive a Jefferson Award for Public Service from the American Institute of Public Service for that year. He was also the first Chinese American to receive the award.

Other notable people who received the award that year were Walter Haas Jr., President, Chairman and CEO of Levi Strauss; and Matson Roth, shipping executive, special ambassador for trade, a member of the ACLU executive committee, and the man who is credited with preservation of Ghirardelli Square in San Francisco. Also honored was co-founder of the San Francisco Caregiver Association and organizer of the San Francisco Alzheimer's Association, Anne Bashkiroff.

On February 24, 1978, H.K. received a letter from *San Francisco Examiner* publisher, Reg Murphy, that read: "The *Examiner* is honored to recognize your outstanding dedication, sacrifice and accomplishment for this community. Realizing that the call to public service is one of the highest individual challenges, we attempt with this recognition to reward those who have served us with distinction."

With characteristic humility, in response to his Jefferson Award for Public Service, my dad said, "The community event is bigger than the man. I am not a glory hunter. I believe in doing what you can in the sense of being able to help, particularly when something can enhance life for all of us."

Maple Leaf Award

In 1978, the *Chinatown News*, a biweekly magazine published by the

Chinese Publicity Bureau in Vancouver, British Columbia, awarded H.K. a Maple Leaf Award. It was the highest award made by the organization to recognize civic involvement and professionalism. From 1953 to 1956, the publication had used the name *Chinatown,* after which the name changed to *Chinatown News.* Its last publication was a special "souvenir edition," released on April 8, 2007.

Cultural Integrity and World Harmony Awards

One of the more unusual awards my dad received was from the San Francisco Center for the Transcendental Meditation program, located on Laguna Honda Boulevard.

On September 6, 1977, Evelyn Hsiang Chinn, Teacher of Transcendental Meditation, wrote to H.K.: "On behalf of the 7,000 practitioners of the Transcendental Meditation Program in San Francisco, it is a great pleasure to inform you that you and your colleague, Mr. Thomas Chinn, have been selected as recipients of the Maharishi Award in the Category of 'Cultural Integrity, Invincibility, and World Harmony.' The presentation will take place at the San Francisco Autumn Festival for the Age of Enlightenment, to be held Tuesday, September 20, 1977. The awards are the highlight of the Festival and will be presented to ideal citizens whose personal qualities have led to success in their chosen fields of law, education, cultural integrity, spiritual development, art, business, music, science, government, and health.

"The award for 'Cultural Integrity and World Harmony' goes to individuals whose activities have contributed most toward preserving and strengthening his own culture and establishing a harmonious relationship between different levels of society and with men of other cultures and ways of life.

"The award is highly appropriate to your work as co-founders of the Chinese Historical Society in San Francisco. The Society has been instrumental in inviting the Chinese community to take interest and pride in its heritage in this country, and in informing the public at large of both the more obvious and the more subtle and profound influences of Chinese culture to American life."

The Age of Enlightenment Award, scribed in beautiful calligraphy, read: "Through the window of science, we have seen that the orderly influence of a few individuals in any society is enough to change the direction of the times toward all harmony, happiness, and progress. On the basis of scientific validation, and of the experience of over one million people participating in the Transcendental Meditation program, we feel comfortable in inviting all to join hands, to proclaim the 'Age of Enlightenment,' and recognize the outstanding achievement of H.K. Wong in the field of 'Cultural Integrity and World Harmony,' recorded this 20 day of September 1977 in San Francisco, the first city of the 'Age of Enlightenment' declared by Maharishi Mahesh Yogi."

Honorary Mayor of Marriott's Great America

As previously mentioned, in 1978 my dad was appointed Honorary Mayor of Marriott's Great America in Santa Clara, California, because of his work in establishing the Chinese Moon Festival and participating in its pageant. As H.K. would laughingly say when his accolades were mentioned at the Jefferson Awards, "I am also the Crown Prince of the August Moon."

H.K. had been asked to help the Women's Auxiliary Chinese Hospital Fund with the event, and the organization had been short one candidate for its emperor contest. My dad willingly complied to run for emperor of the contest. Each candidate had to raise a contribution, and the highest contribution was crowned emperor. My dad painted and offered his watercolors for sale. He garnered second place by selling 132 paintings and receiving donations from numerous friends and relatives, garnering his rightful place as Crown Prince of the August Moon festival.

Posthumous Honors

In 1987, H.K. was recognized in the *San Francisco Examiner* Centennial

Issue as one of 101 "Most Notable San Franciscans" in the past 100 years. This distinction was shared by such notables as the DiMaggio Brothers (sports); A.P. Giannini (founder Bank of America); Joseph Strauss (builder of the Golden Gate and Bay Bridges); Dianne Feinstein (San Francisco's first female mayor); George Christopher (former S.F. mayor); George Moscone (respected S.F. mayor); Harvey Milk (gay activist, S.F. supervisor); Steve Jobs (personal computer pioneer); Charles de Young (the *S.F. Chronicle's* former publisher); Andrew Halliday (father of cable cars); Willie Mays (San Francisco Giants); Levi Strauss (blue jeans empire); Domingo Ghirardelli (chocolate czar); Cecil Williams (pastor of Glide Memorial Church); Ansel Adams (internationally known photographer and environmentalist); Lawrence Ferlinghetti (beat poet and publisher); Imogen Cunningham (internationally known photographer); Isadora Duncan (acclaimed dancer); Bill Graham (music promoter); Lana Turner (actress); Yehudi Menuhin (composer and violinist); Janis Joplin (rock and roll singer); Sally Stanford (legendary madam and former Sausalito mayor); and Herb Caen (newspaper columnist), among others.

In recognition of his profound contribution to the world of tennis in America, in 1992, my dad was posthumously inducted into the Northern California Tennis Association Hall of Fame. My mom accepted his induction plaque at the Mark Hopkins Hotel on Nob Hill in San Francisco. The other tennis figures inducted to the Hall of Fame that year included Dick Gould of Menlo Park, the most successful coach in collegiate tennis history; George Rice of Napa, CA, a notable Northern California tennis player and shop owner for over sixty years; and Erik Van Dillen of San Mateo, a world top-ten tennis professional who was partnered with the renowned tennis great, Stan Smith.

In 1997, my dad was posthumously inducted into the California Tourism Hall of Fame by Governor Pete Wilson for his exceptional contribution to California Travel and Tourism as the Director of the Empress of China and Director of the San Francisco Convention and Visitors Bureau. An official certificate was presented to my mother on February 5, 1997 by the State of California Travel and Commerce Agency, Division of Tourism.

Keys to the city of Honolulu and the island of Maui presented to H.K. by Mayor Neal Blaisdell and Mayor Eddie Tam, April 1957.

The 1977 Jefferson Award for outstanding public service presented to H.K., March 1978.

Honey admired the silver Jefferson Award medal that was presented to H.K. by Mildred Hamilton from the *San Francisco Examiner*, March 1978.

H.K. was congratulated by San Francisco Mayor George Moscone after he received the Jefferson Award, March 1978.

20

LEGACY

"Remember him for his humor,
his sensitivity, and his love of mankind;
and on the tennis court, he always
played the best shot he had."

– Honey Wong

An article published on September 30, 1958, written by journalist Donald Canter for the *San Francisco News* was entitled: "Things happen when H.K. Wong strolls down Grant Avenue." It captures a snapshot of the wonderful legacy my dad left behind.

"When the 100 delegates to the National Homebuilders Hardware Convention in Chicago walked into the dining room of the Sherman Hotel this morning, as guests of San Francisco's Schlage Lock Company, they rubbed their eyes. This did not look like Chicago, this looked like San Francisco's Chinatown. To enter the room, they walked through the Moon Gate, the colorful archway flanked by reproductions of Grant Avenue's famous Oriental lamp posts. The walls were colored with multi-colored scrolls and on the tables were incense sticks, Chinese spoons, and chopsticks. Who sold Schlage Lock on the idea? In Chinatown, they told me: Must be H.K. Wong. Who else would think of it?

"His full name is Henry K. Wong. Everybody calls him H.K. If you are lucky, you can find him in his 1123 Grant Avenue furniture store. Or maybe in his Ti Sun Company Hardware store. If you do not find him, just walk down the street, and keep asking, 'Seen H.K.?' Somebody always has. He will find you before you will find him. His greeting is always, 'What's doing, boy?' You ask him if he knows anything about that Schlage Lock

H. H. Wong

deal in Chicago and he gives you a big grin.

"(*H.K. answers*) 'Met a Dallas Smith of that outfit a few months ago,' he beams. 'Just about where we stand now. Asked him what he was doing. Nothing much was his reply. But you sit down with them over a cup of coffee – and you make them talk. Once they are here on Grant Avenue, they all seem to talk. So, he tells me about the convention and about the breakfast the company wants to give the delegates and about the theme they are trying to find to decorate the room. So, I take a paper and pencil and I make a couple of sketches on the back of an envelope. You know, an archway and an Oriental lamppost and things like that.'

"H.K. takes another envelope out of his pocket and makes the sketches again. Just a few lines, but you get the idea. And that is how there is a valuable promotion stunt for Chinatown in Chicago today. That is how tens of thousands of people pour into Chinatown on Chinese New Year to watch the giant parade; that is why Chinatown organizes the Miss Chinatown USA contest – just because somebody ran into H.K. somewhere on Grant Avenue and left with a pocket full of ideas. Why does H.K. do it? Why doesn't he stick to his two stores? Why doesn't he just mind his own business?

"(*H.K. answers*) 'Here is where my mother stood – this very corner. It was Chinese New Year, maybe 50 years ago, maybe more. She just stood here and watched the crowd. A young boy saw her standing here. He was Kim Wong. He asked his friends if they knew the girl, and they said her name was Shee Gee. A few days later, Kim Wong's friends went to see Shee Gee's parents. A month afterwards, Kim Wong and Shee Gee met for the first time. That was the day they were married. They had twelve children. I was one of them. Our parents are dead now. Mother was the last to go. But never can I forget her words: On Grant Avenue, you do not have to look for things to happen. They just happen to you.'"

My dad approached life with vigor and zest. A Renaissance man and pioneer in many ways, his imagination, natural ability to connect with people, and energy always inspired innovation. Things did happen to him. He made everything he touched "decorated." If H.K. was involved, it became livelier, more interesting, and better. But his bright candle would eventually burn out. At 77 years old, on January 11, 1985, H.K. lost his life to cancer. The following week, in the January 18, 1985 issue of *Asian Week*, a full-page spread honored his life. In addition to the headline, "Mr. Chinatown H.K. Wong Dies at 77," other articles were, "H.K., I'm Glad We Knew You," "Over Half a Century of Community Works," "H.K. Wong: A Man for All Seasons," and "Chinatown's Ambassador."

Justice Harry Low wrote, "Writer, publicist, historian, restaurateur, artist, family man, tennis player, community leader – H.K. was all these and much more. He was my friend, and I enjoyed his company because he was a truly jovial, compassionate, and generous person. He had a fine sense of humor and we were often interrupted by a hearty laugh coupled with a cackle and a slap on the back. He had a special talent to think new and good ideas, a real visionary, yet he had humility and wisdom. He worked hard and played hard, and his unique human warmth and compassion made him even more enjoyable...he leaves a rich legacy to the community...H.K. had a zest for life and we all sensed his vibrance. He loved the grandeur of the human spirit...and had a flair for all that he undertook as we watched in awe. H.K.'s death is an occasion for mourning. His having lived is a cause for rejoicing."

An open letter in the same issue written by Gerrye Wong began simply, "Goodbye my friend." Gerrye wrote, "H.K. Wong was San Francisco Chinatown's best press agent. In the 10-block radius adjoining his beloved Grant Avenue where he grew up, he knew the inside stories behind each obscure door-front, and he loved sharing the history with the outside world. And the outside world loved hearing about his Chinatown from his enthusiastic lips which never tired nor ceased to give whomever he met, his own inimitable smile. We will not forget you, my friend. You were always proud to be a Chinese American, and you always instilled in us the feeling that we too should be proud of our rich heritage. San Francisco at large always thought of you as Mr. Chinatown, and we Chinese were proud to have you as our representative because you always showed a dignified and down-to-earth quality to all who met you. We will miss you, my friend."

A memorial service was held at the Grace Cathedral on Nob Hill, San

Francisco. H.K.'s two closest friends, Dr. Walter Wong and Donald Canter, delivered the eulogy to a crowd of over 300 of my dad's friends. My dad's ashes were scattered over the Sierra Nevada foothills in the Mother Lode, a region that he cherished during his years searching for artifacts and oral histories from the Chinese pioneers.

Seven years later, almost to the day, on January 12, 1992, my mom lit a candle for my dad. She wrote, "There's so much to be grateful for – my good health, my home, my friends, and financial income. Meeting and marrying H.K., my life became an exciting adventure as his shadow. Despite all the favorable above, I cannot fully enjoy the sunshine without my dear H.K. to share the ups and downs of daily living. Last Saturday, the Chinese Historical Society of America honored me, but this again was a result of his initial doings. But being remembered is a credit to his living."

ACKNOWLEDGMENTS

I am eternally grateful to Dr. LaVay Lau, without whom I would not be who I am today. She was instrumental in arranging my adoption as a puny five-year-old and provided my case files and notes from the orphanage and the adoption process. We were able to maintain contact all these years through my parents' friendship with her brother Merton.

Being a historian, my dad kept all his writings, clippings, photos, and notes, often making copies of them. My mother was also a packrat. After my mother passed away, I had the monumental job of clearing out my parents' house. Thanks to my parents, I was able to collect 60 years' worth of source materials packed into 40 boxes. There was so much material, much of which I had never seen before, that it was a tough task deciding what to include in the book. I am grateful to my co-author, Catherine Lenox, for her help in this decision.

Sue Fawn Chung, my distant cousin and Professor Emerita of History, encouraged me for many years to write this book about my dad. She provided details on the early years of the Chinese Historical Society of America, and some lovely anecdotes about visits with my mother.

My wife Rebecca was a great help in reviewing the many versions of the manuscript and offering suggestions to make it read better. My daughter Allison, with a B.A. degree in Industrial Design from the Rhode Island School of Design, created the fabulous design for the book cover.

Senator Dianne Feinstein was a good friend of my dad during her tenure as President of the Board of Supervisors and Mayor of San Francisco. She took time from her busy schedule and provided the foreword to the book. My dad valued his friendship with Mayor Feinstein and enjoyed working with her on many community projects for San Francisco.

Ada Tom was a fellow director during the final years of the Empress of China. We had a good working relationship, and she was supportive during my time on the board. She provided many insights into the beginnings of the restaurant and its operations.

June Gong Chin, the first Miss Chinatown USA, is a close family friend. Our family enjoyed many visits to their country cabin, and her husband P.Q. Chin lent us his Jaguar sedan on several occasions for jaunts around California. June provided many stories and photographs of the early days of the Chinese New Year Festival and the Miss Chinatown USA pageant.

Anita Anderson provided tremendous copyediting support on the manuscript. She was very thorough and working with her was delightful. Sonja Gerard did a masterful job designing the book, arranging all the photographs, and adding the graphic elements including the sprouting bamboo shoots at the start of each chapter.

This book is a result of a fortuitous reunion with my co-author, Catherine Lenox, who crafted a wonderful life story about my dad. Catherine captured his spirit, integrity, charisma, and humility, bringing his colorful personality to life. She was a joy to work with, and I appreciated all of her hard work to guide this book to fruition.

ABOUT THE AUTHOR

Wesley R. Wong is the adopted son of Honey and H.K. Wong. He is an Eagle Scout and Silver Beaver with the Boy Scouts of America, and recipient of the Bronze Pelican and Saint George Emblems for his service to the National Catholic Committee on Scouting. He holds a Bachelor of Science degree in Computer Science from the University of California, Santa Barbara, and a Master of Business Administration from Santa Clara University. After 34 years in the computer industry developing and managing software, he took an early retirement to focus on his passion for glass art. Wesley creates stained glass, mosaics, and fused glass art and develops new techniques from his Glasstastique Studio in San Jose, California. He travels to various studios around the country to teach workshops in glass art. He is married to Rebecca, with son Nathaniel and daughter Allison. During the statewide lockdown due to the Coronavirus pandemic, Wesley has revived his juggling skills, a hobby that began in the 1980s but had gone dormant for over 30 years.

Regarding what inspired him to write *Mr. Chinatown: The Legacy of H.K. Wong*, Wesley says, "I was always proud to call H.K. my father. Nathaniel and Allison never had a chance to meet their grandfather H.K., as he had passed away many years before they were born. This book is an opportunity to bring my dad's spirit and personality to life and to share some of his stories and accomplishments as a prominent businessman and civic leader in Chinatown and San Francisco, a legacy for which they can be proud of the grandfather they never met."

ABOUT THE CO-AUTHOR

Owner and founder of Write Contact, LLC., co-author Catherine Lenox ghostwrites creative nonfiction books and legacy memoirs. She holds a Bachelor of Arts degree in English and Publications from San Francisco State University, and lives near Seattle, Washington. A former radio news reporter and writer/editor for numerous magazines, newspapers, and corporate and government publications, she enjoys helping others tell their stories. Catherine's father, Lionel "Bud" Lenox, and H.K. Wong were lifelong friends, so she has particularly enjoyed helping Wesley tell H.K.'s story.

To learn more about the legacy of H.K. Wong,
additional fun facts, and photos, please visit:

www.MrChinatown.com

CPSIA information can be obtained
at www.ICGtesting.com
Printed in the USA
LVHW021203100921
697438LV00013B/896